Status
Envy

Status Envy

The Politics of Catholic Higher Education

Anne Hendershott

Transaction Publishers
New Brunswick (U.S.A.) and London (U.K.)

Library of Congress Catalog Number: 2008029622
ISBN: 978-1-4128-0817-0
Printed in the United States of America

Library of Congress Cataloging-in-Publication

Hendershott, Anne B.
    Status envy : the politics of catholic higher education / Anne Hendershott.
        p. cm.
    Includes bibliographical references and index.
    ISBN 978-1-4128-0817-0
        1. Catholic universities and colleges—Political aspects—United States.
    2. Catholic Church—Education (Higher)—United States. I. Title.

LC501.H43   2008
378'.071273—dc22   2008029622

Contents

Acknowledgments

Of the many who helped me with this book, I am most indebted to my students at the University of San Diego. Their observations and insights about Catholic higher education are reflected throughout these pages.

I am grateful to Rosemary Getty, who recently retired from the University of San Diego School of Law. Her willingness to check facts, look for primary sources, and make theoretical connections went well beyond the call of friendship. I am especially grateful to Shelley Siegan, who encouraged me to contact Irving Louis Horowitz at Transaction about this project. Professor Horowitz has been a kind and generous editor whose patient reading and re-reading of the manuscript is greatly appreciated. I feel most fortunate to have had the honor to work with him.

Thank you to San Diego Attorney, Charles LiMandri, of the Thomas More Law Center, and Professor Gerry Bradley of Notre Dame's Law School who both read drafts of the first chapters of this manuscript. Their suggestions helped to begin to shape the work at the earliest stages. While they may not agree with all of my conclusions, I am grateful for their help.

And, finally, thank you to my new colleagues at The King's College in New York City. They have welcomed me as a contributor to the commitment they have made to providing students a biblically based curriculum in a faithful environment that both challenges and nurtures them. I am happy to be a part of this mission.

Introduction

More than fifty years ago, an obscure Catholic college professor published an essay in a long forgotten journal accusing faculty on Catholic campuses of "perpetuating mediocrity" by giving too great a priority to the moral development of students instead of scholarship and intellectual excellence.[1] Within six months, as historian Philip Gleason points out, more than 3,500 reprints had been distributed: it had been commented on in the Catholic press, noted by *Newsweek*, read aloud in the refectories of many religious communities, and discussed at meetings of Catholic educators, including two sessions at the National Catholic Education Association's 1956 convention.[2] The author, Monsignor John Tracy Ellis, became a Catholic celebrity—and Catholic higher education has yet to recover.

Looking back on these early days of what can only be viewed as the "revolution" in Catholic higher education, it is difficult to understand how such a bitter little essay could have generated such emotional debate among faculty and administrators on Catholic campuses. With further reflection, we can begin to see that Ellis's analysis may have, as one historian recalled, "popped the cork on long-suppressed discontents."[3] Ellis noted the absence of Catholic scholars from the national dictionaries of science and letters and decried the dearth of scholarship on Catholic campuses. He accused Catholic faculty members of "living within a ghetto mentality" that prevented them from "mingling as they should with their non-Catholic colleagues" and lamented the undue emphasis placed upon the virtue of humility for Catholic faculty without compensating warnings against the "evils of intellectual sloth." But, most importantly, Ellis concluded that Catholic academics would never achieve parity with their counterparts on secular campuses unless they overcame their sense of inferiority and began to act like scholars.[4]

Others joined the fray including Rev. John J. Cavanaugh, former president of Notre Dame whose own essay asked, "Where are the Catholic Salks, Oppenheimers, and Einsteins?" Cavanaugh, like Ellis, suggested

1

that Catholic faculty do not have a sense of dedication to an intellectual apostolate. Both concluded that "cultural and attitudinal factors were the most important causes of Catholic intellectual backwardness."[5]

The debate over the perceived absence of Catholic intellectualism dominated discussions among Catholic faculty and administrators on Catholic campuses for decades, and in some important ways the sentiments contained in the Ellis essay are disputed even today. Still reeling from the accusations of mediocrity and moralism, and working through a defensiveness that characterized campus conversations following the essay's publication, the sense of faculty inferiority was gradually replaced by feelings of anger and resentment that now permeates the faculty culture on many Catholic campuses. Faculty are reminded of the perceived inferiority of Catholic colleges and universities each year when the *U. S. News and World Report* surveys on higher education include few of the 224 Catholic colleges and universities on their lists of the top schools in the country with only Notre Dame in the top twenty and only Georgetown and Boston College included in the top fifty in 2006. The prestigious *Fisk Guide to Colleges* contains only a handful of Catholic colleges on its listing of the "Best 300" colleges in the country; and while the *ISI Guide to Choosing the Right College* lists a few more Catholic colleges, there are qualifiers and warnings about the loss of Catholic identity on most. Notre Dame is described as the "Land O' Lapsed" to refer to the undermining of the Catholic identity of the school in 1967, when Catholic college and university officials gathered at Notre Dame's retreat in Land O' Lakes, Wisconsin and decided that the Catholic identity of their schools was a liability in achieving upward mobility in an increasingly secular age.[6]

Notre Dame's recently retired president, Fr. Edward Malloy, had been a longtime critic of Church interference in university governance. But, faithful Catholic supporters of Notre Dame were encouraged when Fr. Malloy's successor, Fr. John Jenkins, seemed to be willing to confront the anti-Catholic culture growing on campus when he expressed uneasiness with the annual campus production of *The Vagina Monologues*, and the celebration of the Notre Dame Queer Film Festival. In an address to the faculty on January 23, 2006, Fr. Jenkins cited concerns that "the portrayals of sexuality in *The Vagina Monologues* stand apart from, and indeed, in opposition to, Catholic teachings on human sexuality." Fr. Jenkins invited "dialogue" from the Notre Dame community to help him make his final decision on whether these events should continue on the Catholic campus.

It is likely that the newly appointed Notre Dame president may not have realized just how embedded in the campus culture these events had become. Fr. Jenkins may not have realized that Notre Dame had joined more than thirty other Catholic colleges in presenting *The Vagina Monologues* each year for the past five years—and the Queer Film Festival had become institutionalized on the campus. And, each year these productions have caused concerns among faithful Catholics because of their graphic and celebratory descriptions of behaviors contrary to Catholic moral teachings. But, any hopes that Notre Dame's president would cancel *The Vagina Monologues* were dashed when two months later, he announced that "after extensive consultation with faculty on campus" he decided that he "saw no reason to prohibit the performances." In fact, Fr. Jenkins became so concerned about the status of women on campus after his discussions that he thanked the faculty for pointing out the "need" for such a play. And, in a final capitulation to the feminist lobby on campus, Fr. Jenkins announced that he would form and chair an ad hoc committee composed of faculty, administrators, and students charged with fostering a wide-ranging discussion of gender relations and roles.[7]

David Solomon, Director of Notre Dame's Center for Ethics and Culture, believes that the presidential surrender to the angry faculty on *The Vagina Monologues* and the Queer Film Festival raises questions about whether Notre Dame has the will to retain its Catholic distinctiveness in the face of a hostile culture and whether it can do so with a faculty that seems largely out of sympathy with Catholic tradition. In an opinion piece in *The Wall Street Journal*, Solomon wrote, "Those faculty members who had been plotting Father Jenkins's removal from the office of Presidency for even discussing possible restrictions now congratulated him, and his former student critics praised him as a champion of personal freedom."[8] In an open letter to Fr. Jenkins, the Rev. Wilson Miscamble, a distinguished historian and former rector of the campus seminary, advised the president that, "You were called to be courageous and you settled for being popular." To avoid sacrificing status, Fr. Jenkins chose the status quo at Notre Dame as he joins most Catholic college administrators in their pursuit of upward mobility—even when such status seeking compromises the Catholic identity.

Attempting to please a hostile faculty has become even more difficult since 1990 with the release of *Ex Corde Ecclesiae*, the papal document identifying the centrality of Catholic higher education. Literally translated as "from the heart of the Church," Pope John Paul II's *Ex Corde Ecclesiae* called for Catholic colleges to be accountable to local bishops. A key component of this accountability led to a controversial requirement within the papal document that all theologians obtain a mandatum, or a certificate from the local bishop, attesting that their teaching was *in communio* or in keeping with official Church teachings.[9] Yet, more than a decade later, *Ex Corde* continues to be resisted by most of the nation's Catholic colleges and universities because the faculty and administrators on these campuses claim to view it as a threat to their academic freedom and independent governance. In a commentary in the Jesuit magazine, *America*, Notre Dame's then-president, Fr. Malloy, and Fr. Donald Monan, chancellor of Boston College, warned of "havoc" if it were adopted and called the mandatum requirement "positively dangerous" to Catholic institutions in America—and the faculty senate at Notre Dame voted unanimously for the guidelines of *Ex Corde* to be ignored.[10]

At the same time faculty and administrators have resisted the tenets of *Ex Corde*, Catholic colleges and universities have been eager to comply with whatever terms are suggested by the secular accrediting associations. For example, when the Western Association of Schools and Colleges (one of six regional associations throughout the country that accredit public and private colleges and universities) simply "recommended" that the University of San Diego further diversify its faculty and student body in terms of race and ethnicity, the university created a major in Ethnic Studies, hired a Latino professor to direct it, and provided a generous budget that allowed him to hire support staff as well as Black, Latino, and Native American faculty members. In contrast, when faculty wanted to create a Catholic Studies major, there were no university funds allocated to hire a director or provide release time for a current full-time faculty member to direct the major. As a result, Catholic Studies languishes without funding for programming, faculty, or support staff while Ethnic Studies was given department status, a reduced teaching load for the full-time director, full-time, tenure-track faculty members, dedicated office space, support staff, and a generous budget to invite Ethnic Studies "celebrities" to campus for conferences and speaking engagements. Likewise, when the secular accrediting association suggested that the University of San Diego increase its assessment procedures to measure academic outcomes more accurately, university administrators created a special campus office of assessment and hired personnel to staff the assessment initiative.

Of course, this is to be expected as in the upside-down world of Catholic colleges and universities, there is status in hosting a Department of Ethnic Studies or an Office of Assessment, while there is no status derived from activities related to strengthening the Catholic identity. In fact, many faculty and administrators believe they have themselves lost status by "settling" for a faculty position at a Catholic college or university rather than a higher-status position at a secular institution. Blaming the "Catholic identity" for their low status rather than any possible personal and professional inadequacies, this resentment has driven a form of status envy among faculty and administrators. Envy combines with a hostility to Catholic teachings that threatens to destroy what is left of the Catholic identity of these institutions.

Concerns about status affect us all—but the resentment that drives status envy seems especially prevalent among college professors. In his book on the role of envy in the professions, Joseph Epstein writes, "My own candidate for a large group existing in a state of *resentment* would be American academics: Sometimes this will reveal itself in a general sourness; sometimes it takes the form of hopelessly radical political views. These political views, it does not take long to recognize, usually feature a complex shifting and reorientation of society so that people like themselves will be allowed a justly deserved role of power."[11]

This type of status seeking should not be surprising as Christopher Jencks and David Riesman predicted these kinds of academic strivings in their 1968 study of higher education, in which they described the "Harvard-Berkeley model" of the research university as the academic pacesetter. While Jencks and Riesman acknowledged that nearly all colleges and universities aspired to higher status, their book, *The Academic Revolution*, still held out hope that Catholic higher education might be able to provide an ideology or personnel for developing alternatives to the Harvard-Berkeley "model of excellence." Still, the authors acknowledged, "the ablest Catholic educators will feel obliged to put most of their energies into proving that Catholics can beat non-Catholics" at the Harvard-Berkeley game.[12] And, sadly, they were correct as many Catholic college administrators believe it is necessary to emulate their secular counterparts. One new faculty administrator at the University of San Diego suggested at his first faculty meeting that he thought that the College of Arts and Sciences should strive to follow the example of Haverford College, "because a number of Nobel Prize winners have emerged from there."[13]

Of course, to be fair, most of us would have to acknowledge that we would like to be viewed with respect. In fact, author, Tom Wolfe believes that "every living moment of a human being's life, unless the person is starving or in immediate danger of death in some other way, is controlled by a concern for status."[14] From sports to education, we are all captivated by rankings and everyone wants to be the best. Founded in 1949, my own academic home for more than fifteen years, the University of San Diego, was born of the founder, Most Rev. Charles F. Buddy's, well-documented "dream" of a "Notre Dame of the West." Sadly, in ways that Bishop Buddy could not have anticipated—and most likely would have deplored, the dream has been realized as the University of San Diego has joined Notre Dame in its slide toward secularization.

This loss of the Catholic identity is occurring on Catholic campuses throughout the country as faculty and administrators pursue upward mobility by shedding much of their Catholic culture to conform to status expectations. The students have paid the highest price. Indeed, for those who are committed to the value of Catholic higher education, the news about the student culture at Catholic colleges and universities, as reported a few years ago by the Higher Education Research Institute at the University of California at Los Angeles, was discouraging. The institute compared the results of a survey administered to 7,200 incoming first year students at thirty-eight Catholic colleges and universities with a survey given four years later to those same students as graduating seniors. The results indicated that Catholic seniors at Catholic colleges showed sizeable increases in support for legalized abortion, premarital sex, and same sex marriage. After four years at a Catholic college, Catholic student support for legalized abortion increased from 37.9 percent to 51.7 percent, for premarital sex from 27.5 percent to 48.0 percent, and for gay marriage from 52.4 percent to 69.5 percent. These increases for Catholic students on Catholic campuses were greater than the increases exhibited by Catholic students attending secular colleges and universities.[15]

With the release of the data, liberal Catholic organizations attempted damage control. Others dismissed the findings outright. Monika Hellwig, then President of the Association of Catholic Colleges and Universities said, "The real question is whether the task of higher education in our pluralistic, changing society is to lock students into rules, or to teach them critical thinking." For Hellwig and most liberal Catholic scholars, one is apparently not supposed to direct one's critical thinking against the reigning politically correct support for abortion and gay marriage. While Hellwig correctly maintained that Catholic colleges and universities must "allow freedom of thought and freedom of debate," she failed to acknowledge that there is very little debate allowed on these campuses.[16] The debacle surrounding Fr. Jenkins at Notre Dame is just one example of what can happen to any student, faculty member, or administrator who dares to question the liberal orthodoxy on campus. As a result, from the moment the first-year student steps on most Catholic college campuses, the re-education begins—and few dissenting voices are allowed.

The following chapters will look at some of the ways in which this hostility manifests itself in the classrooms and the culture of Catholic colleges and universities. On some campuses, as the faculty and administration attempts to distance itself from all things Catholic, the curriculum and the student culture has become so degraded that local bishops have actually declared the colleges "no longer Catholic" and have removed the names of these colleges from the directories listing Catholic colleges and universities. Since *Ex Corde Ecclesiae* was issued in 1990, Marist College, Marymount Manhattan College, Nazareth College, and Saint John Fisher College have all been stripped of their designation as "Catholic colleges" by the bishops. Others will surely follow as Archbishop Michael Miller, Secretary of the Vatican's Congregation for Catholic Education recently told a gathering at the University of Notre Dame that the newly elected Pope Benedict XVI would likely favor "evangelical pruning," rather than maintaining ties to Catholic institutions that have become too secular. In his address to the faculty, Archbishop Miller said he challenged American academics to come up with ways to measure their Catholic identity and to think broadly about what it means to be a Catholic institution.[17]

More than thirty years ago, Jencks and Riesman offered a challenge to Catholic colleges and universities when they asserted in *The Academic Revolution* that although "there is as yet no American Catholic University that manages to fuse academic professionalism with concern for questions of ultimate social and moral importance," Catholics may have the ability to make this "distinctive contribution to the over-all academic system."[18] Today, Jencks and Riesman may be encouraged with some signs of hope as the following chapters will introduce a few Catholic colleges that have begun to reclaim their Catholic identity and a few more orthodox Catholic colleges that have been created in places as diverse as Naples, Florida, San Diego, Phoenix, Sacramento, and New York.

We have yet to see what effects the competition will have on the existing Catholic colleges. One thing that is for certain is that many of the bishops have already promised that the status quo cannot continue for Catholic colleges and universities. The bishops know that the Catholic Church itself is threatened by relativism and a growing secularism. They also know that Catholic colleges and universities have aided and abetted this process—and a growing number of them have said that they are not willing to tolerate it any longer. They are now being led by Pope Benedict XVI who has called on Catholics to resist what he has described as the "dictatorship of relativism" and has suggested that the time may have come for a "mustard seed Church," suggesting as the biblical mustard seed suggests, "a much smaller presence but with a faith whose dimensions could move mountains."[19]

Some of the most faithful members of this "mustard seed Church" are introduced in recent books like *God on the Quad* by Naomi Schaefer Riley and *The New Faithful* by Colleen Carroll. Both books reveal that this new generation of college students is very different from the last in terms of embracing a new religious orthodoxy. A survey cited in Carroll's book suggests that this new generation of young Catholics embrace "key tenets of an orthodox Catholic faith."[20] Many of these young Catholics are seeking a traditional religious experience on their campuses. Most recently, a group of students at Georgetown University have asked the Director of Campus Ministry to add a Catholic Tridentine Mass for the "more than 50 students who support this request." The Tridentine Mass is a traditional Mass that is said in Latin, and allows more time for private prayer, reflection and contemplation. The use of the Tridentine Mass nearly disappeared after the Second Vatican Council and the creation of the new Mass in the vernacular, but Pope Benedict XVI reaffirmed the legitimacy of the Tridentine Mass in a recent apostolic letter. An article published in *The Hoya*, indicated that some Georgetown students are already attending the traditional Mass at St. Mary, Mother of God Church in Chinatown and claim that they are "already excluded from the Georgetown community."[21]

And, it is not only Catholic students who are drawn to religious colleges in a search for meaning in their lives. In an interview published in *The New Faithful*, Ethics Professor Jean Bethke-Elshtain noted that "the rebellion against relativism" among her students is quite noticeable. Elshtain has detected among her students "a sort of quest for some kind of purpose or meaning . . . I think something is afoot."[22] A recent University of California, Los Angeles survey on spirituality in higher education found 75 percent of all undergraduates were "searching for meaning or purpose in life," and 78 percent claim to discuss religion openly with their friends. There seems to be a seeking for something more from religion—not just an empty spirituality, but strong moral direction. Schaefer Riley calls those who seek out religious colleges the "missionary generation" because they refuse to accept the sophisticated ennui of their contemporaries. "They snub the spiritual but not religious answers to life's most difficult questions. And, they rebuff the intellectual relativism of their professors and the moral relativism of their peers."[23]

Whether this missionary generation will have an impact, remains to be seen because at the same time the "new faithful" are arriving on Catholic campuses, they are finding an increasingly faithless faculty culture in which Christian professors are discriminated against and religious viewpoints have been crowded out by feminism and multiculturalism.[24] In a recent interview for *The Chronicle of Higher Education*, George Marsden, a professor of history at the University of Notre Dame and the author of *The Soul of the American University: From Protestant Establishment to Established Nonbelief*, acknowledges that "conservative religious views can be a strike against you if you are early in your academic career." Yet, Marsden maintains that it is not the religious views themselves that eliminate people from the academy, rather it is politics that are the primary factor.[25]

And, while it is difficult to claim widespread discrimination against faithful faculty members, it is clear that the academy itself can be a difficult place for any committed Christian. A 2006 national survey of professors published in *The Chronicle of Higher Education* revealed that while most professors believed in at least the possibility of God's existence, "they were more than twice as likely to be skeptics or atheists as the general population."[26] Citing the surge in successful books celebrating atheism, including the *New York Times* best selling *God Is Not Great: How Religion Poisons Everything* by Christopher Hitchens, as well as Daniel Dennett's *Breaking the Spell*, Richard Dawkins' *The God Delusion*, and most recently, *The End of Faith* by Sam Harris, Professor Carlin Romano recently wrote that "atheism is on a roll, if not a holy roll." Romano describes the success of such books as "a sign of widespread resentment among nonbelievers over the influence of religion in the world.[27] Religion writer Rachel Zoll writes that "atheists like Hitchens are tired of believers using fairy tales posing as divine scripture to justify their lust for power. . . . a lot of people in this country are fed up with endless lectures by bogus clerics and endless bullying."[28] Romano suggests that "when believers start to use sacred texts to oppress, the atheist must attack and reject the 'divine' aspect of their books out of self defense and because it interferes with the individual's freedom and conscience and behavior."[29]

Even among Catholics themselves there remains great diversity of opinion on such issues as homosexuality, women's ordination, and abortion. While official Catholic teachings prohibit these activities, these teachings are contested by Catholics who are themselves gay or lesbian, advocates of women's ordination, or pro-choice on abortion. For these Catholics, doctrine is viewed as a social construct contingent on the specific historical, cultural, and institutional contexts in which it emerges. For this group of Catholics, Catholicism is grounded in the view that interpretive authority is diffuse: "It is not located solely in the official hierarchical power structure, but is dispersed, seen in the everyday interpretive activities of ordinary Catholics."[30]

The belief that Catholic doctrine is a "site of contested knowledge" emerged with the Second Vatican Council. Convened by a beloved Pope John XXIII, the council met between 1962 and 1965, caused a revolution in Catholic parish life and liturgy—and what some have called an "epoch-making act of liberalization" within the Church.[31] As Yale sociologist, Michele Dillon points out, "the strong consensus among sociologists, historians and theologians is that Vatican II redefined the Church from a rigidly hierarchical, authoritarian, imperialist, anti-modern institution to one that has become more relevant to and engaged in the modern world."[32] The documents of Vatican II stressed that the Church is not merely the clergy, but the entire People of God. But, for orthodox Catholics, the reforms of Vatican II opened the door to a dismissal of the authority of the Church itself.

All of this has contributed to what has become a protracted culture war on Catholic campuses. And, like all culture wars, as sociologist, Herbert Blumer often reminded us, it is the interaction among people that defines the situation. The campus culture war is a reflection of the greater culture war between those who assert that there are no truths—only readings—and those who still believe that the truths have been revealed and require constant rereading and application. It is a war between those who believe that the Church is a site of oppression for women, gay men, and lesbians—and those who are faithful to the Church's teachings on abortion and sexual morality. But, most importantly, it is a war between those who are dedicated to the negation of the authority of scripture and the hierarchy of the Church, and those who are proposing a renaissance of the Catholic intellect and a renewed appreciation for the continued contributions of the Catholic Church itself. The following chapters will analyze some of the battles in this culture war—the casualties and the triumphs—as one side seeks liberation from an oppressive past, and the other side remains committed to reclaiming a traditional Catholic identity on their campuses.

Notes

1. John Tracy Ellis. "American Catholics and the Intellectual Life." *Thought* 30 (Autumn, 1955): 351-388.
2. Philip Gleason, *Contending with Modernity: Catholic Higher Education in the Twentieth Century.* (New York: Oxford University Press, 1995): 290.
3. Ibid.
4. Ellis. "American Catholics and the Intellectual Life."
5. Gleason. *Contending with Modernity,* 290.
6. *ISI Guide 2006: Choosing the Right College.* (Wilmington, DE: ISI Books, 2006): 696.
7. Rev. John I. Jenkins. C. S. C. "Closing Statement on Academic Freedom and Catholic Character." April 5, 2006: http://president.nd.edu/closingstatement/
8. David Solomon. "A President's Retreat." *The Wall Street Journal.* (April 14, 2006): www.opinionjournal.com/taste/?id=110008239
9. Burton Bollag. "Mourning a Pope Who Stressed Orthodoxy." *The Chronicle of Higher Education* 51 (April 15, 2005): A-1.
10. Ibid.
11. Joseph Epstein. *Envy.* (New York, New York: Oxford University Press, 2003), 80.
12. Christopher Jencks and David Riesman. *The Academic Revolution.* (New Brunswick, NJ: Transaction Publishers, 1968), 405
13. Administrative presentation to meeting for the Sociology faculty. University of San Diego. September, 2006.
14. Joseph Rago. "Status Reporter: The Weekend Interview with Tom Wolfe." *The Wall Street Journal.* (March 11, 2006).
15. Beth McMurtrie. "Catholic Colleges Fail to Impart Church's Teachings, Study's Author Says." *The Chronicle of Higher Education* 49 (March 21, 2003): A 38.
16. Ibid.
17. Scott Jaschik. "Evangelical Pruning Ahead?" *Inside Higher Education.* (November 3, 2005): www.insidehighered.com
18. Jencks and Riesman. *The Academic Revolution,* 405.
19. Michael Rose. *Benedict XVI: The Man Who Was Ratzinger.* (Dallas, TX: Spence, 2005).
20. Cited by Collen Carroll. *The New Faithful: Why Young Adults are Embracing Orthodoxy.* (Chicago, IL: Loyola Press, 2002), 5.
21. Elizabeth Blazey. "Students Push for Addition of Latin Mass." *The Hoya.* (October 23, 2007): www.thehoya.com/news/102307/news3.cfm
22. Cited by Carroll. *The New Faithful,* 7.
23. Naomi Schaefer Riley. *God on the Quad: How Religious Colleges and the Missionary Generation are Changing America.* (New York: St. Martin's Press, 2005), 8.
24. Thomas Bartlett. "Some Evangelicals Find the Campus Climate Chilly—But is That About Faith or Politics?" *The Chronicle of Higher Education* 54 (September 28, 2007): B-6.
25. Ibid.
26. Neil Gross and Solon Simmons. "How Religious Are America's College and University Professors?" Working Paper published October 5, 2006 online at: www.wjh.harvard.edu/soc/faculty/gross/religions.pdf, *The Chronicle of Higher Education.* (October 20, 2006).
27. Carlin Romano. "Are Sacred Texts Sacred? The Challenge for Atheists." *The Chronicle of Higher Education* 54 (September 21, 2007): B-11.

28.   Ibid.
29.   Ibid.
30.   Michele Dillon. *Catholic Identity: Balancing Reason, Faith, and Power.* (New York: Cambridge University Press, 1999), 10.
31.   Philip Jenkins. *The New Anti-Catholicism: The Last Acceptable Prejudice.* (New York: Oxford University Press, 2003), 49.
32.   Dillon. *Catholic Identity,* 47.

1

Early Concerns about Secularization and Status

It is difficult, looking back over the history of Catholic higher education, to be able to say exactly when the culture wars emerged on Catholic campuses. Some historians point to the 1960s as the beginning of the end for Catholic higher education—mostly because of the residual effects of major cultural changes that affected all institutions. The sixties ushered in a new religious pluralism, the sexual revolution, the civil rights movement, the protests over the war in Vietnam, and most importantly, the questioning of the authority of social institutions like the Church. It was a time when Catholics, formerly part of an inner city "immigrant Church," began to move out of Catholic ghettos and achieve upward mobility and higher status in the suburbs. And, as Catholic historian, David O'Brien points out, it was when a popular pope, John XXIII, assembled Church leaders in 1962 for the Second Vatican Council. As this council, with its call to renewal and reform, intersected with the social transformation of what had been the American immigrant Church, the pace of change was astonishing—and unsettling—as Catholics began to question their own relationships with the Church, and the Church's relationship with its colleges.[1]

All of these events surely had an impact on Catholic colleges. Still, it is far too easy to blame the liberalizing trends within society and the Church that began in the sixties for all of the problems with Catholic higher education today. The truth is that concerns about secularization and status surrounded the earliest Catholic colleges. Patterned on the sixteenth century Jesuit plan of study, *Ratio Studiorum,* the curriculum at Georgetown, founded in 1789, the first Catholic College in the country, was comprised of three successive stages: humanistic, philosophical, and theological. Students were required to develop the ability to speak Latin fluently and "with persuasive power" as it was a practical necessity for advancement in lay, as well as clerical, careers.[2] But even in these early days, the stress on philosophy and the classical languages including Greek and Latin was viewed dismissively by secular academic leaders. In his book on the history of Catholic colleges, Philip Gleason recalls that in 1896, the President of Harvard, Charles W. Eliot, publicly humiliated Catholic colleges by publishing an article in *Atlantic Monthly* that compared the Catholic college curriculum to the most backward educational system of the Moslem countries: "where the Koran prescribes the perfect education, to be administered to all children alike." Eliot complained that in this type of education, "the only mental power cultivated is the memory." Having instituted a system of electives at Harvard more than a decade before, Eliot was especially critical of the "uniform education found in the curriculum of the Jesuit colleges, which has remained almost unchanged for four hundred years, disregarding some trifling concessions made to natural science." And, in a mocking attack on Catholicism, Eliot concludes: "That these examples are ecclesiastic is not without significance . . . Direct revelation from on high would be the only satisfactory basis for a uniform, prescribed school curriculum."[3]

While the Harvard president's article contained the most publicly devastating attack of Catholic colleges at the time, the sentiments it contained were part of a common response from secular academic leaders. What was somewhat more surprising was the attack on Catholic colleges from Catholic college leaders themselves. Even today, assessing the progress of Catholic colleges, Rev. Theodore Hesburgh, President Emeritus of the University of Notre Dame, acknowledges that while some Catholic colleges come close, "there has not been in recent centuries a truly great Catholic university, recognized universally as such." While Fr. Hesburgh, who stepped down in 1987 after thirty-five years as head of Notre Dame, acknowledges that although some Catholic colleges have made progress, "one would have hoped that history would have been different when one considers the Church's early role in the founding of the first great universities in the Middle Ages: Paris, Oxford, Cambridge, Bologna, and others."[4]

Unlike Harvard's Charles Eliot, who was critical of the Catholic college plan of study, Fr. Hesburgh is most critical of the Catholic college's historic relationship to the Church itself. In Fr. Hesburgh's opinion, the early European universities in the Middle Ages were great because they encouraged a culture of freedom and independence from the state as well as from the authority of the Catholic Church. Claiming that, unlike

American Catholic universities, these early colleges provided "an atmosphere of free and often turbulent clashing of conflicting ideas, where a scholar with a new idea theological, philosophical, legal, or scientific, had to defend it in the company of peers, without interference from the pressures and powers that neither create nor validate intellectual activities."[5] In Hesburgh's book, *The Challenge and Promise of the Catholic University,* the theme of independence from the "external authority" of the Church is clear. For Hesburgh, "The best and only traditional authority in the university is intellectual competence . . . It was great wisdom in the medieval church to have university theologians judged solely by their theological peers in the university . . . A great Catholic university must begin by being a great university that is also Catholic."[6]

Fr. Hesburgh's status strivings are clear in the first pages of his book on Catholic higher education as he states that in order to become a "great" Catholic university, the university must first be a "great university" that happens to be Catholic. Few questioned this statement of distancing from the Church because until recently, Fr. Hesburgh's musings were simply accepted as "fact" because of his own high status in the academy and beyond. The recipient of more than 150 honorary degrees, the most ever awarded to one person, Fr. Hesburgh became the first person from higher education to be awarded the United States Congressional Gold Medal in 2000. Fr. Hesburgh has held sixteen presidential appointments over the years involving him in civil rights, peaceful uses of atomic energy, campus unrest, and immigration reform—including the United States policy of amnesty for immigrants in the mid-1980s. Fr. Hesburgh was the first priest ever elected to the Board of Directors at Harvard University and served two years as president of the Harvard Board. He also served as a director of the Chase Manhattan Bank. A longtime champion of nuclear disarmament, Fr. Hesburgh has served on the Board of the United States Institute of Peace and helped organize a meeting of scientists and representative leaders of six faith traditions who called for the elimination of nuclear weapons.

On many occasions, Fr. Hesburgh found himself the first Catholic priest to serve in a given leadership position on boards of secular organizations. Much of his success can be viewed as stemming from his ability to distance himself from the authority of the Church and sometimes from its teachings. Such was the case during the years he served as a trustee, and later, Chairman of the Board of the Rockefeller Foundation, a frequent funder of causes counter to Church teachings.[7] His appointment as ambassador to the 1979 UN Conference on Science and Technology for

Development was the first time a priest had served in a formal diplomatic role for the United States government.[8]

One of the ways in which Catholic college faculty and administrators have achieved higher status has been to take the route chosen by Fr. Hesburgh—by publicly embracing the social gospel on civil rights and social justice and by distancing themselves from those teachings less acceptable to the liberal establishment on sexual morality and reproductive rights. But, this distancing was not always the case. Long before Fr. Hesburgh became the authority on Catholic higher education, the founders of the earliest Catholic colleges were not willing to disregard the moral underpinnings of the Church to achieve higher status. In fact, in their founding years, the primary aim of Catholic colleges was to keep the faith alive and spread the faith to others. Not unlike the founding mission of Harvard, Yale, and Princeton, the basic purpose of the first Catholic colleges included preparing young men for the clergy, creating centers for missionary activity, and cultivating the moral virtues.[9] It was not that the earliest Catholic colleges were unconcerned about academic excellence, it was just that the intellectual life of the university was always assumed to be connected to the moral mission of the university.

Although the founding purpose of Catholic colleges did not differ significantly from the earliest American colleges, including Harvard, Yale, Dartmouth, Williams, and Bowdoin (all founded before 1800 by the Congregationalists) historians maintain that there were essential differences in structure and curriculum. While other American colleges followed the English model, which separated secondary and collegiate work, the Catholic college adhered to the French and German models that combined secondary school and college. Strongly Jesuit, this model promoted the basic purpose of Catholic higher education.[10] In terms of status, however, such a model was "so definitely out of date as to mark such places as behind the times and academically inferior."[11]

In an attempt to address these issues of inferiority, the Catholic University of America was founded in 1889 to serve as a national center for scholarship, teaching, research, and the integration of faith and science. Yet, from the outset, political turmoil and conflict overshadowed the university. Most historians maintain that the main cause for the division related to the tension within the Church over the issues of Americanism and modernism.[12] Americanism, one of the emerging strains of intellectual thought at this time, suggested that the Church should accept the best of modern thinking, integrate it with traditional belief, and use the newly constructed belief system for the Church's evangelical mission. Modernism attempted to examine philosophy, theology, and biblical exegesis in light of modern thought and research.[13] The Church rejected both Americanism and modernism and in some ways "galvanized American Catholic higher education around a new unifying purpose: the promotion of Scholasticism and the formulation of an American Catholic culture as an antidote to modernism."

Throughout the first century of Catholic higher education, the philosophy of St. Thomas Aquinas was the "official philosophy" of American Catholic higher education.[14] Confronted with the question, "How are we to reconcile reason with revelation, science with faith, philosophy with theology?" the scholastics responded with reason. They applied dialectic to the study of nature, of human nature, and of supernatural truth. Scholasticism provided a synthesis of faith and reason that made Catholic education distinctive. Far from deprecating reason, the scholastics went as far as one can go in applying reason to the discussion of the dogmas of faith. They acknowledged the authority of revelation yet this authority did not undermine reason. Rather, in philosophy and in natural science the scholastics taught that the argument from authority is the weakest of all arguments as the scholastic were critical of anyone who "styled philosophy as the handmaid of theology."[15] Because it offered salvation from the erosion of spiritual, intellectual, and human values, Scholasticism provided a "unity of purpose in Catholic colleges not present at other church-related institutions."[16] Catholic University dedicated a School of Philosophy to Aquinas in 1895 in the midst of the high point of the Catholic Scholasticism. And, even today, orthodox Catholic colleges like Thomas Aquinas College in Santa Paula, California draw from Scholasticism to inform their classic curriculum.

In his history of Catholic colleges, Gleason points out that structural differences followed philosophical differences between secular and sectarian colleges as the early model of Catholic higher education rejected the idea of electives, claiming that a Scholastic classical education stressing philosophy was the only path to excellence. However, the pressure to conform to the demands of secular accrediting agencies and secular graduate schools became intense at the turn of the century. By 1898, President Eliot's Harvard dropped several Catholic schools from its approved list of institutions whose graduates could be admitted to its law school without taking an entrance examination. Boston College and Holy Cross were among the schools affected. Catholic colleges continued to decline in public esteem, even among Catholics, while the world of secondary and higher education was becoming transformed.[17] A major reason for

this was due to the fact that by the mid-1890s, Harvard's entrance requirements began to be expressed in "points" and the New York Regents
began using "academic counts" about the same time. "Unit" became
the standard term for high school and college requirements after it was
adopted by the Carnegie Foundation for the Advancement of Teaching,
which was established in 1905. Carnegie exerted a powerful influence on
colleges and universities by refusing to extend funding through its grants
program to Catholic colleges since they did not meet its standards by using
"units." Gleason maintains that Carnegie's actions directly contributed
to the secularization of higher education by this discriminatory policy.
For Gleason, "one could hardly ask for clearer evidence of the linkage
between modernization and secularization than that policy."[18]

The shift to quantitative standards rather than qualitative measures
of a student's academic progress prevalent in Catholic colleges was
promoted also by the regional accrediting agencies. The North Central
Association of Colleges and Secondary Schools as well as accrediting
agencies in New England, the Middle Atlantic States, and the South concerned themselves with the problem of articulation between secondary
and collegiate institutions. In 1901, North Central created a Commission
on Accredited Schools, and by 1913 the machinery of accreditation had
become bureaucratized and the standards heavily quantified. All of this
forced Catholic colleges to rationalize and coordinate their educational
operations.[19] Although high schools began to be separated out as a distinct
institutional stage before Catholic colleges could achieve parity with their
secular counterparts, the far greater change in Catholic higher education
was the restructuring of the curriculum to allow electives. At one of the
first meetings of the newly created Catholic Educational Association,
Notre Dame graduate Fr. James Burns, a member of the Congregation
of the Holy Cross, echoed Harvard's accusation that "Catholic colleges,
in their adamant resistance to the system of electives, were in the company of the nation's most backward institutions of higher education."[20]
By 1919, Fr. Burns moved to the presidency of Notre Dame where in a
single three-year term, he is viewed by Gleason as "guiding an academic
revolution that put the university on the path to pre-eminence."[21] The
cost of that pre-eminence was the adoption of the elective system and
the beginning of the abandonment of the Scholastic classical emphasis.
The Jesuits were resistant to moving to the elective system but allowed
each province to adapt their curriculum to local conditions. Ironically,
unlike today's strong liberal leanings, the Jesuits affiliated with Catholic
higher education in the 1800s and early 1900s were aligned with the

conservatives in the Church, while Catholic University and the other non-Jesuit schools were viewed as "bastions of Americanist liberalism."[22] Not surprisingly, eventually it was status concerns that brought the Jesuits closer to the American model as "the Jesuits leaders belatedly awoke to the realization that, in terms of true collegians, their schools were in most cases well nigh deserted."[23]

Concerns about secularization and loss of identity re-emerged, however, as one of the speakers at the meetings of the Catholic Educational Association lamented that to most Catholics, scholastic philosophy had become a name and nothing more.[24] By 1926, the Association of Catholic Colleges was so concerned about the loss of a Catholic identity that the group called for a revitalization of Scholastic philosophy as the means to reinforce Catholic religious identity. The association was especially concerned that colleges were beginning to move away from their Catholic roots by engaging too much with the modern world. One of those with the most public concerns was Notre Dame's own Fr. Burns. Considering the leading role he played in encouraging upward mobility through the movement of modernization, the abrupt turnaround by Fr. Burns is of particular interest to historians. Gleason points out that "writing in 1926, Fr. Burns revealed his concern that having adopted the ideals of the big secular colleges in almost all matters outside religion, Catholics were in danger of losing their distinctive insight or instinct as to the fundamental character of higher cultural education."[25]

In a two-part article on the triumphs and failures of Catholic colleges published in the Catholic journal *Commonweal,* Fr. Burns described what he saw as the over-emphasis on the social aspect of Catholic college life and warned against the application of materialism. But, most surprising to historians like Gleason was Fr. Burns' newly discovered appreciation for the importance of classical studies as the best curricular means of preserving the cultural goals of a Catholic college education. Concerned about the impending slide to secularization, Burns recalled that, "In Scholasticism, the medieval universities had produced a philosophical justification for faith and a defense against skepticism that dominated higher education for as long as Europe was Catholic. Its displacement paved the way for educational trends that were gravely at variance with Catholic principles of life and morality."[26]

Gleason views the "recovered" scholastic, Fr. Burns, as "coming closer than any of his contemporaries to providing an explicit articulation of the systemic relationship that evolved in the 1920s between the Catholic intellectual revival and Catholic higher education." So great was its influence that, by 1930, it had become commonplace for Catholic educators to stress the ideological function of Scholasticism and its role in providing a rational justification for faith. And, as a result, there were the beginnings of what Gleason calls a "Catholic Renaissance" as Scholasticism once again became regarded as providing the rational ground for faith—and education was the means to the end—for Catholics that end is the salvation of souls. The role of philosophy was to "guide the students in the right way of thinking about the truths necessary to reach that end."[27] Theology or religious studies, on the other hand, had not yet achieved the status of a full-fledged academic subject. In fact, until the middle of the twentieth century, the purpose of theology was as an aid in spiritual formation for students through prayer and devotional practices. All of this was viewed as much more important than intellectual mastery of doctrine—and in stark contrast to today's critical and comparative perspective in most Catholic college theology departments. While there were courses in "apologetics" or "evidences of Christianity" the real goal of theology throughout the first half of the 1900s was to help students integrate their lives around identification with Christ.

While some historians view the period from 1930 to 1960 as "the heyday of the institutional Church" for its numerical growth, organizational vigor, and spiritual vitality—including movements for workers and the poor—other historians point to signs of trouble on these campuses.[28] In 1934 Xavier and the University of Detroit both lost their accreditation and although the Jesuits protested against the North Central accrediting body for their decision, status concerns continued to mount, and Catholic colleges attempted to gain upward mobility by adding graduate programs. As Sr. Alice Gallin, a Catholic college administrator, summarized the search for status: "Just as the way for the academic man to get ahead was to earn the doctorate, the way for an institution to get ahead was to offer it. There is no man who does not need to climb. Neither apparently are there many institutions. In the educational system, climbing means getting into the big leagues of graduate, and especially doctoral study."[29]

By 1940, twenty-four Catholic institutions enrolled a total of 7,258 graduate students. World War II had an even greater impact on the institutional side of Catholic higher education as the requirements of a wartime mobilization dictated concentration on scientific and technical education. Electives continued to be added as philosophy declined. At the same time, "the triumph of totalitarianism in Europe confirmed the need for humanistic education that would deepen in young Americans an understanding of, and respect for, the intellectual and moral traditions on which western civilization rested."[30] These events led to a growing interest and attraction to the liberal arts and what came to be called "general education" on all campuses. As might be expected, upwardly mobile Catholic campuses became attracted to the argument put forward in the 1947 *Harvard Report: General Education in a Free Society.* The dean at Catholic University called for "a redefinition of the aims and methods of liberal arts education," hinting broadly that such a statement should take realistic note of the fact that young people had to prepare themselves for gainful employment—beyond the clergy.[31]

The commitment to Scholasticism once again began to lose favor as anti-Catholic sentiments grew throughout the 1950s. Gleason believes that such sentiments were best understood as a "backlash against what was regarded as undue Catholic influence in politics, public morality, and general social policy."[32] By 1955, with the publication of Monsignor Ellis' essay on the inferiority of Catholic colleges, there was a renewed focus on the failure of Catholics to contribute to American intellectual life. And, in 1958, the decision was finally made to remove the course of studies in Latin at Boston College, and permission was given by Jesuit Provincials to eliminate the classical language requirement in any of the twenty-seven Jesuit colleges and universities that thought it best.[33] This ended the last vestige of the classical tradition that defined Catholic colleges.

By the end of the decade of the fifties, Scholasticism had been so thoroughly discredited on Catholic campuses that any academic who dared "speak its name" risked ridicule. In fact, the chairman of DePaul University's philosophy department made *Time* magazine by deriding "the closed system Thomists who still shadowbox the ghosts of the 13th century."[34] It is possible that Scholasticism itself became a casualty of the pursuit of upward mobility as even Gleason suggests that "a too exclusive emphasis on Thomism could still count heavily against a Catholic institution seeking approval for a chapter of Phi Beta Kappa."[35] Notoriously biased against Catholic applications, Phi Beta Kappa gave the "disproportionate place of philosophy," which effectively reduced the number of electives students might take, as the grounds for turning down Boston College for membership as late as 1962.[36] It is also possible that Scholasticism became an inconvenient reminder of moral absolutes in an emerging sixties culture of tolerance for diversity in lifestyle and a growing cultural relativism. As the new decade dawned, Scholasticism became more inconvenient than ever because it provided an embarrassing reminder of what increasingly became viewed as provincial Catholic teachings on sexual morality. The emerging liberation movement for women's rights—including reproductive rights, along with the demands from an increasingly politically powerful gay rights movement—could not easily co-exist with a philosophy that stressed moral absolutes.

Upward mobility and status concerns began to affect individual Catholics. By the early sixties, the Catholic Church was no longer predominantly an immigrant Church—and Catholicism began to contain diverse social classes. While Catholics still remained underrepresented in top business and professional jobs, they occupied many of the same occupations as Protestants.[37] For these newly middle-class Catholics, the religion itself had promoted much of the self-denial and disciplined attitudes required for success in a highly organized society as the Church in general and Catholic education in particular had been vehicles of Americanization and upward mobility. Sociologists Christopher Jencks and David Riesman pointed out that "a Catholic elite began to emerge that was American first and Catholic second."[38] Anti-communism in the fifties had given Catholics an evil to defeat—and an opportunity to show they were real Americans. While Hungarian, Polish, and German Catholics may have been anti-communist because of what they had experienced in their homelands, Jencks and Riesman wrote in 1968 in *The Academic Revolution*, "the Irish Catholics seemed more often to be anti-communist because it was a useful club with which to beat the Anglo-American Establishment, made up of men like Acheson, Marshall, and Hiss."[39] Indeed, Daniel P. Moynihan suggested that "anti-communism gave the Fordham men in the FBI a chance to get even with the Harvard men in the State Department and the White House."[40]

Once they had established their American credentials, the next generation was ready to move on. Indeed, Gleason points to a "perfect storm" in the sixties of academic, social and Church currents that rocked Catholic colleges. "The priority of individual conscience over the law diffused itself . . . Catholics may have been particularly susceptible to the message because of the modernizing trends at the Second Vatican Council. It legitimated change, it reinforced assimilative tendencies, with its emphasis on religious freedom, collegiality, ecumenism, pastoral approaches and openness to the modern world."[41] These changes intersected with faculty demands for academic freedom, fewer clergy and women religious groups on campus, coeducation, more faculty, and student participation in university governance, growing liberation movements on campus and off, and the complete abandonment of the Scholastic approach. While

Catholic colleges had been accused of being "too Catholic" in the fifties, the charge in the sixties and beyond was that the institutions were not Catholic enough.

In 1967 Gleason's "perfect storm" reached maximum strength at the meeting of Catholic academic leaders in Land O' Lakes, Wisconsin where a crucial statement on the nature of the Catholic University emerged. The opening paragraph of the 1500-word statement began: "To perform its teaching and research function effectively the Catholic university must have a true autonomy and academic freedom in the face of authority of whatever kind, lay or clerical, external to the academic community itself."[42] While liberal academics, like Holy Cross College historian David O'Brien, nostalgically look back on the Land O' Lakes gathering with great fondness—as a kind of "Catholic Woodstock" for professors and administrators anticipating independence from the authority of the Church—Gleason described the Land O' Lakes statement a "symbolic manifesto" that marked a new era in Catholic higher education.[43] Within the next few years most Catholic colleges moved to laicize their boards of trustees. Some colleges went even further. Manhattanville College of the Sacred Heart and Webster College publicly and officially declared themselves "no longer Catholic." Manhattanville promptly dropped part of their name, deleting the now too-Catholic sounding "College of the Sacred Heart." Webster, under the direction of the Sisters of Loretto, was not only the earliest Catholic college to announce that it was choosing to relinquish its Catholic identity, its president, Sister Jacqueline Grennan, S. L., renounced her religious vows and withdrew from her own religious order to become a lay leader so that she too could function as president of the now secular institution "without the embarrassment of being subject to religious obedience."[44] Described as "the media's favorite new nun," and by Jencks and Riesman as belonging to the "unusually magnanimous Sisters of Loretto," Grennan pronounced that "the very nature of higher education is opposed to juridical control by the Church."[45]

Indeed, concerns about upward mobility were so high during the sixties and seventies that any hint of obedience to the authority of the Church became an embarrassment. And although many of the Jesuit colleges and, of course, Notre Dame, maintained that members of their founding religious orders would continue to hold the office of the president of what became increasingly secular institutions, many of those colleges that had been founded by women from religious congregations were more than eager to turn the leadership over to lay leaders as women's colleges increasingly merged with men's and co-education became the norm. Having abandoned their earlier preoccupation with integrating the curriculum around a core of philosophy and theology, Catholic colleges entered the final decades of the twentieth century by devoting themselves to the pursuit of academic excellence.[46] Unfortunately, as Gleason points out, "excellence" became increasingly defined as the way things were done at Harvard. This was a fateful decision for Catholic higher education.

Notes

1.   David J. O'Brien. *From the Heart of the American Church: Catholic Higher Education and American Culture.* (Maryknoll, NY: Orbis Books, 1994), 21.
2.   Philip Gleason. *Contending With Modernity: Catholic Higher Education in the Twentieth Century.* (New York: Oxford University Press, 1995) 5.
3.   James Turnstead Burtchaell. *The Dying of the Light.* (Grand Rapids, MI: Eerdmans, 1998), 569.
4.   Theodore M. Hesburgh (editor). *The Challenge and Promise of a Catholic University.* (Notre Dame, IN: University of Notre Dame Press, 1994), 1-2.
5.   Ibid.
6.   Ibid. 5.
7.   The Rockefeller Foundation remains one of the top ten US funders of population, reproductive health, and reproductive rights work throughout the world. Concentrating on international initiatives that focus on contraception, abortifacients, sterilization, and abortion legalization—all counter to the teachings of the Catholic Church, the Rockefeller Foundation, under the leadership of Fr. Hesburgh and beyond, has attempted to change the moral and religious values and practices of people, especially Catholic people, throughout the world.
8.   University of Notre Dame Website. Hesburgh Biography: www.nd.edu/aboutnd/about/history/hesburgh bio.shtml
9.   E. J. Power. *A History of Catholic Higher Education in the United States.* (Milwaukee, WI: The Bruce Publishing Company, 1958), 34.
10.   Patricia Hutchison. "The Purposes of American Catholic Higher Education: Changes and Challenges." December 30, 2001:http://home.comcast.net/~erozycki/Hutchison708F01.html
11.   Gleason. *Contending With Modernity,* 22.
12.   Hutchison. "The Purposes of American Catholic Higher Education."
13.   Gleason. *Contending With Modernity,* 13.
14.   Hutchison. "The Purposes of American Catholic Higher Education."
15   The Catholic Encyclopedia: Scholasticism: www.newadvent.org/cathen/13548a.htm.
16.   George Marsden. *The Soul of the American University: From Protestant Establishment to Established Non-Belief.* (New York: Oxford University Press, 1994): 275.
17.   Gleason. *Contending With Modernity,* 32.
18.   Ibid., 35.
19.   Ibid., 38.
20.   Ibid., 45.
21.   Ibid., 45.
22.   Ibid., 170.
23.   Ibid., 55.
24.   Ibid., 137.

25. Ibid., 139.

26. Ibid., 138.

27. Ibid., 141.

28. *National Catholic Reporter.* "Scholar traces history of Catholic identity of Universities." Catholic News Service. 2005: www.findarticles.com/p/articles/mim1141/is 2 42 /ai n15954415/print.

29. Alice Gallin. *Negotiating Identity: Catholic Higher Education Since 1960.* (Notre Dame, IN, 2000), 98.

30. Gleason. *Contending With Modernity,* 247.

31. Ibid., 249.

32. Ibid., 261.

33. James Turnstead Burtchaell. *The Dying of the Light.* (Grand Rapids, MI: Eerdmans, 1998), 576.

34. Gleason. *Contending With Modernity,* 298.

35. Ibid., 298.

36. Burtchaell. *The Dying of the Light,* 578.

37. Andrew Greeley and Peter Rossi, *The Education of Catholic Americans*, (Chicago, IL: Aldine, 1966), 28.

38. Christopher Jencks and David Riesman. *The Academic Revolution.* (New Brunswick, NJ: Transaction Publishers, 1968), 338.

39. Ibid., 338.

40. Ibid., 338.

41. *National Catholic Reporter.* "Scholar traces history of Catholic identity of Universities." Catholic News Service. 2005: www.findarticles.com/p/articles/mim1141/is 2 42 /ai n15954415/print.

42. Gleason. *Contending With Modernity,* 317.

43. David J. O'Brien. *From the Heart of the American Church: Catholic Higher Education and American Culture.* (Maryknoll, New York: Orbis Books,1994), 58; Also, Gleason. *Contending With Modernity,* 317.

44. Gleason. *Contending With Modernity,* 317.

45. Gleason. *Contending With Modernity, 317.* See also, Jencks and Riesman. *The Academic Revolution*, 346.

46. Philip Gleason. "What Made Identity a Problem?" Included in Theodore Hesburgh, editor. *The Challenge and Promise of a Catholic University.* (Notre Dame, IN: University of Notre Dame Press, 1994), 96.

2

Defining Down the Catholic Identity

As the number and influence of upwardly mobile Catholics grew, one of the most important questions confronting the Catholic colleges was whether the colleges would begin to mirror their Protestant predecessors—remaining Catholic in name only. In 1968, Jencks and Riesman's *The Academic Revolution* pointed out that Catholics were no longer interested in the old ethnic, religious wars of the past or in a Church whose main function was to help them fight on these fronts. Rather, Catholic colleges had two alternatives: One was to change relatively little, continuing to concentrate their resources on first generation collegians from the Catholic ghetto or, attempt to emulate their better-known Protestant predecessors, turning their attention mainly to educating second- and third-generation collegians and to developing a Catholic intelligentsia.[1]

While Jencks and Riesman could not have known in 1968, just how far Catholic colleges were willing to go to achieve upward mobility, they predicted that in order to achieve higher status like the Protestant colleges, Catholic colleges would likely choose to stop being Catholic in any significant sense because ". . . the Catholic upper-middle class may only be willing to enroll in large numbers if their colleges moved from sectarian separatism to denominational secularism, just as the leading Protestant colleges did one hundred years ago."[2] And, although Catholic college administrators denied that it was occurring, the Catholic identity began to be defined down in earnest in 1967—in the days following Land O' Lakes—and has continued unabated until today as Catholic colleges continue to revise their mission statements, the most public pronouncements of their goals, values, and very identities, by first tinkering with the wording and eventually completely deleting references to the Catholic identity of the college itself.

In 1991, after two years of conversations among faculty, staff, Jesuit leaders, students, and members of the board of trustees, the College of the Holy Cross issued a new mission statement that addressed all of the progressive themes of diversity, tolerance, and social justice—but it deleted any reference to the College of the Holy Cross as a "Catholic College." Omitting the word "Catholic" when describing Holy Cross and instead, affirming Holy Cross as a Jesuit college, the new mission statement maintains that "Shared responsibility for the life and governance of the College should lead all its members to make the best of their own talents, to work together, to be sensitive to one another, to serve others and to seek justice within and beyond the Holy Cross community."[3]

History Professor David O'Brien, one of the faculty authors of the Holy Cross mission statement pointed out that the decision to highlight the Jesuit nature rather than the Catholic heritage was a conscious one. In a chapter in his book on Catholic higher education, O'Brien acknowledged the fact that the faculty and staff of Holy Cross are now "religiously and culturally diverse" and claimed that the authors of the new mission statement needed to address this pluralism: "Dialogue requires us to remain open to that sense of the whole which calls us to transcend ourselves and challenges us to seek that which might constitute our common humanity."[4] O'Brien suggests that "for a variety of reasons, I think it better to avoid attaching the word Catholic to the word college. The combination inevitably crates confusion about institutional relationships that inhibits rather than encourages projects that forward its central function—building bridges between faith and culture."[5] For O'Brien, Vatican II opened the door to "other ways in which the word Catholic can be understood."[6]

In an article emphasizing the contrast between the vision of Holy Cross as "a potential Catholic Amherst" held by faculty leaders, with "the defensive posture" of those wishing to maintain the status quo, O'Brien claimed that there were a few members of the Jesuit administration who "insisted that Holy Cross remain visibly Catholic and Jesuit." But, O'Brien was critical of the campus traditionalists' refusal to acknowledge the dramatic changes that were taking place within the Jesuit community itself—in particular, "the commitment to the service of faith and promotion of justice in the context of a preferential option for the poor."[7]

In 1995, Georgetown University attempted to "relate Georgetown's new promise as an academic institution to its heritage as a school founded and administered by Jesuits" by issuing a document intended as a basis for discussion on the Jesuit and Catholic identity of Georgetown.[8]

Claiming that Georgetown had reached a point in its development where it needed to become more reflective about its mission, the report was presented by the authors as "reflecting the view shared by those who participated in the seminar and addressing issues we think need to be addressed by the University as a whole."[9] Entitled "Centered Pluralism" the report makes it clear with the opening paragraph that the Catholic identity is being redefined: "An institution that is increasingly populated by people who are not themselves Catholic can hardly be expected to function in the same manner as one that was largely a Catholic enclave. Either it will redefine its historic role in terms that make sense to a broader range of people, or it will cease playing that role." While the document still stated that Georgetown welcomed "scholars who take the intellectual traditions of Catholicism seriously," the authors made it clear that this "does not mean that Catholic ideas—or the people who advocate them—would be permitted to have a limiting influence on scholarly inquiry and discourse."[10]

Under the Centered Pluralism rubric at Georgetown, Catholic ideas and teachings were no longer allowed to interfere with the work of the faculty, and the Catholic intellectual tradition cannot be privileged any more than any other philosophical perspective—with the exception, of course, of the Catholic traditional commitment to social justice. Like the Holy Cross mission statement, Centered Pluralism reminds readers that "ever since the late 19th century, Catholic teaching has been closely associated with ideas like the living wage." The document also directly addresses Catholic teachings on "morally responsible" university management, which would not allow for downsizing the workforce or contracting out jobs that are related to the academic mission of the university. The authors advocate that from the Centered Pluralism perspective, Georgetown "needs to become more attentive—not less—to the moral claims on its material resources coming from its religious heritage, and it should be prepared to make the resulting policies a defining part of its identity." And, in an obvious nod to faculty concerns, Centered Pluralism reminds others of the strong emphasis in recent Catholic teaching on the importance of participation in governance.[11]

Like the College of the Holy Cross, when issues are favored by the Georgetown faculty—especially issues that favor an increased faculty role in university governance and the imposition of a living wage—there is often a Catholic social teaching that is cited to support it. Yet, when controversial moral issues like the annual production of *The Vagina*

Monologues or a pro-choice honorary degree recipient or dissident graduation speaker is invited to campus, Catholic moral teachings are ignored—or denigrated. In fact, when Cardinal Francis Arinze, a Nigerian prelate and head of the Vatican Congregation for Divine Worship and Discipline of the Sacraments, gave the commencement address at Georgetown in 2003, several faculty members left the stage in protest and many of Georgetown's gay and lesbian students, faculty, and staff walked out of the graduation ceremony. The reason for the protest was that Cardinal Arinze offended the Georgetown community by speaking of the importance of the family to the Catholic Church and cautioned the audience that "In many parts of the world, the family is under siege. It is oppressed by an anti-life mentality as is seen in contraception, abortion, infanticide, and euthanasia. It is scorned and banalized by pornography, desecrated by fornication and adultery, mocked by homosexuality, sabotaged by irregular unions and cut in two by divorce."[12]

Following the graduation, seventy faculty members sent a letter to university officials protesting the cardinal's "inappropriate remarks," and one professor, a former Jesuit priest who now presents himself as a priest of "the American Catholic Church" who blesses gay marriages, was especially offended. A Georgetown dean replied that the cardinal "had not tried to hurt anyone but that doesn't mean it didn't happen" and promised to meet with all those who might have been hurt by the cardinal's words.[13] It would seem that a campus that truly values "Centered Pluralism" might have been open to what is a diverse message of authentic Catholic teachings as a form of pluralism. But, the reality is that pluralism on the Georgetown campus means respect only for the Catholic teachings that the Georgetown faculty agree with.

While it is easy to understand how an increasingly non-Catholic (and sometimes anti-Catholic) upwardly-mobile faculty might have been attracted to the idea of the secularization of the mission statement, it is more difficult to understand how the trustees of Catholic colleges and universities, the very people who have been entrusted with maintaining the mission, allowed such dramatic changes in the mission statements of dozens of colleges like Holy Cross and Georgetown. To understand this redefinition, it is helpful to look closely at the years following Land O' Lakes when status-seeking Catholic college faculty and administrators decided that they needed autonomy from the Church to achieve academic excellence. It was the time when the secularization of Catholic campuses began through the laicization of the leadership—when Catholic colleges like Holy Cross transferred their charters and their property to independent boards of trustees, composed of a majority of laypeople, and shaped a set of statutes that guaranteed academic freedom and independence from the Church or the founding orders.

St. Louis University, founded in 1818 as the second Catholic college in the country, was the first major Catholic university in the country to give laypersons a dominant voice on its board of trustees. The thirteen Jesuit priests who comprised the board of trustees at St. Louis voted to institute the laicization process in 1967 by electing five of the thirteen to remain on the board, including the president and the four vice-presidents, and voted to give equal membership to eighteen laypersons representing various faiths and to five Jesuits from other institutions. They stipulated that the chairman of the board must be a layperson. Reflecting on the first year of lay control, Fr. Paul Reinert, S. J., the president of St. Louis University at the time, found that the new lay-dominated board "surpassed our most optimistic hopes . . . The fourteen businessmen on the board deliberate on the future of the University as seriously as they do on that of their own companies . . . They have made decisions that have helped to strengthen it and keep it on course."[14] When reflecting on the choice of laicization, Fr. Reinert maintains that "We did not change the character of the University as an institution affiliated with the Catholic Church. The move was not one of secularization, under which the university would become a non-sectarian institution, but a drastic reorganization aimed at better achievement of the academic objectives of the university."[15]

While Fr. Reinert can be forgiven for his optimism on the benefits of the laicization since he was writing his book, *The Urban Catholic University,* in 1970, before the destructive effects of secularization were apparent, it is difficult to understand why he thought laypersons could do a more effective job at achieving higher academic status than the Jesuit founders themselves. Some historians believe that it is likely that the potential for new revenue streams offered by affluent lay trustees with business and governmental ties played a more important role than others seem to acknowledge. Like the laicization that occurred in Protestant colleges during the previous century, Jencks and Riesman point out that "businessmen who joined the board were expected to make greater efforts to raise money from their friends than businessmen who were merely members of the alumni association. Conversely, the alumni and other laymen were expected to give more generously to a college controlled by sound business and professional leaders than to one run by presumptively fuzzy minded and financially naïve preachers."[16]

Fr. Reinert echoes this need to enlist affluent and influential business-men. In a section in his book entitled, "Exploitation of Every Source of Financial Support," Fr. Reinert is clear that private colleges and universities had to seek financial support from every source possible—including federal, state, local, and private funding.[17] Complaining that in the past, "crucial financial decisions and projections were being made by a group of men (Jesuits) who typically had little or no direct experience in business transactions, and who, as a matter of fact, had taken the vow of poverty," Fr. Reinert joined Notre Dame's Fr. Hesburgh in the process of laicizing the leadership Catholic higher education.[18] Other Catholic colleges closely followed.

To be fair, many Catholic colleges were indeed faced with a number of challenges during the sixties and seventies—especially financial challenges. Bankruptcy threatened several campuses, especially those women's colleges that resisted co-education and suffered from declining enrollments. Even more alarming, there was an imminent danger that government aid in the form of grants and financial aid to "sectarian" colleges and universities might be declared unconstitutional. Catholic colleges, like their secular counterparts, had grown to depend upon government largesse and the threat of losing such support was a major concern. In *Contending with Modernity*, Philip Gleason suggests that the threat of losing government money was "directly relevant to the trustee question because the kind of formal control exercised over an educational institution by a religious organization was one indicator of sectarianism or its absence."[19] In 1966, the Maryland Court of Appeals ruled in *Horace Mann League v. Board of Public Works of Maryland* that two Catholic women's colleges and a Methodist college were "legally sectarian" and therefore ineligible under the First Amendment to receive aid. The United States Supreme Court declined to review the case, so *Horace Mann* governed legal cases until 1971, when the Supreme Court's decision in *Tilton v. Richardson*, a case involving four Catholic colleges in Connecticut, established a considerably less stringent standard for eligibility. In *Tilton*, the Court ruled in a 5 to 4 decision that the four Connecticut colleges were not "pervasively sectarian" because they were open to non-Catholic students and faculty, that their theology courses were academic and not intended to indoctrinate, and that students were not required to attend religious services.[20]

A final Supreme Court decision related to the perceived need to secularize was again the result of a Maryland case, *Roemer v. Board of*

Public Works and included the three colleges from the *Horace Mann* case together with Loyola and Mount Saint Mary's College. At issue were annual grants to be given by the state of Maryland to qualified private colleges for each student who was a resident of the state. The funds could not be used for sectarian purposes.[21] In another 5 to 4 decision, the Supreme Court ruled once again that church-related colleges and universities were found indistinguishable from other institutions in the independent sector of American higher education and thus eligible for state and federal funding.[22] Catholic college leaders, now intent on secularizing their campuses, interpreted these Supreme Court victories as support for the movement to secularization. Attributing the victory to the fact that between the *Horace Mann* case in 1966 and *Roemer* in 1976, the Catholic colleges had moved their governance structures away from religious community authority, faculty and administrators felt vindicated in their decision for secularization.

Still, in some states, challenges remained and these challenges gave those pursuing secularization more reason to go even further. During the 1960s, many of New York State's private colleges were experiencing financial difficulty and appealed to then Governor Rockefeller for relief. Rockefeller suggested that an unrestricted capitation grant large enough to allow them to survive would also relieve the state of the much larger costs—perhaps ten to twenty times larger—it would incur if private college students transferred to state schools.[23] To help manage the grants, Governor Rockefeller appointed the Select Committee on the Future of Private and Independent Higher Education in New York State, commonly known as the Bundy Committee. A problem arose, however, when the Bundy funds began to be disbursed to Catholic colleges because the New York Constitution's "Blaine Amendment" forbade public appropriations to schools that are "wholly or in part under the control or direction of any religious denomination, or in which any denominational tenet or doctrine is taught."[24] The committee resolved the issue by observing that the majority of private colleges and universities in America "had moved away from their original religious connection, first by replacing clerical control with lay control, then by shifting from denominational to nondenominational until finally becoming plainly secular . . . They noted with satisfaction that Catholic colleges were now moving rapidly through this same evolutionary process from a narrow to a broader self understanding, like Harvard, Columbia, and Cornell."[25]

A trustee at New Rochelle, a New York State Catholic women's college that was desperate for Bundy Committee funds because of their dire financial straits through the sixties and seventies, made what one critic of secularization described as "the most remarkable observation . . . In the midst of an extended board discussion about secular and sectarian issues at New Rochelle, Sr. Borgia, one of the trustees, concluded that their own self understanding was, after all, more important than their public vocabulary." In her observation, Sr. Borgia was simply giving clear voice to what is today a widespread belief that "institutions can maintain one identity privately and another publicly. The college's self-presentation as a secular school infused with a faint religious scent was of course, a bit of a scam, but a scam which would in a brief time dissolve because what was said publicly actually became true . . . The trauma of the Bundy struggle seemed to guarantee that the adjective 'Catholic' would never again precede the noun 'College' at New Rochelle."[26] While one of the leaders of New Rochelle claimed several years later that the only "compromise" New Rochelle made in qualifying for the state funds was to refrain from calling itself a "Catholic College," Notre Dame's former provost, Fr. Burtchaell, responded caustically that "This remark in retrospect sounds like 'peace in our time' in 1938."[27]

In some ways the public-private ploy continues today on many Catholic campuses as they proclaim a Catholic identity for their Bishops, Catholic donors, and concerned Catholic alumni and parents of their students, yet publicly renounce most ties to a Catholic identity in their day to day activities. Many of those who promoted such secularization blame the movement on the need to secularize because of the threats to funding. But Fr. Burtchaell is especially critical of those who continue today to claim that the reason for the slide to secularization was a financial necessity because of concerns about the separation of church and state. His book, *The Dying of the Light: The Disengagement of Colleges and Universities from Their Christian Churches,* points out that on many Catholic campuses, like New Rochelle, the waning centrality of theology and philosophy, the desire to recruit more non-Catholic students and faculty, and the embarrassment about the old ways all were under way long before Bundy funding was even imagined.[28]

Christopher Jencks and David Riesman were saying the exact same thing more than thirty years ago in their important book on the culture wars already evident in Catholic higher education. Indeed, their *Academic Revolution* provides even greater support for Burtchaell's views on the fact that financial concerns did not play the major role in the laicization of the boards of trustees. Writing in the midst of the earliest challenges to state and federal funding in the sixties, Jencks and Riesman write that:

> The logic leading to greater lay control over Catholic education is similar to the logic that led so many Protestant colleges in the same direction over the past century and a half. One of the reasons why Protestant colleges began adding laymen to their boards was that clergymen were frequently identified with one or another side of a sectarian squabble in which the college did not want to take sides. A layman was a safe choice, for his theological views were usually unknown and his bank account non-sectarian. Most Protestant colleges were under financial pressure to attract students from as wide a spectrum of Protestant belief and disbelief as possible, and a lay board played down the sectarian image of the college. Theological disputes among Catholic clerics have seldom reached the same intensity as among nineteenth century Protestants and have never involved appreciable numbers of Catholic laymen. No Catholic college has had to worry about the effect on recruitment of appointing a progressive as against a conservative priest to its board.[29]

While Jencks and Riesman can be forgiven for underestimating the fallout from Vatican II and its unintended consequence of emboldening dissident religious and lay leaders in 1968, their ideas about the reasons for lay leadership have been confirmed by several others. Philip Gleason acknowledged that eligibility for state and federal funds may have played a minor role but, like Jencks and Riesman, maintains that it was surely not the most important role in laicizing the Catholic College. There were several much more important reasons that had more to do with changes in the culture and the Church. In fact, David Riesman and Robert Hassenger pointed out that following the Second Vatican Council, a certain "anti-authoritarian romanticism" emerged among Catholic academics: "They appeared to believe that all of the problems of Catholic universities would disappear if only they were laicized."[30] Dissident religious and lay leaders became increasingly ready to air their views in public and to recruit lay faculty to Catholic colleges for the purposes of expressing views not yet sanctioned by the official Church. Jencks and Riesman echo this perception: "Laymen who would, in an earlier day, have left the Church . . . are today inclined to feel that the Church is not so monolithic, that they can find outspoken clerical allies, that their place in the Church is tolerable, and that they should therefore fight from within."[31]

These conflicts caused deep divisions. Even a supporter of laicization like David O'Brien acknowledges that some of today's problems with Catholic higher education arose with the rapid changes of the sixties and seventies: "In an act of unprecedented trust, religious orders of men and women gave their schools to lay dominated boards of trustees. But, so far there has not been a lot of attention given to the criteria for the selection of trustees, their orientation to Catholic higher education, and their continuing education on issues of importance to Catholic mission and identity."[32] O'Brien points out that the presidents who first laicized their boards admit that, "even though they understood the change as a sharing of responsibility with lay Catholics in the spirit of Vatican II, they selected laypeople on the basis of the skills or experience they could bring to the school: lawyers, benefactors, key alumni, businessmen who could offer specialized advice, such as on investments or insurance."[33] Wealthy donors were highly favored.

This remains true today as a 2005 survey of private college trustees (including all private colleges—not just Catholic colleges) revealed that 52 percent were business executives, 21 percent were professionals including lawyers and physicians, 13 percent were employed in education, and 12 percent were described as "other."[34] A 2007 *Chronicle of Higher Education*-commissioned survey of trustees confirms the continued attempt to recruit wealthy donors to the board. The survey, which gathered data from 1,478 trustees from colleges located in every state and the District of Columbia, revealed that one-fifth of the trustees report incomes of $500,000 or more a year, and an additional 18 percent report yearly incomes of between $250,000 and $500,000.

The average term length for trustees at private colleges is 3.7 years, significantly less than the average term length of 5.4 years for trustees of public colleges. Two trends that are evident indicate that the percentage of trustees at private institutions who are over the age of 50 is now 80 percent, up from 72 percent in 1985. And 13.3 percent of the trustees at private institutions are over the age of 70.[35] Richard Ingram, president of the Association of Governing Boards of Universities and Colleges, believes that the trend toward older trustees is probably inevitable, and not just because society is aging. "Many institutions have come to count more heavily on the philanthropy of board members, an emphasis that has probably influenced institutions to seek out big donors as trustees, many of them older or retired. A governing board's focus on fund raising and the finances of a college has also enhanced the attraction of business savvy trustees. There is a 5 percent increase in the number of trustees who claimed a business affiliation since 1985."[36] While business leaders bring valuable management skills to the position, and attorneys may be able to consult with administrators on personnel and policy issues, they may not necessarily understand or share the mission and values of the founders of the university.

Perhaps the most revealing finding of the 2007 Trustee Survey is that "many board members feel unprepared for the job." Fewer than 15 percent of the trustees considered themselves "very well prepared for what they faced when they joined the board." Four in ten board members described themselves as "slightly" or "not at all prepared" for the job. Among those feeling the least prepared were new and somewhat younger board members, a finding that the survey designers assert "could point to a looming leadership crisis on governing boards as older and more experienced members leave."[37]

The 2007 *Chronicle* survey also indicated that "status concerns" were especially salient for trustees as they gave improvement in their institution's *U. S. News and World Report* rankings significantly more importance than did college presidents in a similar survey. Trustees who are alumni of the college they serve worry significantly more than non-alumni trustees about quality of faculty and higher *U. S. News and World Report* rankings. And, since alumni are significantly over-rep-resented on boards of trustees (comprising 66 percent of the boards of private non-denominational colleges, and 54 percent of private, religious colleges) it is easy to understand how status conscious trustees might pay less attention to the wording of the mission statement than to the published rankings in *Princeton Review* or *U. S. News and World Report*. Considering the fact that many board members indicate that they were unprepared for the position, it is possible that some do not have a clear idea of the mission itself.

Survey designers and analysts warn that "the findings on preparation and the gap between trustees and presidents on key issues may be one reason why so many campus chief executives are under fire these days . . . The presidents don't communicate with their boards enough and in some cases, the boards haven't selected the right person to be president."[38]

Perhaps in an effort to address this need for informed and prepared trustees, one trend among Catholic colleges is the increasing practice of appointing current and former college presidents to the board. In fact, the percentage of current and former college presidents on Catholic col-lege boards is much higher than at other private college boards because Catholic colleges have actually sought such leaders out as members for several decades. This practice cannot help but have some influence on the decisions made by the board. The idea of appointing current college presidents to sit on another institution's governing boards has raised a number of questions especially when the colleges are competitors—drawing from the same demographic pool of potential students. In some cases, it can even raise legal questions. While Richard Ingram claims that "It's an interestingly increasing practice . . . There is a certain measure of comfort that comes from having someone on the board on sticky issues involving the culture of the academy or the nuances of faculty thinking," others question whether the practice is a positive one for creating a truly independent board.[39] Ingram's choice of the word "comfort" is revealing as it suggests that the university president who helps stack the board with presidential colleagues with similar status strivings will have comfortable and congenial allies on the board who will educate the rest of the board on the issues that are "just too complex" for non-academics to understand.

Ideally a board member is going to ask hard questions—but too often, the board members of Catholic colleges and universities have become rubber stamps for the president. This can be a huge problem as the recent corporate scandals involving executives at Enron, Tyco, Adelphia, and others have shown us what can happen when governance fails. The corporate scandals of the past five years have shown us that in too many cases, board members are not independent, as they have been chosen by the very people they are supposed to oversee—the chief executives. In an effort to give investors a greater role in corporate governance, the Securities and Exchange Commission has proposed a number of changes to increase the independence of corporate board members. The move to corporate shareholder democracy, which began with the Sarbanes-Oxley Act of 2002, mandates dozens of new rules and procedures that are intended to strengthen corporate governance. They include more regularly scheduled meetings of independent directors separate from company management, more careful oversight of accounting by the board audit committees, and more potential liability for board members if things go awry. A consensus has finally emerged within the corporate world that board members must be "more informed, more skeptical and more independent."[40] This is just not true with Catholic college oversight.

While they do not have to answer to the same kinds of creditors and investors, there are indeed "stakeholders" in higher education—including donors, faculty members, students, administrators, alumni, and Catholic Church members who have invested their money or time and sometimes even their careers in a college. They too want a return on their investment—or at least they want to know that the institution will not misuse or squander their contributions. When the colleges do not provide this accountability, stakeholders are increasingly demanding that the board of trustees respond.

Too often, however, the board becomes isolated and ends up being micromanaged by the president of the college rather than providing independent oversight. At general board meetings, the president often sets the agenda—including the time allotted to discussion of sometimes uncomfortable topics related to the Catholic identity or the mission of the university. This became clear at an annual retreat for a Catholic college board of the trustees in the late nineties. As was their custom, the mid-winter board retreat was held at a resort in Palm Desert, California, and the long weekend included organized board recreational activities including golf, tennis, barbeques, and dinners. Scheduled for discussion was the outcome of a university-wide values survey that was administered to the faculty, staff, and students the previous fall. The survey had been commissioned by the vice-president of Mission and Ministry in an effort to begin to determine whether the university was fulfilling its mission as a Catholic university. The goal of the survey was to evaluate whether the university was meeting its goals and objectives in terms of its claims to be a "values-based" university. It was the vice-president's intention that the university's board of trustees would be given a complete report and presentation on the outcome of the survey.

Unfortunately, the survey data revealed some disturbing facts for the administration. A significant number of the respondents found the Catholic identity lacking—and some found it altogether absent. Students and staff members were much more likely than faculty to express disappointment in the lack of a Catholic culture on campus. Although most faculty members had little interest in enhancing the Catholic identity, significant numbers of students and staff wanted to see the identity be "more visible."

At the conclusion of the data analysis, the values survey committee prepared a report for the university community and the chair of the values survey committee, a faculty member from the College of Arts and Sciences, prepared an executive summary of the data for the board and a presentation for the board at the Palm Desert retreat. The president of the university scheduled the presentation of the survey data during the hour before lunch and afternoon golf. This would not have been a problem if the president had not spent so much time leading an interactive computer simulation that required the board members to respond to hypothetical challenges that they might someday face in their role as board members. As a result, there was less than thirty minutes left in the morning session to present the outcome of the real (rather than hypothetical) data. Worse, at the start of the faculty presentation on the values survey results, a member of the golf resort staff announced that the box lunches for the golfers were available for pick up in the lobby, and about half of the board members left to prepare for their afternoon golf outing. There was little time for the presentation and no time for questions or discussion.

In addition, there was no time for informal follow-up after the presentation because the faculty presenter was not invited to interact with the board members throughout the weekend. In fact, while the board members and the university administrators, including the president, vice-presidents, and deans, were all housed at the exclusive Palm Desert golf resort, the faculty member was assigned with other university support staff to rooms at a Palm Desert motel three miles away. In this case, by strategically scheduling the presentation and then running out the clock, the president effectively managed to control the information that the board was allowed to hear. And, as any student of management and board relations knows, the trustees will only rise to the level of expectation of the chief executive.

While this is true, the ultimate responsibility must lie within the trustees themselves. While trustees can claim that they are not always given all of the information needed to make decisions, the reality is that under American civil law, the board holds in trust the purposes for which the institution was founded. They need to pursue evidence that the Catholic identity and mission of the university is being implemented. In his book on *The Moral Responsibilities of Trusteeship*, David H. Smith suggests that "the trustee form of governance is defined by loyalty to the purpose for which the organization was created . . . This loyalty is personalized as identification with the particular objectives of the donor or founders. It is a conservative principle in the sense that it inevitably leads to concern with the history of the organization, which should become what Robert Bellah and his colleagues call a 'community of memory.'"[41] Smith maintains that the fiduciary principle establishes the organization's own particularity, slant, or vision and then based on that mission the trustee acts on behalf of the entruster for the benefit of the beneficiary. The trustee is always constrained in some way by the will of the founder or by the purpose for which the organization was created.

Yet, Smith points out that while the fiduciary principle establishes the organization's vision, the trustee is also constrained by general concern for the common good. This principle of the common good forces the trustee to ask whether the organization's purpose is morally worthy and whether the organization is using morally worthy means to accomplish its mission. And, in a surprising move away from the fiduciary principle, Smith proposes that there are times when a Catholic college trustee must move away from the founders' vision in the direction of the common good. As an example of this, Smith describes Catholic University of America's conflict over dissident Catholic theologian Charles Curran.

Smith writes that "Curran was an extremely well known Catholic moral theologian who began teaching at Catholic University in 1965. During the late '60s as Vatican II came to a close, Curran's controversial views on sexual ethics became a major focus of controversy at Catholic University. Favoring liberal views on reproductive and homosexual rights, Curran brought attention to himself through his writings and public speeches. In response to such dissidence, the Catholic University trustees voted not to renew his contract in 1967." [42] But, the faculty was furious about what they interpreted as a violation of Curran's academic freedom. They protested, a strike was called, and the university was effectively shut down. The trustees responded by renewing Curran's contract and giving him a promotion. A year later, when Curran publicly rejected the papal encyclical on birth control, *Humanae Vitae,* the trustees began a second unsuccessful attempt to remove him from the faculty. Smith writes that "Partly in response to these events, Catholic University reformed its policies to clarify and reaffirm its identity as an American research university."[43]

By 1971 Curran was awarded tenure and was promoted once again at Catholic University but the controversies continued as he escalated his criticisms of Church teachings on sexual morality and reproductive rights. In response, the Vatican's Office of the Sacred Congregation for the Doctrine of the Faith headed by then-Cardinal Ratzinger, investigated, and in 1985 urged Curran to reconsider his views. When this was unsuccessful, Cardinal Ratzinger offered a compromise that would allow Curran to teach moral theology but not in the field of sexual ethics. When the compromise was rejected in 1986, Cardinal Ratzinger wrote to Curran, "The authorities of the Church cannot allow the present situation to continue in which the inherent contradiction is prolonged that one who is to teach in the name of the Church in fact denies her teaching."[44]

The chancellor and the board of Catholic University attempted a compromise in which Curran would teach in other departments in the university—outside of the theology department but this compromise failed also because Curran's only competence was in theology. As Smith writes, "Curran could not pretend he was not a theologian."[45] Curran left Catholic University and, in response, the American Association of University Professors (the AAUP) concluded that Catholic University had "deprived Curran of his tenure without due process . . . violated Professor Curran's academic freedom . . . and that the board, in particular, had failed to exercise their responsibility to protect the university's autonomy and the academic freedom of the faculty."[46] Catholic University remains today on the AAUP list of censured institutions because of what the AAUP continues to define as the university's "blatant" violation of Curran's academic freedom.

In contrast to the AAUP conclusions, a civil suit brought by Curran against the university resulted in total vindication for the university. The judge in the civil suit defined the issue not as one individual's academic freedom, but rather as the freedom of an institution to define its own identity. The judge argued that "Professor Curran could not reasonably have expected that the University would defy a definitive judgment of the Holy See that he was unsuitable and ineligible to teach Catholic theology . . . the University was bound to accept the declaration of the Vatican as a matter of religious conviction and pursuant to its long standing unique and religious conviction."[47]

In this case and every other case beyond *Horace Mann* that has been brought before the courts regarding the right of a religious institution to define and maintain its identity, the courts have supported the institution. Still, David Smith agrees with the AAUP and criticizes the trustees at Catholic University for their decision by pointing out that being an American university carries a "price." Instead of privileging the fiduciary principle, Smith believes that concern for the common good and respect for the university as a university demands that allegiance to Rome cannot trump the American value of academic freedom:

> Identifying oneself with the common purpose of higher education comes at a price. The Catholic University of America is an American university, entitled to the recognition, privileges and resources of the sort accorded to other American universities . . . Sponsorship of an academic institution entails giving up something, namely the right to act in ways contradictory to the institution's identity as an institution of higher education. If the sponsor means to maintain an American college or university, it must recognize the rules of the game in which it has chosen to play . . . Sponsored higher education cannot both claim the rights and privileges the community offers to an academic institution because of its commitment to certain values and violate the community's accepted standards derived from those values. Rights entail responsibilities.[48]

Smith maintains that while the religiously sponsored college must take seriously the mission of its sponsor, it must also acknowledge that it is first a college with a broader dependent clientele that properly expects it to provide educational services. But if the Catholic college continues to accommodate those like Charles Curran who redefine Catholic teachings to suit their own ideology or politics, how can it possibly maintain its Catholic identity? There will always be contested terrain on Catholic campuses and there will always be those like Curran who try to redefine Catholic teachings—and define down the Catholic identity. Yet, Smith dismisses such redefinitions by simply describing Charles Curran's vision of the Catholic Church as a "broader one in which his views were one of several acceptable options."[49] It was clear that the Vatican and the Catholic University of America believed otherwise.

It is difficult to know how to address the need for informed individuals, who are committed to the mission, to be appointed to the governing boards of Catholic colleges. The lessons learned at Dartmouth during the past few years provide a cautionary tale. Dartmouth is unique because since 1891, alumni, or those that *The Wall Street Journal* calls "the school's financial underwriters," have held the right to elect half of its non-administrative or *ex officio* trustees who oversee the school and hire and fire its president. The remaining seats are filled by appointment and typically go to big donors. Until a few years ago, the candidates for election to Dartmouth's board had been vetted by a small board committee, in an effort to "ensure quiescence." However, four years ago, four reform-minded candidates won seats on the board using a provision allowing nomination by petition. These proactive alumni have challenged what *The Wall Street Journal* has called "Dartmouth's bureaucratic bloat," its academic standards, and the campus threats to free speech.[50] The alumni trustees have been remarkably successful in overturning coercive and unconstitutional speech codes on campus and in beginning to address what one of the new alumni trustees called a "shortage of teaching" in some departments.[51] And, as a result, their presence has been perceived as a threat to a faculty and administration unaccustomed to oversight from their alumni donors.

A few years ago, in response to this threat, the administration gathered a small committee of alumni to alter the petition process to make it less likely that outsiders could win. But, they lost in an alumni referendum. Not to be deterred, in 2007, four years after the reform minded trustees won seats on the board, administrators decided to expand the eighteen-member board with eight more trustees selected by the board itself. Negating the 116 years of open elections for trustee openings at Dartmouth, administrators demonstrated how much power over their "oversight" boards they actually had. With the influence of elected trustees thus diluted, power was further consolidated in a small executive committee that will control the agenda. The college also declared that it will run future trustee elections on its own terms. In a follow-up essay published in *The Wall Street Journal*, the designers of this new, more concentrated form of governance stated that "because of divisiveness . . . We do not believe that having more elections is in the best interests of the College."[52]

The editors at *The Wall Street Journal* assert that "elite academia loathes oversight or accountability," and they accuse college presidents—both on secular and religious colleges—of being "a product and wholly owned subsidary" of the faculty. Whether this is true remains to be seen. But, what cannot be denied is the warning Dartmouth has provided to those who may attempt to encourage governing boards to actually govern.

To be fair, we must acknowledge that, in some cases, foundation and federal grants and contracts hastened the secularization process in the past, and it appears that these pressures continue today but in an entirely different climate. During the spring of 2007, St. Louis University found itself forced to reaffirm publicly that "it is not controlled by the Catholic Church or by its Catholic beliefs" in a case heard before the Missouri Supreme Court. A lawsuit filed against the University by the Masonic Temple Association argued that the $8 million in tax increment financing that St. Louis University received for its new sports arena violated state and federal constitutions. The Missouri Constitution prohibits public funding to support any college, university, or other institution of learning controlled by any religious creed, church, or sectarian denomination.[53]

In response to the lawsuit, the university assured the court that: "with 42 trustees, it would take 22 of them to conduct the university's business. With 22 trustees assembled, it would take at least 12 votes to approve a corporate act of the board. Thus the nine Jesuit trustees on the board do not have the numerical authority to take any action on behalf of the university." The school also pointed out to the court that despite its Jesuit tradition, "the school does not require employees or students to aspire to Jesuit ideals, to be Catholic or to otherwise have any specific religious affiliation."[54] Fewer than half of the students who attend St. Louis University identify themselves as Catholic. In a friend of the court brief filed on behalf of the Masonic Temple Association, the American Civil Liberties Union wrote that "it was surprising the University would sell its heritage for $8 million."[55] It can be argued that St. Louis University, like many other Catholic Universities, had sold its heritage many years before.

Notes

1. Christopher Jencks and David Riesman. *The Academic Revolution*. (New Brunswick, NJ: Transaction Publishers, 1968), 342.
2. Ibid.
3. Holy Cross Mission Statement. Included in David J. O'Brien. *From the Heart of the Church: Catholic Higher Education and American Culture*. (Maryknoll, New York: Orbis Books, 1994), 125.
4. O'Brien. *From the Heart of the Church,* 125.
5. Ibid., 153.
6. Ibid., 154.
7. Ibid., 127.
8. Bruce Douglass. "Centered Pluralism: A Report of a Faculty Seminar on the Jesuit and Catholic Identity of Georgetown University. Included in *Enhancing Religious Identity: Best Practices from Catholic Campuses*. (Washington, D C: Georgetown University Press, 2000), 69.
9. Ibid.
10. Ibid., 76.
11. Ibid., 82.
12. James Hitchcock, "The New Orthodoxy of Dissent: Cardinal Arinze's Georgetown Address." May 25, 2003. www.wf-f.org/JFH-Georgetown%26Dissent.html
13. James Hitchcock, "The New Orthodoxy of Dissent: Cardinal Arinze's Georgetown Address." May 25, 2003. www.wf-f.org/JFH-Georgetown%26Dissent.html
14. Paul C. Reinert, S. J. *The Urban Catholic University*. (New York, NY: Sheed and Ward, 1970), 74.
15. Ibid., 75.
16. Jencks and Riesman. *The Academic Revolution*. (New Brunswick, NJ: Transaction Publishers, 1968), 348.
17. Reinert, S. J. *The Urban Catholic University ,* 89.
18. Ibid., 74.
19. Philip Gleason. "What Made Identity a Problem?" Included in Theodore Hesburgh, editor. *The Challenge and Promise of a Catholic University.* (Notre Dame, IN: University of Notre Dame Press, 1994), 315.
20. Alice Gallin. *Negotiating Identity: Catholic Higher Education Since 1960.* (Notre Dame, IN, 2000), 38.
21. Ibid., 38.
22. Ibid., 39.
23. James Turnstead Burtchaell. *The Dying of the Light.* (Grand Rapids, MI: Eerdmans, 1998), 646.
24. Ibid., 647.
25. Ibid.
26. Ibid., 655, 662.
27. Ibid., 662.
28. Ibid., 664.
29. Jencks and Riesman. *The Academic Revolution,* 346.
30. Burtchaell. *The Dying of the Light,* 664.

31.   Jencks and Riesman. *The Academic Revolution,* 346.
32.   O'Brien. *From the Heart of the Church,* 76.
33.   Ibid.
34.   Paul Fain. "Surveys Find Governing Boards are Older and Slightly More Diverse." *The Chronicle of Higher Education 51* (July 1, 2005): A-21.
35.   Ibid.
36.   Ibid.
37.   Jeffrey Selingo. "The Chronicle Survey: What Trustees Think." *The Chronicle of Higher Education* 53 (May 11, 2007): A-11.
38.   Ibid., A-12.
39.   Julianne Basinger. "More Presidents Recruit Ex-Presidents for Their Institution's Boards." *The Chronicle of Higher Education* 48 (February 8, 2002): A-29.
40.   Carol Hymowitz. "How to Be a Good Director." *The Wall Street Journal* (October 27, 2003): R-1.
41.   David H. Smith. *Entrusted: The Moral Responsibilities of Trusteeship.* (Bloomington, IN: University of Indiana Press, 1995), 5.
42.   Ibid., 75.
43.   Ibid.
44.   Ibid., 76.
45.   Ibid., 78.
46.   Ibid.
47.   Ibid.
48.   Ibid., 79.
49.   Ibid., 87.
50.   "The Illiberal College." The editors of *The Wall Street Journal.* (September 1-2, 2007): A-6
51.   Joseph Rago. "Mr Rodgers Goes to Dartmouth." The Weekend Interview. *The Wall Street Journal* (September 1-2, 2007): A-7
52.   "Dartmouth Diminished." The editors of *The Wall Street Journal.* (September 1-2, 2007): A-6
53.   Tim Townsend. "Did St. Louis University Sell Its Jesuit Soul for a Sports Arena? *St. Louis Post-Dispatch.* April 21, 2007.
54.   Ibid.
55.   Ibid.

3

Secularizing the Mission

Status concerns are most visible in the ways in which Catholic colleges and universities choose to present themselves on their websites and in their published catalogue descriptions. Proudly proclaiming their inclusion on Princeton Review's listings of "Top Colleges," "Best Value Colleges," "Most Beautiful Campuses," or even "Colleges with a Conscience," Catholic colleges highlight this status on their website homepages—often accompanied by photos of attractive smiling students and bucolic campuses. What is less visible on each website is the Catholic affiliation. In fact, a systematic review of the mission and values statements of more than two-hundred Catholic colleges and universities reveals that a substantial number have carefully constructed their college descriptions to downplay their ties to Catholicism—and some have deleted the word "Catholic" from their own websites, catalogues, and bulletins.

Fr. Richard Neuhaus, editor of *First Things,* recalls a colleague telling him that "when a school is haggling over its mission statement, it is a sure sign that it has already lost its way."[1] And, while that may be too strong a statement, the truth is that decision makers on Catholic campuses have made a conscious, and some cases, well-documented effort to create ambiguity when describing the Catholic identity of their schools.

While some have moved away from defining themselves as Catholic, others have taken a more selective approach to describing their Catholic identity—claiming to value the aspects of the Catholic heritage they find appropriate. For example, the statement of Catholic identity of The College of St. Catherine in St. Paul, Minnesota maintains that the college has been "dedicated as a campus community to our Roman Catholic heritage and identity." But, in the next sentence, the college seems to distance itself from that heritage by stating that St. Catherine's affirms the aspects of the Catholic identity that are "appropriate to higher education," values

47

the "rich and diverse history of the Church and the vision of Vatican II," and claims to "reach out to those who have been marginalized by our society and our churches."[2]

For those students considering attending St. Catherine's, the college provides a listing of the aspects of the Catholic heritage that they find appropriate:

> From the Church's intellectual tradition, which has equated the search for truth with true liberation, we value an open atmosphere of critical inquiry, cross cultural studies and interdisciplinary teaching. From its social tradition, with its consistent commitment to the poor and outcast, we value and reach out to those marginalized by our society and our churches, and in particular, we seek to promote women's leadership. From its sacramental tradition, which has emphasized ritual, symbol and the use of material things as signs of grace, we value the integration of the material and spiritual, and the use of creative rituals for prayer and celebration. And, from the tradition that has stressed both communal participation and the worth of the individual, we value dialogue, respect for diversity and the nurturing of personal conscience.[3]

Like St. Catherine's creative approach to its Catholic identity, St. Joseph's College in West Hartford, CT looks "critically" at the Catholic Church—in an ecumenical manner. Describing itself as having been "founded by the Sisters of Mercy in the Roman Catholic tradition," the "Core Values" section of the St. Joseph's website states, "Saint Joseph College is grounded in its heritage as a Catholic institution expressing the Catholic tradition in an ecumenical and critical manner."[4]

One of the strategies that many Catholic colleges like St. Joseph's have used is to refer to a Catholic "heritage" or "tradition" or to replace the word "Catholic" with the name of the founding religious order. Like the College of the Holy Cross, neither the College of Santa Fe nor Holy Names University describe themselves as Catholic colleges in their mission statements. Rather, they each draw upon their founders' heritage to describe their mission. The College of Santa Fe refers to its "LaSallian Tradition" rather than its Catholic heritage. And, when describing its culture, the College of Santa Fe refers only to its location in Santa Fe, New Mexico—"a region steeped in culture and history," rather than to refer to any Catholic culture or identity.[5]

Likewise, in its description of its history, Holy Names states that it was founded in 1868 when six sisters of the Holy Names arrived in California from Montreal, Canada. There is no indication that they were Catholic sisters throughout the description of the history of the university. And, although the "spiritual tradition" section of the Holy Names website acknowledges that Holy Names University is "rooted in the Catholic tradition," the reference to "Catholic" is used as a way to show their inclusiveness, or what they call their universality:

> Rooted in the Catholic tradition, Holy Names demonstrates a respect for others' values and customs. This is evident in holiday displays that incorporate symbols for Kwanzaa, Muslim, Jewish and Christian celebrations. Students experience the universality of a catholic education at Holy Names University.[6]

There is no reference to a Catholic identity throughout the Holy Names University self-description. The fact that Holy Names includes symbols of "Christian celebrations" on campus is revealed at the end of a list of alternative religious celebrations. And, in a section on the website that lists "The Top Ten Reasons to Attend Holy Names University," not a single one of the top ten reasons mentions that it is a Catholic university. Rather, status concerns drive the top ten list with "reputation" listed as the most important reason to attend Holy Names. Other top ten reasons to attend Holy Names include "location, heritage, faculty, size, innovation, diversity, resources, and alumni." Yet, the fact that Holy Names is a Catholic University is never mentioned. Even within the "heritage" section—where Catholic heritage might have been most appropriately included—Holy Names mentions only that "Since our founding in 1868, we have continually put students at the heart of everything we do." There is not a word in the top ten reasons to attend Holy Names that mentions Catholic heritage, Catholic identity, or Catholic culture. Words like God, Jesus, Christian, or religion are noticeably absent from the top ten list.[7]

The College of Notre Dame of Maryland's mission statement claims that the college "educates women as leaders to transform the world." And, like most colleges founded by women religious groups, the mission statement highlights the founders rather than the Catholic identity: "Embracing the vision of the founders, the School Sisters of Notre Dame, the College provides a liberal arts education in the Catholic tradition."[8] Likewise, the University of St. Mary in Leavenworth, Kansas described itself as having been "shaped by the educational mission of the Sisters of Charity of Leavenworth."[9] Claiming that their mission is to "educate students of diverse backgrounds," St. Mary's focuses on the founders rather than the Catholic identity. Never mentioning its Catholic heritage or founding, Ohio's Ursuline College describes itself as offering an education "within a Catholic tradition marked by the Ursuline heritage of educating women."[10] And, while Stonehill College in Bedford, Massachusetts describes itself as a Catholic institution, it reassures potential students and faculty members that the College has a "long tradition of free inquiry."[11]

Barry University in Miami Shores, Florida does not mention its Catholic affiliation, tradition, or heritage in its statement of purpose or its vision statement. While Barry describes itself as an "independent, co-educational Catholic international institution of higher education" within the "nature" section of the website, it does not cite its Catholic identity or culture when describing the "purpose" of Barry University. In fact, the purpose of the university is presented as any other state sponsored school might: "The primary purpose of Barry University as stated in the Charter, is to offer its students a quality education."[12]

The combined mission statement of the College of Saint Benedict and Saint John's University in Minnesota claims that their "liberal arts education is rooted in the Catholic university tradition and guided by the Benedictine principles of the colleges' founders and sponsoring religious communities."[13] And, although the colleges do not refer to themselves as Catholic colleges, they claim to draw upon their Catholic heritage to assist their colleges to "excel in the study of the intersection of global cultures and community sustainability, leavened by the commitments of the Catholic intellectual life." And, like Holy Names, the College of St. Benedict and St. John's draw from Catholic social teachings to "value ecumenism and respect for diverse cultures."[14]

In reviewing each of the more than two hundred mission statements, one of the most striking features is the prevalence of the word "rooted" when referring to Catholic tradition or Catholic heritage. Rather than referring to the Catholic identity, colleges are increasingly describing themselves as being "rooted" in the Catholic tradition or in the tradition of their founders. Like the Benedictine colleges in Minnesota, Mount St. Vincent of Riverdale, New York "provides to qualified students an excellent values oriented education rooted in its Catholic heritage and in the liberal arts tradition."[15] And, although they acknowledge this heritage as part of their mission statement, none of the goals that Mount St. Vincent's has identified to fulfill their mission addresses this Catholic heritage. In fact, not a single one of the eight goals even mentions the word Catholic.[16] Marymount College of Palos Verdes, California states, "Marymount's philosophy is rooted in Christian tradition."[17] St. Vincent College, of Latrobe, Pennsylvania, describes itself as "an educational community rooted in the tradition of the Catholic faith, the heritage of Benedictine monasticism, and the love of values inherent in the liberal approach to life and learning."[18] Rosemont College is "rooted in Catholicism and guided by the educational principles of Cornelia Connelly and the Society of the Holy Child Jesus." And, rather than stating that it values its Catholic heritage, Rosemont states that its values include, "Trust in and reverence for the dignity of each person; diversity in human culture and experience; and persistence and courage in the promoting of justice with compassion."[19]

Indeed, the values and goals statements of Catholic colleges are especially revealing as many have revised them to delete any mention of valuing a Catholic identity. While the University of San Diego's newly revised mission statement continues to describe the university itself unambiguously as a "Roman Catholic institution," two years ago the faculty and administrators made a conscious decision to delete "Catholicity" from its listing of the university's five major core values. Replacing the core value of Catholicity with the values of "Community, Ethical Conduct, and Compassionate Service," the revised mission statement also contains a revised core values statement on academic excellence to proclaim that in its pursuit of academic excellence, "The University promotes the institutional autonomy and integrity necessary to uphold the highest standards of intellectual inquiry and academic freedom."[20] In other words, although the university continues to acknowledge that it was founded as a Roman Catholic institution, the newly revised statement of core values claims "autonomy" as one of its most important core values. One can only surmise that autonomy from the Church may have been what the authors had in mind. Also omitted from the San Diego mission statement were any references to God, Christ, or faith—all included in the mission statements of the past. And like Holy Cross's highly ideological mission statement, San Diego's mission statement contains the inherently subjective but increasingly obligatory Catholic mission statement promise to "foster peace and to work for justice."[21]

Many colleges couple the claim that they are rooted in the Catholic tradition with the statement that they are inspired by or guided by their founders. For example, the mission statement of Marymount College of Fordham University in New York describes the college as "an independent liberal arts college in the Catholic tradition which empowers women to participate fully in the multicultural workplace of the 21st century."[22] In a recent national survey of 124 senior administrators from 33 Catholic colleges and universities, many senior administrators disclosed that they were ambivalent about exactly which cultural emphasis should dominate in their institutions—the Catholic culture or the culture of the sponsoring religious congregation.[23] This ambivalence is reflected in the mission and values statements of Catholic colleges and universities—and the ways in which these Catholic colleges and universities describe themselves on their websites. Choosing to highlight their "rich Dominican commitment to education," or their "Benedictine tradition of hospitality," rather than their Catholic identity is quite common. Interview data with the senior administrators involved in the survey revealed that many of them thought it "strategically best for faculty, staff and administrators to emphasize and be well informed about the founding religious orders." The administrators surveyed believed that the focus on the religious order was "more particular to their institutions and more inclusive."[24]

Most administrators polled believed that the stories and cultures of the Vincentians, the Mercies, the Charities, the Dominicans, the Benedictines, the Franciscans, or, of course, the Jesuits, are "stirring and can easily be shared in appropriate ways with students." The authors of the survey support this claim that the culture of the founding religious orders is "easily accessible to people with many different backgrounds." They find that "laypersons are enthusiastic about congregational heritage and goals, and equally enthusiastic about sharing this information with students."[25] Such a nostalgic reverence for the founders provides a rich cultural backdrop for a Catholic campus—and great photos for the website of pious and heroic leaders pictured in prayerful contemplation dressed in the religious garb of long ago.

What is left unsaid by the senior administrators is that the emphasis on the sponsoring religious order and its culture helps the university ignore the Catholic Church itself. Even the authors of the study suggest that focusing on the founders rather than the Church, "means the university is convinced that Catholic culture on campus is best captured through the prism of the sponsoring religious congregation, not through the teachings and practices of the Catholic Church itself . . . By downplaying the Catholic connection, the strong links between the sponsoring religious congregation and the Catholic Church are neglected."[26] The authors conclude: "While it is possible for Catholic universities to give precedence to transmitting congregational culture over Catholic culture, this approach clouds the religious cultural issue on campus."[27] But, then again, it is most likely that clouding the religious cultural issue on campus is the real reason for the focus on the founders. Some decision makers on Catholic college campuses do not even make an attempt to recall their Catholic heritage or the inspiration of their founders at all.

While the College of the Holy Cross mentions its Jesuit heritage in its mission statement, a conscious decision was made by the faculty and administrators to purposely delete any reference to a Catholic identity for the mission statement.[28] In describing such decisions, former *New York Times* religion editor, Peter Steinfels, has likened the focus on the founders rather than the Catholic identity to "taking off your wedding ring when traveling."[29]

Aquinas College in Grand Rapids, Michigan describes itself as "an inclusive educational community rooted in the Catholic Dominican tradition."[30] Likewise, Assumption College is "rooted in the Catholic intellectual tradition," but, more positively, the College also maintains that it is "enlivened by the Catholic affirmation of the harmony of faith and reason."[31] Quincy University's website simply states, "founded by Franciscans, Quincy is an independent, coeducational, primarily undergraduate institution rooted in the Catholic tradition."[32] Notre Dame de Namur University's mission statement describes the university as "Founded upon the values of the Sisters of Notre Dame deNamur and rooted in the Catholic tradition." Notre Dame de Namur also joins other San Francisco Bay Area Catholic colleges like Holy Names in its commitment to "the values of social justice and global peace." And, like Rosemont, not a single one of its "core values" even mentions the word Catholic. Rather, Notre Dame's core values are described on the website as "listed in alphabetical order to imply no ranking: community, diversity, excellence, integrity, justice, learning and service."[33]

Focusing on the founders rather than the Catholic identity, Silver Lake College is "based on the principles and truths of Franciscan Catholic tradition." And, although the college does not mention the word Catholic within the description of their four identified goals, they claim "to foster commitment to Christian values, service, and leadership in the world community."[34] This is a common practice, yet, St. Francis University in Loretto, Pennsylvania promises "higher education in an environment guided by Catholic values and teachings."[35] St. Francis College in New York claims in its mission statement that "Both the Franciscan heritage and the Catholic tradition establish a cornerstone of academic excellence, responsibility and mutual respect throughout the entire College community."[36] And, Briar Cliff University describes itself simply as a "community committed to higher education within a liberal arts and a Catholic perspective."[37]

Distancing itself further from its Catholic identity, the College of New Rochelle describes itself in its mission statement simply as "an independent College which is Catholic in origin and heritage."[38] Mount Marty College describes itself as "an academic community in the Catholic, Benedictine liberal arts tradition."[39] And, the mission of St. Michael's College aims to "contribute through higher education to the enhancement of the human person and to the advancement of human culture in the light of the Catholic faith."[40]

In a stronger description of the Catholic identity, St. Anselm College acknowledges itself as "a Benedictine, Catholic, liberal arts college that offers access to the educational process that encourages students to lead lives that are both creative and generous."[41] Some Catholic colleges appear to selectively publish different versions of their mission and goals. For example, St. Joseph's University recently published a job advertisement seeking "diverse faculty members" that makes no reference at all to a Catholic or a Jesuit identity. Published in *The Chronicle of Higher Education's* special supplement on "Diversity," the ad was entitled "A Rewarding Career is Waiting for you at St. Joseph's University." Rather than describing St. Joseph's as a Catholic or a Jesuit University, the description of the university is simply that "St. Joseph's University located in Philadelphia, Pennsylvania, is committed to the principles of diversity and embraces the understanding that a multicultural environment will positively contribute to the enrichment of campus life for students, faculty and staff."[42]

This is an increasingly common practice—to publish different descriptions of the university based upon the targeted audience. Several Catholic colleges publish one mission statement on its own website and yet another in its self description for the online version of *U. S. News and World Report: America's Best Colleges 2006.* While the university homepage claims that Mount Aloysius is a Catholic College founded and sponsored by the Religious Sisters of Mercy, the mission statement published by Mount Aloysius in the online version of *U. S. News and World Report* does not mention its Catholic identity and instead claims that "The mission of Mount Aloysius College is to respond to individual and community needs with quality programs of education in the tradition of the Religious Sisters of Mercy."[43]

The mission statement for Carroll College of Helena, Montana, states that it is a "Catholic, diocesan, liberal arts college in the ecumenical tradition of the Second Vatican Council." In drawing upon the Vatican Council, Carroll allies itself with the new more open and pluralist post-Vatican II Catholic Church yet later in the mission statement still appears to acknowledge that "As a Catholic college, Carroll is obligated to treat judgments concerning ultimate reality and decisions concerning ultimate value at both an academic and a pastoral level." To its credit, Carroll College acknowledges that the college is obligated to teach faithfully: "This obligation involves the College's relationship to the Magisterium of the Catholic Church defined as the perennial, authentic and infallible teaching office." Yet, within the same paragraph, Carroll seems to soften such fidelity by pointing to the "special role of the theologian . . . who makes available to the Magisterium his or her scientific competence while acting as a mediator between religion and culture by carrying on an academic dialogue with philosophy, science, the liberal arts, the believing community and the secular society."[44]

The Catholic heritage is often cited by Catholic college and university descriptions as something to "honor" yet the same colleges that claim to honor the heritage, often refuse to call themselves Catholic. For example, D'Youville College never describes itself as a Catholic college and instead claims it is an "independent institution of higher education that offers baccalaureate and graduate programs to students of all faiths, cultures and backgrounds." D'Youville also states that it "honors its Catholic heritage and spirit of St. Marguerite d'Youville by providing academic, social, spiritual and professional development in programs that emphasize leadership and service."[45] Likewise, the mission of The College of St. Elizabeth is "a community of learning in the Catholic liberal arts tradition for students of diverse ages, backgrounds and cultures."[46] And, Iona College stresses the American Catholic Church, rather than citing the Roman Catholic Church, by describing itself as "a diverse community of learners and scholars dedicated to academic excellence in the tradition of the Christian Brothers and American Catholic higher education."[47]

The claims to honor or cherish the Catholic heritage are common. Chicago's DePaul University does not describe itself as a Catholic university yet maintains that it "treasures its deep roots in the wisdom nourished in Catholic universities from medieval times."[48] To its credit though, DePaul's website states that "the principal distinguishing marks of the university are its Catholic, Vincentian and urban character."[49] Dominican University of California describes itself as an "independent international, learner centered university of Catholic heritage which interweaves Dominican values, the liberal arts and sciences, and the skills and knowledge necessary to live and work in an interdependent world."[50] Likewise, Dominican College of Orangeburg, New York describes itself as "an independent institution of higher learning, Catholic in origin and heritage."[51] Lewis University is "guided by its Catholic and LaSallian heritage."[52]

Sometimes, in their pursuit of upward mobility, just as turn-of-the-century European immigrants to America changed their foreign-sounding names to the higher status Americanized names, some Catholic colleges have actually chosen to delete a "Catholic sounding" portion of their name. For example, as pointed out in the previous chapter, Manhattan-ville College of the Sacred Heart deleted the descriptor "College of the Sacred Heart." More recently, "Our Lady of the Elms College" decided to drop the reference to the Virgin Mary in the "Our Lady" portion of the name and instead, advertise the college simply as "Elms College." And, on their website, they claim to be "proud to be one of New England's finest liberal arts colleges . . . rooted in the Catholic tradition, we prepare our students for roles of service and leadership in their careers, in their communities, and in their families."[53]

While at first glance, it might seem that New York's Catholic colleges and universities were more likely to delete references to their Catholic identity, perhaps in response to the New York Bundy Commission controversy of the past, the truth is that there are still a few high status and very successful Catholic colleges and universities in the state that have maintained a strong mission statement. For example, the high-ranking St. John's University of Staten Island New York states clearly, "St. John's University is Catholic, Vincentian and Metropolitan." St. John's commits itself to "create a climate patterned on the life and teaching of Jesus Christ as embodied in the traditions and practices of the Roman Catholic Church."[54] In contrast, St. Joseph's College in Brooklyn, New York has no references to its Catholic identity in its mission statement or in any of its eight goals statements, and acknowledges only that it is "rooted in the liberal arts tradition."[55] Likewise, the mission of Thomas Aquinas College in Sparkill, New York maintains only that it is "continuing its Catholic heritage and the spirit of its founders, the Dominican Sisters of Sparkill."[56]

Even those colleges like New York's Nazareth College and St. John Fisher, which have been deleted from the *Directory of Approved Catholic Colleges* by their bishops, appear to want to create ambiguity about their identities by continuing to describe their "rich Catholic heritage" in their marketing materials. Nazareth College describes itself as "historically rooted in the Catholic tradition of its founders, the Sisters of

Saint Joseph."[57] Likewise, in a mission statement that was revised by St. John Fisher College and approved by its board of trustees in 2003, after the college's removal by their bishop from listings of approved Catholic colleges and universities, the college continues to claim that it is "guided by its Catholic heritage, as expressed in the motto of its founders, the Basilian Fathers: teach me goodness, discipline, and knowledge." The website also includes pictures of campus statues of their patron saints, and in many ways it is comparable to many of the websites of those Catholic colleges still approved by the bishop of New York.[58] In fact, the claims that Nazareth and St. John Fisher make about their Catholic heritage or tradition do not differ from those of most approved Catholic colleges and universities.

Indeed, although the majority of Catholic colleges and universities create ambiguity about their continued Catholic identity within their mission statements, there are several that continue to clearly proclaim themselves as Catholic colleges. King's College of Pennsylvania describes itself as "a Catholic college in the Holy Cross tradition."[59] Anna Maria College describes itself as "a Catholic institution of higher learning."[60] Aquinas College of Nashville, Tennessee not only describes itself unambiguously as a Catholic institution of higher education, it also maintains that the mission of Aquinas is "to bring the message of salvation to bear on ethical, social, political, religious and cultural issues."[61] Alvernia College states that it is "a Catholic co-educational college sponsored by the Bernardine Sisters of St. Francis."[62] Avila University is "a Catholic university sponsored by the Sisters of St. Joseph of Carondelet."[63] Likewise, Caldwell College, Christian Brothers University, Clarke College of Dubuque, Iowa, the College of Mount St. Joseph, College Misericordia, the College of Mount St. Joseph, Cardinal Stritch Calumet College of St. Joseph, Magdalen College of Warner, New Hampshire, the University of Dallas, Franciscan University of Steubenville, Ohio, the University of St. Thomas of Houston, and the University of San Diego all describe themselves unambiguously as "Catholic institutions." Some of the newest Catholic colleges include the descriptor "Catholic" in their titles. For example, Southern Catholic College, Wyoming Catholic College, and John Paul the Great Catholic University are among the newest Catholic colleges.

Some of the strongest mission statements not only mention a Catholic identity, but also proclaim faithfulness to the Magisterium. DeSales University has one of the strongest mission statements analyzed. Not only does DeSales claim faithfulness to Catholic teachings, it also proudly proclaims that *Ex Corde Ecclessiae's* requirement of the Mandatum is important to DeSales University and made it a point of honor that the theology faculty was granted the Mandatum by the bishop of the Allentown Diocese "even before it was necessary."[64] DeSales also states that it is "firmly and publicly committed to the principles of Roman Catholic doctrine and morality."[65] Likewise, Ave Maria University in Naples was "founded in fidelity to Christ and His Church," and describes itself as "committed to Catholic principles."[66] Christendom College describes itself as "A Catholic co-educational college institutionally committed to the Magisterium of the Roman Catholic Church." Christendom also maintains that its "particular mission" is "to restore all things in Christ by forming men and women to contribute to the Christian renovation of the temporal order."[67] In the same spirit, Thomas Aquinas College of Santa Paula, California describes itself as "responsible first and foremost for helping its students perfect their intellects under the light of the truths revealed by God through the Catholic Church."[68]

Some colleges have taken an even more creative approach to describing their mission. For example, Thomas More College in Merrimack, New Hampshire, one of a few dozen Catholic colleges that have remained institutionally faithful to the Magisterium posted a letter from its president on its website to remind prospective students and their parents of the evangelizing purpose of a Catholic college. In the section of the website entitled, "The Purpose of a Catholic Education," the president's letter states: "The purpose of a Catholic College . . . is to help transform the heart and mind of each student who, almost miraculously, appears in the classroom."[69]

Thomas More's presidential statement reminds readers that the mission of Catholic higher education has always been evangelization—to help transform the hearts and minds of students. What has changed on some campuses, however, is the goal of the transformation. While the Classical Jesuit goal at Georgetown, the earliest Catholic college in the country, was to transform students' hearts and minds in order to bring as many as possible to the knowledge of the truth of salvation and the Kingdom of God, the radical changes within the Jesuit Order in the sixties and seventies resulted in a radical change in the mission and goals of today's Catholic colleges.

A review of the mission statements of the twenty-eight Jesuit colleges and universities shows the movement away from evangelization—and toward social justice. This movement is really a reflection of the changing mission of the Jesuit order itself—it is a reflection of what St. Joseph's University website calls the "evolving world view of the Society."[70] In his bestselling book about the Jesuits, Malachi Martin points out that the reversal of the evangelizing mission occurred in the seventies:

> The "Kingdom" being fought over now was the "Kingdom" everyone fights over and always has: material well being. The enemy was now economic, political and social: the secular system called democratic and economic capitalism. The objective was material: to uproot poverty and injustice which were caused by capitalism. The weapons to be used now were those of social agitation, labor relations, sociopolitical movements, government offices . . . The poor who were good, were being trampled by the non-poor who were evil. The preferential option for the poor absolutized revolutionary thought and divinized political action.[71]

The movement away from evangelization and toward social justice is reflected in the mission statements on each of the Jesuit campuses—and was eventually included in the mission and goals statements of many of the more than two hundred Catholic colleges and universities. Indeed, a "commitment to social justice" or to "creating a more just society" now joins "appreciation for diversity" as the most popular phrases for Catholic college mission, values, and goals statements. On many of these campuses, it is a phrase with the power of a command. During a public debate at the Jesuit St. Joseph's College of Philadelphia, the dean of the faculty stated, "a student who did not believe in social justice would not qualify for a degree at his school."[72]

The mission statement of St. Joseph's University claims that it "instills in each member of its academic community, "a love of learning and other highest intellectual and professional achievement; moral discernment reflecting Christian values; and a transforming commitment to social justice . . . St. Joseph's espouses the educational priorities of the Society of Jesus which include: searching for God in all things, pursuit of the greater good, the service of faith together with the promotion of justice and effective compassion for the poor and those in need."[73]

Like St. Joseph's University, Fairfield University's mission statement makes the promotion of justice "an absolute requirement." "Fairfield University, founded by the Society of Jesus is a coeducational institution of higher learning whose primary objectives are to develop the creative intellectual potential of its students and to foster in them ethical and religious values and a sense of social responsibility. Jesuit education, which began in 1547 is committed today to the service of faith, of which the promotion of justice is an absolute requirement."[74]

Like the other Jesuit colleges' commitment to justice, Le Moyne College "seeks to prepare its members for leadership and service in their personal and professional lives to promote a more just society."[75] Loyola Marymount, Los Angeles, declares its purpose to be: "the encouragement of learning, the education of the whole person and the service of faith and the promotion of justice."[76] Loyola University Chicago is "a diverse community seeking God in all things and working to expand knowledge in the service of humanity through learning, justice and faith."[77] And, St. Louis University "encourages programs which link the University and its resources to its local, national, and international communities in support of efforts to alleviate ignorance, poverty, injustice, hunger, to extend compassionate care to the ill and needy, and to maintain and improve the quality of life for all persons."[78]

Many of the Jesuit colleges and universities claim to be "inspired" by the vision of Saint Ignatius Loyola, founder of the Society of Jesus in 1540, in their pursuit of social justice. Such inspiration is necessary because the reality is that the social justice movement within the Jesuit Order emerged from the thirty-second meeting of the General Congregation in 1975. Ignatian Spirituality, with its focus on the spiritual exercises, is not overtly related to "social justice." Yet, Jesuit colleges and universities refer, as Canisius Colleges does, to the "*contemporary* Jesuit mission of the promotion of justice." Others claim that the Ignatian spiritual exercises "inspire" a need for social justice.[79] For example, John Carroll University's mission statement holds that "commitment to the values which inspired the Exercises promotes justice by affirming the equal dignity of all persons."[80]

Creighton College "is directed to the intellectual, social, spiritual, physical, and recreational aspects of students' lives and to the promotion of justice."[81] Likewise, Georgetown University claims to embody the Jesuit principle "in our commitment to justice and the common good . . ."[82] And, Loyola University of New Orleans, which claims to be "inspired by Ignatius of Loyola's vision of finding God in all things . . . prepares students to lead meaningful lives with and for others; to pursue truth, wisdom and virtue; and to work for a more just world."[83] The University of Scranton's goals are to "educate men and women for others who are committed to the service of faith and promotion of justice."[84] Wheeling Jesuit University "endeavors to produce intelligent, moral leaders who will champion the Jesuit values of faith, peace and justice."[85] And, Xavier "shares in a worldwide Jesuit commitment to a creative and intelligent engagement with questions of peace and justice."[86]

Advocacy in the service of the transformation of society to a more just society is encouraged in the mission and goals statements of each of the twenty-eight Jesuit colleges and universities. Marquette "strives to develop men and women who will dedicate their lives to the service of others, actively entering into the struggle for a more just society."[87] Santa Clara University maintains "a commitment to fashioning a more humane and just world."[88] The University of San Francisco's newly revised 2001 vision, mission, and values statement promises to "educate leaders who will fashion a more humane and just world."[89]

Regis University distances itself from Rome by declaring itself to be "standing within the Catholic and United States traditions . . . we encourage the continual search for truth, values and a just existence . . . and we further encourage the development of the skills and leadership abilities necessary for distinguished professional work and contributions to the improvement and transformation of society."[90] Rockhurst claims to "devote its resources to enhancing the quality of life of all citizens . . . students must become citizens of the world, conscious that all of their personal decisions have economic and moral implications for themselves and others." Yet, Rockhurst also claims to "express its Catholic liturgical life by its ecumenical openness to other religious traditions."[91] Spring Hill College suggests that "we are enjoined through the process of a personalized education, to protect the rights of all and to work for that peace and justice which is the intent of God's kingdom.[92] And, Seattle University "fosters a concern for justice and the competence to promote it."[93]

Despite the overwhelming institutional support for the social justice mission, there are some individual Jesuits who are beginning to question the ways in which social justice is being defined on their campuses. For a recently published book on the Jesuits entitled *Passionate Uncertainty: Inside the American Jesuits,* authors Peter McDonough and Eugene C. Bianchi interviewed hundreds of current and former Jesuits, many of them working on Catholic college campuses. Many of those interviews revealed ambivalence about the primacy of social justice within the order. Some Jesuits are concerned about the negative effects that the social justice mission has had on the teaching mission and academic professionalism since 1975. A Jesuit professor of theology in a Midwestern Jesuit university claims to be "skeptical of the faith and justice movement" because of the effect that it has had on contributing to a sense of anti-intellectualism:[94]

> To become a very serious contributing scholar in American academic intellectual life, that has to be a lifetime's work. And the Jesuits' lifetime work is peace, justice and

the transformation of society. Some of them make it through to an academic orientation in their lives; most of them simply don't have the desire for it . . . Here among
the faculty at the university, Jesuits who become serious scholars are relatively few.
Most of them are not interested in scholarship.[95]

Others are concerned that integrating faith and justice programs into the
academic life of the colleges has not been a priority:

I am disappointed that the energy of the Jesuits is directed toward social welfare
manifestations of commitment, that is, working with poor neighborhoods. By contrast, there is little discussion of developing spirituality in the core vocational sectors
of the students. It is as if the focus is on training individuals to be social workers or
community volunteers; the Jesuit influence is peripheral to the work life which will
occupy the majority of time and the students' vocations to science, business, engineering, etcetera, which will shape so much of our society.[96]

While others are concerned that in the Jesuit zeal for social justice,
education has been compromised:

When the university administration started emphasizing social justice to the point
where social justice and resource allocation were used in the same sentence, many
faculty in business, science, and engineering were concerned that the Jesuit administration would no longer value basic research that did not have a social justice
component.[97]

Despite these concerns, the ideological commitment to social justice
has not only become institutionalized on Jesuit campuses, it has also
reached far beyond the twenty-eight Jesuit campuses to the majority of
Catholic colleges and universities. Most of these Catholic colleges integrate their commitment to social justice into their mission statements,
and on some, centers for social justice have been created. For example, at
the University of San Diego, the goal of the newly created Oscar Romero
Center for Faith in Action is quite simply "to achieve social justice."
Toward the goal of social justice, students provide direct service to the
poor in the San Diego area—including Tijuana, Mexico as well as through
advocacy efforts and economic boycotts related to economic justice.
Recently, the Romero Center's economic justice coordinator successfully
lobbied the university to require it to serve only "fair trade" coffee—in
an effort to ensure that "producers are getting a fair deal and are able
to earn a fair living." The economic justice coordinator also worked to
"organize an informational fair for social justice organizations to make
sure that the University merchandise is sweatshop-free."[98] And, during
the immigration debates during the spring of 2006, the Romero Center
took the lead in organizing student and community "actions" to protest
what they viewed as the harsh anti-immigration policies proposed by
Congress.

The choice of Oscar Romero, the archbishop of El Salvador from 1977 until 1980, was a calculated one because of his work on behalf of the leftist revolutionary opposition to the El Salvador government and his criticisms of US military aid to El Salvador's government during the Carter Administration. Romero's close ties to liberation theology led him to a confrontation with Pope John Paul II shortly before the assassination of the archbishop himself in 1980. Like many Catholic colleges and universities, the University of San Diego often provides the greatest honors to those with ties to liberation theology—a Marxist movement espoused especially by the Jesuits of Latin America that attempts to "empower the powerless" by seeking justice through challenging the existing economic system of capitalism.

On other campuses, students in pursuit of social justice have partnered with farm workers to win concrete changes in the agricultural and fast food industries. For example, college students organized to prevent or remove Taco Bell from twenty-two different campuses throughout the country. After nearly four years of struggle and amidst the momentum of the "2005 Taco Bell Truth Tour," farm workers from the Coalition of Immokalee Workers allied with students to score a decisive victory in their national boycott of Taco Bell. The fast food corporation agreed to work with the Florida based farm worker organization to improve the wages and working conditions of farm workers in the Florida tomato industry by paying the penny per pound surcharge demanded by the workers.

It has become clear that on Catholic campuses, a commitment to social justice usually ends up critical of the free market as a system that subjugates labor, and the implementation of solutions rooted in socialist intervention. Working at the local, state, and federal levels, the Catholic commitment to social justice is often used to lend moral authority to a variety of progressive causes, exerting an influence in campaigns to enforce a living wage, to help unions organize, and to require employers to expand benefits to their employees—sometimes on their own campuses. At Notre Dame, more than three hundred students, faculty, and staff organized in early 2005 to protest President Bush's proposal for social security—decrying the proposal as "a violation of social justice."

Sometimes, the commitment to social justice can become so distorted that it requires a pro-choice perspective on abortion to ensure social justice for women. During the 2004 presidential election, Mark Roche, dean of the College of Arts and Letters at Notre Dame, wrote an op-ed for *The New York Times* advising Catholics to vote for John Kerry, the Democratic nominee for president, despite Kerry's support for policies supporting abortion. Roche claimed that abortion will decline because of Kerry's commitment to social and economic justice. Maintaining that Kerry's positions (beyond abortion) are "more in harmony with Catholic teachings" on social justice than the Republican's poor record on social justice, Roche writes that Kerry and the Democrats "are more likely to criticize the handling of the war in Iraq, to oppose capital punishment and to support universal health care, environmental stewardship, a just welfare state and more equitable taxes."[99]

This distortion of the concept of social justice provides a good example of the problems that occur when social justice is detached from Catholic moral teachings. Rather than integrating teachings on social justice into the teachings of the Church on the sanctity of life and the importance of marriage, most Catholic colleges have secularized social justice to such an extent that some can now define lobbying for gay and lesbian access to marriage as a form of social justice for same-sex couples. A need for social justice can be cited as a reason to help women gain access to abortion as a way to achieve full reproductive rights. As a commitment to social justice, some Catholic colleges will even award community service credit for volunteering at Planned Parenthood or for acting as clinic escorts at abortion facilities.

This trend toward social justice is not unique within Catholic colleges and universities. While most Catholic colleges promote their commitment to social justice in their co-curricular offerings, most secular colleges do also. Like Catholic colleges, secular colleges also offer community service or service learning opportunities for students to work with poor children and families in dealing with school support, housing, food provision, and other social problems. In fact, the overwhelming majority of those on the Princeton Review list of the top eighty-one "colleges with a conscience" are secular colleges and universities.[100] The Princeton guide offers to "help students to find a socially responsible college" and includes list of questions that students can ask prospective colleges involving opportunities for volunteer work. Interestingly, one of the questions students are encouraged to ask is "what are the university's policies on issues such as fair labor, living wage of its employees and food salvaging operations?"[101]

A commitment to social justice, without a commitment to teaching students about the Church's foundation for social justice, makes a Catholic education no more distinctive than a secular education. Loyola University Chicago School of Law Professor John M. Breen maintains that "Catholic colleges must see it as their obligation to introduce students to the Catholic intellectual tradition—the tradition which Martin Luther King Jr. relied on in his struggle for civil rights, which refuted the evils of European fascism and Soviet totalitarianism, and challenges the individualism and materialism and liberal democracies today—then they will offer students something which secular schools do not . . . Then they can realistically hope to form men and women for others."[102]

Yet, ignoring the religious roots of the concept, the politically correct, secularized social justice has become so important on all campuses that it is now beginning to be used as a screening device for some careers. The National Council for Accreditation of Teacher Education, the nation's largest teacher education accrediting organization was criticized in 2006 for requiring that teacher candidates' "dispositions" must be "guided by beliefs and attitudes such as caring, fairness, honesty and responsibility, and social justice."[103] Representatives from the National Association of Scholars and the Foundation for Individual Rights in Education complained that the phrase, "social justice," was "ideologically freighted and ambiguous," and "simply too vague a term and susceptible to interpretation."[104]

In an effort to reinforce the Jesuit commitment to social justice, over three hundred representatives of the twenty-eight Jesuit colleges and universities gathered in October, 2000 at Santa Clara University to discuss the "Commitment to Justice in Jesuit Higher Education." The Reverend Peter-Hans-Kolvenbach, S. J. Superior General of the Society of Jesus, gave the keynote address, "The Service of Faith and the Promotion of Justice in American Jesuit Higher Education." The conference commemorated the twenty-fifth anniversary of the 32nd General Congregation of the Jesuits when the Jesuit commitment to faith and social justice was formulated. At the conclusion of the conference, delegates from each of the twenty-eight Jesuit colleges signed a pledge endorsing Fr. Kolvenbach's call for more faith-justice work on their campuses. Also featured were speeches by the longtime pro-choice stalwart Leon Panetta, former Clinton White House Chief of Staff and director of the Panetta Institute, and Dr. Claire Guadiani, then president of the secular Connecticut College and founder of a new level of college-community economic partnerships in New London, Connecticut. Several of those who attended the Santa Clara Conference compiled reports on how justice issues are integrated in their home institutions. For example, the conference report by faculty and administrators from Loyola University in Maryland suggests that "Justice can transform the campus culture at all levels" and mandated that "Justice begins at home" by recommending a "living wage" for Loyola employees.[105]

To understand how social justice issues achieved such prominence on Jesuit campuses and beyond, the following chapter will look closely at the ways in which the mission of the Jesuits changed so dramatically following the 1975 meeting of the 32nd General Congregation of the Jesuits.[106] It was a time when the message of the Gospel became so politicized that evangelization was no longer the goal. Rather than saving souls, this was a time when the Jesuits began to believe that the best way to help individuals was to redistribute society's wealth, creating an egalitarian society. This redefined social gospel has moved beyond the twenty-eight Jesuit colleges and has been embraced by Catholic campus leaders whose goals have moved from helping others get into heaven, to creating heaven on earth.[107]

Notes*

1.   Richard John Neuhaus. "A University of a Particular Kind." *First Things*. (April 2007): 32.
2.   http://minerva.stkate.edu/president/nsf/pages/catholicidentity
3.   http://minerva.stkate.edu/president/nsf/pages/catholicidentity
4.   www.sjc.edu/content.cfm/pageid/658
5.   www.csf.edu/csf/about/index.html
6.   www.hmu.edu/abouthnu/richhistory.html see also, www.hnu.edu/abouthnu/spiritualtradition.html
7.   www.hnu.edu/abouthnu/10goodreasons.html
8.   www.ndm.edu/about/missionstatement/
9.   www.stmary.edu/about/default.asp.
10.   www.ursuline.edu/president/mission.htm
11.   www.stonehill.edu/welcome/mission.htm
12.   www.barry.edu/aboutbarry/misision.default.htm
13.   www.csbsju,edu.about/vision/
14.   www.csbsju.edu/about/vision/
15.   www.mountsaintvincent.edu/325.htm
16.   www.mountsaintvincent.edu/325.htm
17.   www.marymountpv.edu/about/mission.asp
18.   www.stvincent.edu/our_mission2
19.   www.rosemont.edu/about/index.php
20.   www.sandiego.edu
21.   www.sandiego.edu
22.   www.fordham.edu

*All college and university websites were accessed during October-November, 2007

23. Melanie M. Morey and John J. Piderit, S. J. *Catholic Higher Education: A Culture in Crisis.* (New York: Oxford University Press, 2006), 206.
24. Ibid., 208.
25. Ibid., 206.
26. Ibid., 208.
27. Ibid., 208.
28. David J. O'Brien. *From the Heart of the Church: Catholic Higher Education and American Culture.* (Maryknoll, New York: Orbis Books, 1994), 125.
29. Ibid., 13.
30. www.aquinas.edu/about/index.html
31. www.assumption.edu/about/overv/facts/facts.html
32. www.quincy.edu/AboutQU/
33. www.ndnu.edu/about-us/president/mission.aspx
34. www.sl.edu/information.htm
35. www.francis.edu/aboutmission.htm
36. www.stfranciscollege.edu/about/history
37. 2005-2007 Catalog. Briar Cliff University.
38. www.cnr.edu/CNR/missta.html
39. www.mtmc.edu/about/mission.asp
40. www.smcvt.edu/about/facts.asp
41. www.anselm.edu/about+us/facts+about+us/College+Philosophy.htm
42. Job Advertisement. St. Joseph's University. *The Chronicle of Higher Education* Diversity Supplement. (September, 2007).
43. www.mtaloy.edu/about_mac. For U. S. News and World Report *America's Best Colleges* 2006: www.usnews.com/usnews/edu/college/director/brief/drmiss_3302_brief.php.
44. www.carroll.edu/about/mission.cc
45. www.dyc.edu/welcome/about.asp
46. www.cse.edu/about_collegeprofile.htm
47. www.iona.edu/about/mission.cfm
48. www.depaul.edu/about/
49. www.depaul.edu/about/
50. www.dominican.edu/about/giving/presidentscouncil/about-dominican.html
51. www.dc.edu/about.aspx?ID=90
52. www.lewisisu.edu/welcome/,ossopm.htm
53. www.elms.edu/about/mletter.htm
54. www.stjohns.edu/about/mission.
55. www.sjcny.edu/page.php/prmID/332
56. www.stac.edu/stacmiss.htm
57. www.naz.edu/trustees/aboutnaareth/mission.html
58. www.sjfc.edu/welcome/mission.asp
59. http://kings.edu/aboutkings/missionstatement.htm
60. www.annamaria.edu/about/mission.php
61. www.aquinas-tn.edu/overview/mission.htm
62. www.alvernia.edu/campuslife/handbool.htm
63. www.avila.edu/admission/mission,htm
64. www.desales.edu/default.aspx?pageid=95
65. www.desales.edu/default.aspx?pageid=95
66. www.naples.avemaria.edu/
67. www.christendom.edu/welcome/mission.shtml
68. www.thomasaquinas.edu/about/catholic.htm

69. www.thomasmorecollege.edu/about/catholiceducation.html
70. www.sju.edu/mission_statement.html
71. Malachi Martin. *The Jesuits: The Society of Jesus and the Betrayal of the Roman Catholic Church.* (New York: Simon and Schuster Touchstone Books, 1987), 479.
72. David Horowitz. "Debating the Academic Bill of Rights." (June 23, 2006): www.frontpagemagazine.com
73. www.sju.edu/sju/mission_statement.html
74. www.fairfield.edu/x2110.xml
75. www.lemoyne.edu/about/mission.htm
76. www.lmu.edu/page16894.aspx
77. www.luc.edu/planning/stratplan_04_09.shtml
78. www.slu.edu/jesuit_slu_mission_statement.html
79. www.canisius.edu/about/mission_statement.asp
80. www.jcu.edu/A&S/jcuniversity_mission_.htm
81. www.creighton.edu/mission/
82. www.georetown.edu/president/mission_statement.html
83. www.loyno.edu/welcome/mission.html
84. University of Scranton. Mission, Characteristics, and Goals. Approved by the Board of Trustees May 4, 2005.
85. www.wju.edu/about/mission.asp
86. www.xavier.edu/mission/
87. www.marquette.edu/about/mission/
88. Santa Clara Mission Statement, Approved by the Board of Trustees February 20, 1998
89. www.usfca.edu/mission/
90. www.regis.edu/regis.asp?sctn=abt
91. www.rockhurst.edu/about/glance/mission.asp
92. Mission Statement of Spring Hill College.
93. www.seattle.edu/home/about_seattle_university/mission/
94. Peter McDonough and Eugene C. Bianchi. *Passionate Uncertainty: Inside the American Jesuits.* (Berkeley, CA: University of California Press, 2002), 228.
95. Ibid.
96. Ibid., 227.
97. Ibid., 225.
98. Kelly Philips. "A Voice for the Voiceless: Achieving Social Justice is the Goal of the Oscar Romero Center for Faith in Action." *USD Magazine.* (Winter 2005).
99. Mark W. Roche. "Voting Our Conscience, Not Our Religion." *The New York Times.* (October 11, 2004).
100. Princeton Review. *Colleges with a Conscience: 81 Great Schools with Outstanding Community Involvement.* (2005).
101. Ibid.
102. Richard John Neuhaus. *First Things.* "The Public Square." (August/September, 2006): 81.
103. Paula Wasley. "Accreditor of Education Schools Drops Controversial Social Justice Language." *Chronicle of Higher Education* 52. (June 16, 2006): A-13.
104. Ibid.
105. Paul Bagley, "Commitment to Justice in Jesuit Higher Education: Conference Report." Santa Clara University. (October 5-8, 2000).
106. Paul Shaughnessy. "Are the Jesuits Catholic?" *The Weekly Standard.* (June 3,

2002): 27-31.

107.   Steven Malanga. "The Religious Left, Reborn. *City Journal.* (Autumn 2007): 76-84.

4

A Pope Away from a Perfect Life

Malachi Martin, author of *The Jesuits,* began his 1986 best-selling story of the Society of Jesus by stating "A state of war exists between the papacy and the Religious Order of the Jesuits—the Society of Jesus."[1] It is a sad story of the decline of the Jesuits, a religious order that was founded more than four centuries ago with the intention of gathering a group of courageous and dedicated religious men whose primary purpose was to defend the Church and the papacy. And, while it is a discouraging story of unfaithfulness and loss, it is an important one because it helps to explain how Catholic colleges lost their way. Although there are only twenty-eight Jesuit colleges throughout the country, the influence of the Jesuits on Catholic higher education remains strong as Catholic college administrators have long looked to the Jesuits for ideas on how to structure the curriculum and culture on their own campuses.

Indeed, from the earliest days of Catholic education, the Jesuits set the standard for the ways these colleges and universities should structure themselves. The Jesuit way was always something to emulate. From its founding, the Society of Jesus had organized itself on military lines "with a military love for a clear chain of command: The Jesuit was to serve as a soldier of God beneath the banner of the Cross and to serve the Lord alone and the Church, his spouse, under the Roman pontiff, the vicar of Christ on earth."[2] The Jesuit mission was to "strive especially for the defense and propagation of the faith and for the progress of souls in Christian life and doctrine." This mission applied to the Jesuit educational initiatives where the task was defined as one of devising methods to "reaffirm the Jesuit ethos in educational institutions."[3] And, while they have been involved in many things, the Jesuits had always been best known as brilliant educators.

The founder, a Basque soldier named Ignatius Loyola, believed the more universal the work, the more divine it becomes.[4] He was successful almost at once. Within thirty years of its founding, the Jesuits were working in every continent and in practically every form of apostolate and educational field. In the first four hundred years, they created colleges and universities in the United States and hundreds of high schools and academies throughout the world. Because of their faithfulness and their zeal to bring the faith to others, the Jesuits provided the Church with 38 canonized saints, 134 holy men already declared "Blessed" by the Catholic Church, 36 already declared "Venerable," and 115 considered to have been "Servants of God." Of these, 243 were martyrs—put to death for their loyalty.[5]

Loyola's intention for the Jesuits was that they be "Pope's Men," supremely faithful to the pope. And, in this defense, the Jesuits "carried the battle" right into the territories of all papal enemies: "They waged public controversies with kings, they debated in Protestant universities, they preached at crossroads and in marketplaces. They were everywhere, showering their contemporaries with their brilliance, with wit, with acerbity, with learning, and with piety. Their consistent theme was that the Bishop of Rome is successor to Peter the Apostle upon whom Christ founded his Church."[6] From the earliest days, the mission of the Jesuits was the defense of papal authority and the propagation of the faith.

But much of that ended in 1965. With the close of Vatican II and the election of Pedro de Arrupe y Gondra as the 27th Father General of the Jesuits, the Jesuits began to wage war with the pope. The war has continued throughout the reign of each of the last three popes, as many within the order have denigrated and deceived them, disobeying them as they waited for each pope to die in the hope that the next pope would leave the order with a free hand to accomplish their new mission of social justice.[7] Believing themselves to be just a pope away from a good life, one Jesuit writer observed that "the Jesuits have become papists who hate the Pope and evangelists who have lost the faith."[8]

Indeed, in a 2002 article on the Society of Jesus, Fr. Paul Shaughnessy, S. J., writes, "Almost overnight the pope's light infantry became a battalion in which every man decided for himself which war he was fighting."[9] The result was an institutional nightmare, "confusion and cowardice at the top; despair, rage and disillusionment in the ranks . . . American Jesuits went from 8,400 members in 1965 to fewer than 3,500 today. Entering novices declined from a peak one-year total of 409 to a low of 38. Worse, the number of priests who leave the order each year roughly equals the number of entering novices; the number of Jesuits who die annually is twice as high as either."[10]

While the demographics are depressing, Fr. Shaughnessy laments that "the real crisis, at its heart, is not one of size but of allegiance." Just as all wars are about power, the current war between the Vatican and the Jesuits involves a power struggle over authority—the struggle over who is in command of the Roman Catholic Church and her institutions, especially her colleges and universities. Yet, in some important ways, the struggle goes much deeper than authority and control, and involves an attempt by the Jesuits to redefine the very purpose of the Catholic Church itself—from one of spiritual otherworldliness with a concern for eternal salvation—to a Church involved in the here and now and the struggle to create a new sociopolitical system by helping to redistribute the earth's resources and goods. Quite simply, the new goal of the Jesuits was to use the Church as a way to help usher in a new socialist society—a Marxist Heaven on Earth. This new goal—antipapal and sociopolitical in nature—continues to have a profound effect on not only the Jesuit colleges and universities, but on much of Catholic higher education. With the Jesuits setting the standard for social justice, the Jesuit mission is reflected in the redefined mission statements on social justice—and in the faculty's antipathy to the authority of the Vatican.

In McDonough and Bianchi's 2002 book on the Jesuits, *Passionate Uncertainty*, the theme of "waiting for the next pope" was a common one. Published prior to the death of John Paul II, the authors interviewed a number of Jesuits who are almost disdainful of the papacy:

> A small minority are enthusiastic about the vision and values of Pope John Paul II and Cardinal Ratzinger; the rest are waiting for a new Pope, who they hope will restore the dynamism and direction of the council {Vatican II}. They are not convinced that this Pope really is committed to the listening necessary for any fruitful dialogue with other Christian churches, with other religions, with scholarly disciplines, with economic, political, and technological forces shaping contemporary cultures. Instead of dialogue, there are various forms of monologue—encyclicals, apostolic constitutions declarations by curial congregations, the Catechism of the Catholic Church . . .[11]

Other Jesuits spoke even more forcefully. One Jesuit history professor declared that Pope John Paul II was "not just one of the worst popes throughout history; he is the worst . . . There's a cutting off of dialogue, a listening to one side . . ."[12] A second Jesuit sarcastically stated that, "The Society has not sold its soul to the Restoration of John Paul II."

And another Jesuit described the pope even more negatively, "I am scandalized by Rome's intransigent refusal to re-examine its doctrines regarding gender and sex (birth control, ordination of women, married clergy, homosexuality, divorce, and remarriage.) I am scandalized by the attempts to quash dissent and any challenge to papal power . . . Frankly, I think the church is being governed by thugs."[13] Still, another actually wishes for his own Society of Jesus to "facilitate" the death of the Catholic Church itself:

> The Church as we have known it, is dying, at least in the West . . . Its growing poverty will make possible many changes; the ordination of women and married men and the ascension of the laity to administrative and magisterial positions of leadership; the growth of local churches, the dismantling of the Vatican and its bureaucracies; the movement to a servant leadership . . . I hope and pray that the Society will help to facilitate this death and resurrection.[14]

While the Jesuit animosity is well documented in *Passionate Uncertainty*, the question remains: How could this happen? How could four hundred years of support for the papacy dissolve so quickly after 1965? While it would be easy to blame "the sixties" and the questioning of authority that characterized the decade, it would only be part of the story. To truly understand the current sad state of the Jesuits, we need to look much more deeply into the years following Vatican II—and we need to look beyond the Church in the United States.

According to historians like Malachi Martin, the war between the papacy and the Jesuits began when a small number of Jesuit priests became involved in the propagation of a new more liberating and empowering theology that coupled theology with sociology and a dominant concern for the "here and now" rather than eternal salvation. A longtime Jesuit commitment to missionary work in Nicaragua became redefined when the Jesuits began to view their mission in more worldly terms. The Jesuits began to see their work as helping the Roman Catholic country defeat the regime led by the Somoza family. Allying with Daniel Ortega y Saavedra and the Marxist Sandinistas, the Jesuits became leaders in what emerged as a violent Sandinista attack on the Somoza regime. The Jesuit alliance also involved alliances with Fidel Castro's Communist Cuba as well as the Palestine Liberation Organization and the Soviet Union: "The Sandinistas also entered into a pact with the Palestine Liberation Organization whereby the PLO would train Sandinistas in guerrilla tactics . . . The overall arrangement was that Nicaragua, as a nation, would be completely assimilated into the Marxism of one party." The Sandinista leaders openly proclaimed their ultimate aim, "to create a Marxist society in Nicaragua to serve as the womb from which Marxist revolution throughout Central America would be born. Revolution throughout the Americas was the slogan."[15]

The Jesuits were important to the Sandinista leadership. With more than 90 percent of the Nicaraguan population belonging to the Catholic Church, the Sandinistas knew that in order to gain the support of the people they needed to enlist the Catholic Church to legitimate their activities. As representatives of the Catholic Church, Jesuits were trusted by the people—they had been present as Catholic missionaries in Nicaragua since the 1600s. For the Jesuits and the Nicaraguan people, liberation theology provided the Sandinista support because this theology "of the people" combined Christianity with the very aim of Marxist-Leninism: "Heaven became the earthly paradise of the workers from which capitalism is abolished. Justice became the uprooting of capitalist gains, which would be returned to the people, to the mystical body of Christ, the democratic socialists of Nicaragua. And, the Church became that mystical body, the people deciding its fate and determining how to worship, pray, and live, under the guidance of Marxist leaders."[16]

Enlisting the Jesuits in the war, the Sandinistas successfully redefined the armed violence of a Marxist-style revolution into a religious action sanctioned by legitimate Church spokesmen. The Jesuits were joined by Franciscan and Maryknoll teachers and lecturers throughout the Catholic schools of Central America and, eventually, throughout the United States: "Scores of religious publications—newspapers, magazines, bulletins, releases—published and distributed in the United States by the Jesuits, the Maryknoll Missionaries, the Sisters of Loreto, the Sisters of St. Joseph of Peace, the Sisters of Notre Dame of Namur, the Leadership Conference of Women Religious, the Conference of Major Superiors of Men, and kindred organizations all defended the Nicaraguan revolution and the role of clerics in it."[17] Many of them alluded to a Marxist utopia in which the "people of God" became the new Church—and made the rules of the Church. Franciscan Liberation Theologian Leonardo Boff, the chief promoter of the dream, dismissed the hierarchical authority of the Church mandating that "the sacred power must be put back into the hands of the people . . . No teaching or directing authority would be allowed from above, from the alien hierarchic Church. In fact, the very symbols of that Church must be firmly rejected. Symbols and all else must come only from below—from the people."[18]

During these early days, few understood what was happening. Pope Paul VI remained uninvolved because he erroneously believed that the superiors of the Society of Jesus would supervise their priests. As a result, the Vatican did not become involved until 1973 when it became apparent that the Jesuits were involved in a revolutionary war that included killings, bombings, bank robberies, kidnappings, torture, and mutilation. But, by then, it was too late.[19] After a prolonged revolution in which 45,000 were wounded, 40,000 children were orphaned, and over 1,000,000 people were reduced to starvation, the Sandinistas—and their Jesuit supporters—marched in triumph into Managua on July 19, 1979.

The Somozas were removed from power by the three factions of the Sandinista Front for National Liberation. The Carter Administration immediately contributed millions of American tax dollars to the Sandinista regime and the president posed for pictures in the Rose Garden of the White House with Sandinista leader, Daniel Ortega y Saavedra, and two other members of his Sandinista junta. Later that year, the Sandinistas assassinated Somoza, his driver, and his bodyguard. By the following year, more than 2,000 political enemies of the Sandinistas had been executed. More than 6,000 were imprisoned—many of them were priests who refused to ally with the Sandinistas. From its first days in power, the Sandinista government included "five loyal and useful priests" in cabinet positions including Jesuit Fernado Cardenal, Jesuit Alvaro Arguello, Father Ernesto Cardenal, Maryknoll Father Miguel D'Escoto Brockman, and diocesan priest, Father Edgar Parrales.[20] The newly elected Pope John Paul II allowed the priests to serve in the Sandinista government "temporarily" until the country recovered from the effects of the armed revolution. Vatican sources reveal that the pontiff regretted this decision soon after.[21]

In a rebuke to the Jesuits in February, 1982 Pope John Paul II reminded the priests that "The ways of the religious minded do not follow the calculations of men. They do not use as parameters the cult of power, riches or politics . . . Your proper activity is not in the temporal realm, nor in that one which is the field of laymen and which must be left to them . . . St. Ignatius was in all instances obedient to the Throne of Peter."[22] The pope's message was ignored.

Later that year, in a letter to the Nicaraguan bishops the pope denounced the "People's Church" in especially harsh terms: "This Church born of the people was a new invention that was both absurd and of perilous character . . . Only with difficulty, could it avoid being infiltrated by strangely ideological connotations along the line of a certain political radicalization, for accomplishing determined aims."[23] This was a strong statement from the John Paul II, who usually spoke in conciliatory terms, but by then it was too late for the pope to have much influence on the Jesuits—they had already stopped listening to directives from the Vatican. The commitment to social justice and the preferential option for the poor continued to be redefined—and although the Sandinistas soon lost power in Nicaragua when, under pressure from the United States, they finally allowed the people of Nicaragua to vote; they remain a formidable threat in the country even today. Two years ago, *The New York Times* reported on Daniel Ortega's return to power in the headline, "Old Foe of the U. S. Trying for a Comeback in Nicaragua."[24] And, in 2006, Ortega was successful in his fourth campaign for the presidency in Nicaragua. There are also renewed concerns about Sandinista ties to Islamic terrorists in the Middle East by revolutionaries. *The New York Times* reported that a "sting operation by the United States and Nicaraguan authorities netted a Nicaraguan group trying to sell shoulder-fired missiles that terrorism experts consider a threat to civilian aircraft."[25]

While the story of the Jesuits' role in Nicaragua may seem tangential to Catholic higher education, it is an important one because of its continued effect on many Catholic colleges and universities. The ideology of the "People's Church" has been embraced by liberation theologians on most Catholic campuses. And the Sandinistas remain romantic role models for faculty on many of these campuses. In fact, at the University of San Diego, Dora Maria Tellez, one of the Sandinista leaders of the revolution, has been an honored guest on campus. In 2001, Tellez received the prestigious Sally Furey award. And, while few faculty were aware of her revolutionary activities, those who championed Tellez as the recipient of the honor knew quite well of her storied past—it was the reason she was invited to campus.

However, in the post-9/11 world of 2005, when Tellez was invited yet again to the San Diego campus, the US State Department denied her a visa to travel to the United States. The general consul in Nicaragua, Luis Espada-Platet, stated in a letter to Ms. Tellez that the Immigration and Nationality Act "prevents persons who endorse or espouse terrorist activity from entering the country."[26] Under the Patriot Act, the federal government has the authority to exclude foreigners who, in the government's view, have used positions of prominence to endorse or espouse terrorist activity—or who have engaged in terrorist activities.

Dora Maria Tellez had been invited to study at the University of San Diego in preparation for her appointment as a Robert F. Kennedy Visiting Professor of Latin American Studies at Harvard. The Tellez faculty position at Harvard was to be a joint appointment in the Harvard Divinity School and the Harvard Rockefeller Center for Latin American Studies. Since Tellez was required to learn to speak English in order to teach at Harvard, she had planned to participate in the University of San Diego English Language Academy for the Summer and Fall 2005 semesters, and then begin teaching at Harvard in January of 2006.

While Tellez states that she "is a scholar and not a terrorist" and claims in published interviews to have "no idea why I have been so labeled," the reality is that, in 1978, Tellez described herself as a "combatant and guerrilla leader" of the Sandinistas. Tellez was one of twenty-five revolutionaries who dressed as waiters and stormed a session of Congress at Nicaragua's National Assembly—holding elected representatives and their staff members hostage. In those days, Tellez called herself "Commander 2" because she served as the "second-in-command" in the takeover of the national palace. In an impressive show of force on August 22, 1978, Tellez and her comrades held two thousand government officials hostage in a two-day standoff. Threatening to kill the hostages, Tellez was in charge of negotiating with representatives of the Somoza regime until the Sandinista demands were met and the Somoza-led government acquiesced to the demands and released hundreds of political prisoners that had been imprisoned since December of 1974.[27]

In 1979, Tellez led guerrilla fighters in the pivotal city of Leon—and is described admiringly in a memoir by one of her own comrades as "one of the fiercest guerrillas during the final offensive."[28] A self-described lesbian, her entire military staff consisted of female guerrilla soldiers. After the revolution, Tellez served alongside Jesuit priests in the Sandinista government cabinet where she remained an advocate for gay and lesbian rights and full reproductive rights for women in the Catholic country.

Despite all of this—or perhaps for some, because of all of this—122 faculty members and administrators from the University of San Diego, Harvard, and Notre Dame signed a letter denouncing the actions of the Bush Administration and demanding that the state department "clear her name by restoring her human rights." It is most likely that the Notre Dame involvement is related to the fact that last year, Tariq Ramadan, like Dora Maria Tellez, was denied a visa under the Patriot Act to teach there. While the faculty claim that Ramadan, a scholar only interested in "social justice," was unfairly linked to terrorist groups simply because his grandfather, Hasan al-Banna, founded the Muslim Brotherhood (the most powerful Islamist institution of the twentieth century) the reality is that Tariq Ramadan seems to have developed his own links. Daniel Pipes has pointed out that Ramadan was banned from entering France in 1996 on suspicion of having links with an Algerian Islamist who had initiated a terrorist campaign in Paris.

The terrorist links are clear in both cases, yet in their zeal to address issues of economic and political justice, Catholic college faculty and administrators often overlook the details that might distract them from fulfilling their mission of social justice. It is likely that, other than those liberation theologians on campus who championed the Tellez invitation, many of the 122 faculty signatories of the state department denunciation were unaware of the Tellez Sandinista activities. Yet, some campus leaders are so attracted to the idea of the anti-American socialism that the Sandinistas represent as a form of social justice. In fact, in the San Diego case, faculty were reminded in a mass-email from a San Diego liberation theology professor that, Dora Maria Tellez could not be a terrorist because she had already been allowed to visit the Catholic San Diego campus in 2001 to administer the prestigious Sally Furey Lecture.[29] Besides, many on the faculty must have known that the University of San Diego has honored other members of terrorist organizations in the past. Luz Mendez, a Guatamalan National Revolution Unity Party member, received the University of San Diego 2004 PeaceMaker Award. The award was given to Mendez for "her work for justice" despite the fact that the state department lists the party as a terrorist organization.

For those outside of academia, it may be surprising to learn that such university honors and awards can be given to Sandinista revolutionary guerrillas or members of documented terrorist organizations. But, anyone who has spent any time working on a college campus learns quickly that in the upside-down world of academia, administrators defer to most faculty decisions—including the hiring and tenuring of faculty, the choosing of commencement speakers and honorary degree recipients, and the recipients of awards like those administered to Dora Maria Tellez or Luz Mendez—or even Larry Flynt, the infamous publisher of "mainstream" pornography who was an honored guest at Georgetown University a few years ago.

Faculty governance, rather than shared governance, is evident on Jesuit campuses where presidential deference to faculty demands reached new heights at the University of San Francisco in 2001. Under pressure from the faculty, Fr. Stephen Privett, S. J., San Francisco's new president, dismantled the St. Ignatius Institute, a Catholic great books program that the powerful progressive faculty members had long disdained because it was viewed as a conservative center of what one faculty member described as "a very narrow understanding of orthodoxy."[30]

Founded in 1976 by Jesuit priest Fr. Joseph Fessio, the St. Ignatius Institute provided a traditional core curriculum that had operated as a separate school within the university—hiring its own faculty, including conservative theologians that would most likely not be invited to teach at the Jesuit-led university because of their orthodoxy. It was an albatross for liberal faculty outside the institute because it provided a reminder of the authentic Catholic intellectual tradition, but it was an "oasis" for San Francisco students seeking an orthodox Catholic educational experience. One former student stated, "It taught me to think. It rooted my spiritual life. It gave me the best friends I could ever ask for . . . The Institute was more than an academic program . . . The St. Ignatius Institute changed my life."[31]

However, after only four months in his new position as president of the university, Fr. Privett acquiesced to his faculty's concerns about the conservative nature of the institute and suddenly—without consulting with the Institute's Advisory Board or following any established procedures or protocol—fired the institute's longtime director, John Galten, along with institute associate director John Hamlon, and merged the institute with the struggling and decidedly non-orthodox Catholic studies program at the University of San Francisco. Claiming that the "restructuring creates efficiencies by consolidating resources," Fr. Privett defended his decision to make sweeping changes in the structure of the institute by indicating that "appointing a new director for the Saint Ignatius Institute provides the requisite academic leadership, promotes synergies between the Institute and other University programs, and creates efficiencies by consolidating resources."[32] Claiming that he fired Galten, in an effort to improve the "credibility and integrity of the program within the University and across the academy in general," Fr. Privett denigrated the long tenure and the accomplishments of the administrators of the institute by saying that "the directors of academic programs must be faculty members . . . neither was qualified to judge the academic qualifications of prospective faculty, shape curriculum or assign courses to the appropriate faculty person."[33] Ignoring the fact that the institute had attracted some of the best students at the university and had received the prestigious Templeton Award, a national honor for its outstanding curriculum, Fr. Privett acted swiftly to dismantle the program.

Galten responded to his dismissal in a statement published in the *National Catholic Reporter*: "Over the past 25 years, the Institute has been assaulted by members of the Jesuit community . . . The Institute had been singled out for punishment by members of the Jesuit community who disagreed with its tone, despite its academic excellence."[34] Following the firings, six Institute faculty members resigned in protest. One of those who resigned was quoted in the *National Catholic Register* pointing out that "the Institute frequently had to fend off attempts by liberal Jesuits in the theology department to try to insert themselves into the teaching staff of the program. They just wouldn't let it be . . . The Institute always had a theological position that said the role of theology is to explain why the Church teaches what she teaches—as opposed to taking a position of what is sometimes called the 'loyal dissent.'"[35]

The controversy achieved national attention when *National Review* writer Stanley Kurtz published several articles in *National Review Online*. The *San Francisco Chronicle* published a full-page statement of protest decrying the destruction of the institute—paid for by prominent conservatives including William Bennett, former US secretary of education; Ralph McInerny, philosophy professor at the University of Notre Dame; Robert George, professor of political science at Princeton University; Michael Novak, religion and policy scholar at the American Enterprise Institute; George Weigel, senior fellow at the Ethics and Public Policy Center; Hadley Arkes, philosophy professor at Amherst College; and Richard John Neuhaus, editor of *First Things*. The *Chronicle* statement read, "When even a nominally Catholic institution like USF refuses to allow one small center of traditional Catholic learning to exist in the form it has for 25 years, we believe it truly is an educational crisis."[36]

Students at the St. Ignatius Institute staged a campus demonstration—including protest chants in Latin—in defense of the program.[37] Lamenting the loss of what one student called "the integration of the academic, social, and spiritual elements," several students said that the "independent orthodox voice" provided by the institute was what attracted them to the school.[38] There were even appeals made to then-Cardinal Ratzinger as the leader of the Vatican's Congregation for Catholic Education. And, although the Cardinal responded with pleas for collaboration from both sides and a request to maintain "the integrity of traditional

Catholic doctrine" at the University of San Francisco, Fr. Privett remained steadfast in his support for the faculty demands to assume control of the institute—and appeared to pay little attention to the Vatican directives.

In fact, Fr. Privett's first faculty appointment for the newly revamped St. Ignatius Institute was Albert R. Jonsen, an ex-Jesuit priest and a pro-choice medical ethicist who has publicly spoken in defense of human cloning, euthanasia, and tissue banks using material derived from elective abortions. Stanley Kurtz suggested that "It is more than obvious that President Privett is bound and determined to wipe out any small remaining center of traditional Catholic teaching at his university—and to do so in direct violation of admonitions from the Vatican itself."[39]

Attempts by the fired institute staff to form an entirely new college—separate from the University of San Francisco were met with a renewed—and personal attack on Fr. Fessio, S. J., the founder of the Ignatius Institute. In fact, Fr. Fessio's Jesuit superior ordered him to sever all of his public and private ties to the newly created college—and transferred him out of Catholic higher education to the post of chaplain at an obscure forty-bed hospital in Duarte, California. Forbidden to have any contact with the fledgling college, Fessio's Jesuit Provincial arbitrarily imposed the punishment on Fessio without any public explanation. As Kurtz said, "Imposing a transfer like that on a man of Fessio's stature is something like sending a purged Communist leader to Siberia."[40] Such a punishment for recalcitrant Jesuit priests who are unwilling to conform to the liberal orthodoxy is not unusual. In fact, Kurtz points out that the obscure hospital in Duarte, California seems to have become the "Devils Island" for Jesuits who don't conform to the order's progressive politics. Fr. Fessio was preceded in his exile to Duarte by Fr. Cornelius Buckley, a longtime Jesuit history professor at the University of San Francisco, deemed insufficiently liberal for the school. Labeling him "divisive," the Jesuits exiled Fr. Buckley to Duarte in 1990—where he remained for many years prayerfully obedient to the vows he took in an order of dissident priests who have defined him as the "disobedient" one.[41]

Indeed, this is the real irony of the Jesuits now that the dissenters in the order, who rose to power through disobedience to papal authority, use their power to repress traditional Jesuits like Fr. Fessio and Fr. Buckley.[42] In theory, Jesuit college presidents like Fr. Privett remain subject to their religious superiors, but in reality, Fr. Shaughnessy writes that "the presidents set the tone by which Jesuit life is lived" and, on the occasion of conflict between university presidents and Jesuit superiors, "the presidents win hands down."[43] What Fr. Shaughnessy left unsaid was that on the occasion of conflict between university presidents and the faculty, the faculty always wins. Like Harvard President Larry Summers, who was forced out after he questioned the feminist faculty orthodoxy on gender differences within the sciences, the fate of Fr. Joseph Fessio, a former student of Pope Benedict XVI and founder of the St. Ignatius Institute and Campion College, provides a good illustration of the power of the faculty, the subservience of the presidents to the faculty, and the weakness of the now-neutralized boards of trustees on Catholic campuses.

Looking closely at the leadership on Jesuit campuses, Fr. Shaughnessy concludes that prestigious positions, like university administrators, are filled for the most part with a group of Jesuit priests informally known as the "Gallery Owners." Adept at fund raising, the Jesuit presidents are described by Fr. Shaughnessy as, "discreet, well-spoken, well-dressed gay priests in their fifties and early sixties:"[44]

> Where the older Jesuits are notable for the heat of their anti-papal passion, the Gallery Owners display a nearly complete apathy toward religion in all its forms. Conventionally liberal, they support condoms and women priests less as a matter of faith than a fashion statement—rather like wearing a baseball cap backwards…The teachings of the Church, being largely an irrelevance, has minimal importance in shaping the opinion of the Gallery Owners, who tend to regard orthodox Catholicism—like boxing or heterosexuality—as one of the coarse amusements of the working class.[45]

It is, of course, impossible to verify Fr. Shaughnessy's provocative perceptions of the high status "Gallery Owners" within the academic administration of Jesuit colleges and universities. What can be verified are examples of Jesuit college presidents openly dissenting from Vatican directives about sexual morality. In 2002, Seattle University president, Rev. Stephen Sundborg, S. J., wrote an opinion piece for the *Seattle Times* urging Catholic bishops to reject the bishop's recent directive on the unsuitability of homosexuals for ordination and, instead, advised priests to "affirm unmistakably the suitability of homosexual persons to be ordained as priests" and to apologize for any statements on the bishops' part that have called their lives of ministry as priests into question. Fr. Sundborg also called on the bishops to affirm that they "seek not to exert external control over Catholic institutions of academic freedom."[46]

The results of such beliefs are evident on Jesuit campuses. In fact, in 2007, Fr. Thomas J. Brennan, a Jesuit priest and assistant professor of English at St. Joseph's University in Philadelphia, announced in the middle of the celebration of a campus mass that he is homosexual. During the mass he was celebrating in front of more than four hundred students and university community members, he spoke of his homosexuality as one of the "worst kept secrets on campus."[47] The reason it is no longer a secret is because according to Fr. Brennan's own writings, he has been "coming out" to the students in his classes for several years now. In fact, in a book entitled, *Jesuit Postmodern*, Fr. Brennan contributes a chapter entitled "A Tale of Two Comings Out: Priest and Gay on a Catholic Campus," in which he describes his decision to "come out" to the students enrolled in his courses and writes that "coming out as lesbian or gay remains a vital faculty contribution."[48]

Since 2002, when the Roman Catholic Church's sex abuse scandal emerged nationwide, the spotlight gradually moved from parish priests to several high profile cases involving gay Jesuit priests working at Catholic colleges and universities. And as more victims came forward, concerns and criticisms that were raised about how dioceses had handled sex abuse cases began to be raised about the Jesuits.[49] These concerns are especially prevalent in the Oregon Province, which had 25 Jesuits "credibly accused" of sexual abuse out of about 250 Jesuits in Washington, Oregon, Alaska, Montana, and Idaho. Since 2002, the Oregon province alone has spent about $8.5 million to settle forty claims, and an additional eighty claims are pending.[50]

In Washington, *The Seattle Times* reported that the former Gonzaga University President Fr. John Leary, who died in 1993, had been accused of abusing male undergraduate students. Father John D. Whitney, currently the head of the Oregon province of Jesuits, acknowledged that Fr. Leary had been accused of abusing minors and young men while he was president of Gonzaga. Male students have also filed sexual abuse allegations against Rev. Michael Toulouse and the Rev. Englebert Axer, both deceased Seattle University professors. A lawsuit that is currently pending in Seattle claims that Jesuit Father Michael Toulouse sexually abused at least one minor in Spokane when he was teaching at Gonzaga High School and abused others after he was transferred to Seattle University.[51] As recently as September, 2006, the Rev. Anton T. Harris, a Jesuit, resigned his position as vice-president of Mission and Ministry at Seattle University after the *Seattle Post-Intelligencer* ran a front page report that he had sent pornographic greeting cards to a twenty-five-year-old Jesuit seminarian. The vice-presidency position in mission and ministry was created to ensure that Seattle remained mindful of its mission as a Jesuit, Catholic institution, yet the young seminarian complained that Fr. Harris and two other Jesuits had made homosexual overtures to him during his time in the seminary. While these examples certainly cannot be generalized, they point to serious problems on Jesuit campuses—and beyond. The following chapter will demonstrate that the problems of dissent that have plagued Jesuit institutions are replicated on Catholic campuses throughout the country—especially within theology departments.

Notes

1. Malachi Martin. *The Jesuits: The Society of Jesus and the Betrayal of the Roman Catholic Church.* (New York: Simon and Schuster, 1986), 13.
2. Paul Shaughnessy. "Are the Jesuits Catholic?" *The Weekly Standard.* (June 3, 2002): 27.
3. Peter McDonough and Eugene C. Bianchi. *Passionate Uncertainty: Inside the American Jesuits.* (Berkeley, CA: University of California Press, 2002), 220.
4. Martin. *The Jesuits.* 13.
5. Ibid., 27.
6. Ibid., 28.
7. Ibid., 36.
8. Shaughnessy. "Are the Jesuits Catholic?" 27.
9. Ibid.
10. Ibid.
11. McDonough and Bianchi. *Passionate Uncertainty.* 268.
12. Ibid., 275.
13. Ibid., 279.
14. Ibid., 278.
15. Martin. *The Jesuits,* 55-56.
16. Ibid., 57.
17. Ibid., 61.
18. Ibid., 59.
19. Ibid., 60.
20. Ibid., 63.
21. Ibid., 112.
22. Ibid.
23. Ibid.
24. Ginger Thompson. "Old Foe of U. S. Trying for a Comeback in Nicaragua." *The New York Times.* (April 5, 2005): www.nytimes.com/2005/04/05/international/americas/05nicaragua.html
25. Ibid.
26. Maria Pilar Aquino. "We are Not Silent: Public Declaration by 122 Members of the Academic Community In Support for Dora Maria Tellez." San Diego, CA. March 29, 2005.
27. Gioconda Belli. *The Country Under My Skin: A Memoir of Love and War.* (New York: Random House, 2002), 194.
28. Ibid.
29. Aquino. "We are Not Silent."
30. Published comments by Sr. Theresa Moser, RSCJ, Assistant Dean, College of Arts and Sciences, University of San Francisco. Included along with the Response by Stephen A. Privett, S. J. President of the University of San Francisco to the charges made on the website of Friends of the St. Ignatius Institute: http://vatican2.org/USF.htm.

31.   Mary Beth Bonacci. "A Great Books Program Bites the Dust." February 1, 2002: www.freepublic.com/focus/news/67543/posts

32.   Response by Stephen A. Privett, S. J. President of the University of San Francisco to the charges made on the website of Friends of the St. Ignatius Institute: http://vatican2.org/USF.htm

33.   Ibid.

34.   Melissa Jones. "Conservative St. Ignatius Institute Revamped. *National Catholic Reporter*. (February 16, 2001): www.natcath.com/NCR_online/archives/021601/021601dhtml

35.   Eve Tushnet. "University of San Francisco vs St. Ignatius Institute." *National Catholic Register*. (April 8-14, 2001): www.catholiceducation.org/articles/education/ed0098.html

36.   Cited by Patrick Reilly. "Society Urges Return of USF's St. Ignatius Institute." Cardinal Newman Society: www.cardinalnewmansociety.org. Cites ad published in the *San Francisco Chronicle*. (March 18, 2001).

37.   Stanley Kurtz. "Firing Fessio." *National Review Online*. (March 13, 2002): www.nationalreview.com

38.   Tushnet. "University of San Francisco vs St. Ignatius Institute."

39.   Kurtz. "Firing Fessio."

40.   Ibid.

41.   George Neumayr. "Jesuits Implode*" The American Prowler*. (March 13, 2002).

42.   Ibid.

43.   Shaughnessy. "Are the Jesuits Catholic?" 30.

44.   Ibid.

45.   Ibid.

46.   Rev. Stephen Sundborg, S. J. *The Seattle Times*. (May 30, 2002): http://www.seattleu.edu/proffice/news/2002/PR_Detail.asp?recordID=5302002101445

47.   John Henry Westen. "Jesuit Priest Comes Out as Gay During Sunday Mass at Catholic University Parish." (November 5, 2007): www.lifesite.net/ldn/2007/nov/07110505.html

48.   Thomas J. Brennan, S. J. "A Tale of Two Comings Out." Included in *Jesuit Postmodern*. Edited by Francis X. Clooney, S. J. (Lanham, MD: Lexington Books, 2006), 193.

49.   Janet. I Tu. "Abuse Cases Put Focus on Jesuits." *The Seattle Times*. (October 16, 2006): http://seattletimes.nwsource.com/html/localnews/2003306651_jesuit16m.html

50.   Ibid.

51.   "Sexual Abuse Scandal Leads to Catholic University Official's Resignation." *Catholic News Service*. (October 17, 2006): www.catholic.org/printer_friendly.php?id=21645&section=Cathcom

5

Theological Confusion

In an essay entitled, "Liberal Catholicism Reexamined," Peter Steinfels, the longtime religion correspondent for the *New York Times,* writes, "one definition of liberal Catholicism is simply papal teaching a hundred years too soon." Reflecting the sentiments of many theologians on Catholic campuses who believe that their dissenting views on the divinity of Christ, the path to salvation, women's ordination, reproductive rights, and sexual morality are the views of the future of the Catholic Church, Steinfels believes that liberal Catholicism "defends the relative autonomy of distinct spheres of human activity, whether of politics or religion or science, art or literature."[1]

In contrast, Cardinal Francis George of Chicago, who was elected president of the National Conference of Catholic Bishops in 2007, argues that liberal Catholicism is "an exhausted project, now parasitical on a substance that no longer exists . . . unable to pass on the faith in its integrity."[2] And Fr. Richard John Neuhaus, editor of *First Things,* warns of the "serious harm that can be done by unbounded criticism, conflict and contradiction . . . the harm of souls misled—and possibly lost . . . and of innumerable persons denied the high adventure of Catholic fidelity." Arguing that a major problem for liberal Catholicism is its inability to come to terms with the requirement of obedience for Catholics, Fr. Neuhaus suggests that intellectual obedience is an inseparable part of what it means to be Catholic.[3]

It is into this debate over change, criticism, fidelity, and obedience that *Ex Corde Ecclesiae,* the most important document affecting Catholic colleges and universities in this century, was released. Pope John Paul II's Apostolic Constitution on Catholic Colleges and Universities is important because it was the first attempt by the Vatican to revitalize what Pope John Paul views as the "authentically Catholic character" of the

Church's colleges and universities. And while *Ex Corde* acknowledges that the Catholic University, as a university, possesses the institutional autonomy necessary to perform its functions effectively and guarantees its members academic freedom, the document reminds those working on Catholic campuses that this freedom must always be viewed "within the confines of the truth and the common good" and that there must be "fidelity" to the Christian message as it comes to us through the Church.

Toward that goal, *Ex Corde* states that the "honour and responsibility of a Catholic University is to consecrate itself without reserve to the causes of truth."[4] And *Ex Corde* holds faculty and administrators at Catholic colleges and universities responsible for pursuing and proclaiming that truth. For Pope John Paul, the pursuit of truth is the university's way of serving both the dignity of man and the good of the Church. *Ex Corde Ecclesiae* maintains that it is in the context of the "impartial search for truth that the relationship between faith and reason is brought to light and meaning."[5]

It is these very constraints that have compelled many Catholic college faculty and administrators to spend more than a decade protesting the document and refusing to comply with the requirements contained within it. Much of the response by college administrators and theologians reveal status concerns. In fact, so alarmed with the demands of *Ex Corde* were Boston College President Donald Monan and Edward Malloy, president of Notre Dame, that they published an article warning that the papal document would threaten the status of their institutions: "The universities' acceptance of the obligations spelled out here would mean the sacrifice of many of those prerogatives that make Catholic universities and their professional staffs the respected and influential members of the higher education community that they are." Concerned about a loss of status in the eyes of their secular peers, the presidents of Notre Dame and Boston College wrote that they desired a document for Catholic colleges and universities that "by reason of its literary style, as well as its content, they would be proud to display to sister institutions of higher education."[6]

Describing the decree as "unworkable and dangerous," the editors of *America* warned that the impact of the norms of *Ex Corde* would be "disastrous" for Catholic colleges and universities.[7] And, in an especially hyperbolic article, one theologian likened the approval of *Ex Corde* to the "Doomsday Clock" for Catholic higher education. Drawing upon the metaphor of the doomsday clock, a vestige of the cold war, the Bulletin of Atomic Scientists showed how close the world was to the midnight of mass nuclear annihilation. Jon Nilson, theology professor at Loyola University, Chicago, warned of a similar annihilation for Catholic colleges:

> If there were a doomsday clock for Catholic higher education in the United States, its hands moved closer to midnight in November, 1999, when the U. S. bishops approved *Ex Corde Ecclesiae*. The hands moved still closer this past November when the bishops accepted draft procedures for implementing the Application's requirement of a mandatum for theologians. The hands are still moving, counting down to the moment when the American experience of independent but church related colleges and university as envisioned and enacted by Theodore Hesburgh, Timothy Healy, Joseph O'Hare, Raymond Baumhart, J. Donald Monan, Raymond Fitz, Alice Gallin, Paul Reinert and so many others, will be terminated.[8]

Nilson was especially critical of "the Vatican's inability to appreciate a system of Catholic higher education independent of the church's juridical control" and described the document as an attempt by Rome to "put theologians on a short leash" in the application of the requirement of a mandatum for theologians.[9] Theologians like Nilson are especially concerned about the fact that *Ex Corde* invokes a canon law (Canon Law 812) requiring that all theology professors on Catholic campuses receive a "mandatum" from their bishop—an acknowledgement by the bishop that the Catholic professor of a theological discipline is a teacher within the full communion of the Catholic Church. The mandate also recognizes the professor's commitment and responsibility to teach authentic Catholic doctrine and requires that the professor refrain from putting forth as Catholic teaching anything contrary to the Church's magisterium.[10]

Ex Corde requires that the Catholic university must have at least four essential characteristics: First, there must be a Christian inspiration "not only of individuals but of the university community as such." Secondly, there must be "a continuing reflection in the light of the Catholic faith upon the growing treasury of human knowledge, to which it seeks to contribute by its own research." Third, there must be "fidelity to the Christian message as it comes to us through the Church." And, finally, there must be "an institutional commitment to the service of the people of God and of the human family in their pilgrimage to the transcendent goal which gives meaning to life."[11] Theologians have a special responsibility for fidelity to the Christian message, but many American academics have considered the provision a threat to academic freedom and an effort by the Church to control the institutions. Many of these academic theologians see the document as a threat to their high status on the Catholic campus—as revealed by their comments about wishing for a document that they would be "proud to share" with their peer secular institutions. And, in response, they spent more than a decade demanding that the document be withdrawn.

When the faculty and administrators began to realize that they could not stop the bishops from implementing *Ex Corde*, they began a series of counter initiatives. Theresa Moser, the former president of the College Theology Society and an assistant dean at the University of San Francisco, dismissed the document as "going against our tradition in the university."[12] Terrence Tilley, chairman of University of Dayton's religious studies department, wrote that the norms of the document "send the wrong message," and suggests, "Implementing *Ex Corde* will discourage the most able Catholic students of theology and religious studies from studying at Roman Catholic institutions."[13]

Some faculty members have simply refused to implement the document. Claiming that *Ex Corde* did not apply to them, the faculty senate at Notre Dame voted unanimously for the guidelines to be ignored.[14] In fact, Fr. Richard McBrien, a theology professor at Notre Dame, declared in *America* that he would "not seek the mandate" because it would "compromise the academic integrity of the faculty and the university." Likewise, theology faculty member Lawrence Cunningham was quoted as saying that he resented the fact that Catholics should have to take an oath of fidelity to their faith.[15]

Others chose a more creative approach to the document. Rather than public dissent, Rev. Raymond Collins, dean of the religious studies department at Catholic University of America, advised faculty members to "selectively dissent" from *Ex Corde* by refusing to implement the parts they disagreed with. In an attempt to avoid outright confrontation with Church authorities, Fr. Collins advised that theologians should "set aside Church teachings they found wanting, but without fuss, thus implementing the *Ex Corde* guidelines selectively—being faithful in their fashion."[16] Many Catholic colleges seem to already be doing this in their mission statements. And, theology professors simply mirror this mission by choosing Catholic teachings they find acceptable, including most teachings on economic justice and the preferential option for the poor, and rejecting others, especially those focusing on the women's role in the Church, homosexuality, and reproductive rights. Most maintain that they—not the pope—are the "alternative Magisterium" or authority on what the Church "really" teaches.[17]

One of the most defiant of the liberal theologians continues to be Daniel Maguire, theology professor at Marquette University in Milwaukee, Wisconsin. Maguire responded to *Ex Corde* by publishing a copy of the open letter of dissent that he wrote to then-archbishop of the Milwaukee Diocese, Rembert Weakland, in *Academe*—the journal of the American Association of University Professors. Stating that he would "neither request a mandate nor an ecclesial blessing," Maguire's letter to his archbishop argues that "The application of *Ex Corde Ecclesiae* for the United States and their Guidelines Concerning the Academic Mandatum in Catholic Universities (Canon 812) are seriously flawed both as theology and as law."[18] Dismissing *Ex Corde* as a document that had "slipped into magic, implying as it does that non-theologian bishops will be miraculously endowed with divine inspiration to make up for their lack of expertise in judging all the complex branches of theology." Ridiculing the Episcopal authority of the Church, Maguire believes that only trained theologians like himself are qualified to understand such complex moral issues.[19]

Maguire has reason to fear the requirements of the mandatum on teaching "authentic" Church doctrine because throughout his career at Marquette he has flaunted many Church teachings—creating his own brand of theology surrounding abortion and euthanasia. Defiantly describing himself in an article for *The Chronicle of Higher Education* as "a pro-choice theologian at Marquette," Maguire maintains that "the university has lived with that for 25 years. I defended mercy death before I had tenure, and I got tenure."[20] Claiming expertise in Catholic moral teachings, Maguire's published writings assert that the Catholic Church not only "allowed" abortion throughout its history, it also celebrates abortion as a "sacred choice" for women. In his book, *Sacred Choices: The Right to Contraception and Abortion in Ten World Religions*, Maguire criticizes what he sees as the current "conservative" Catholic Church teachings on abortion and suggests that the Church's teachings on the evil of abortion today differs from those of the past.

A longtime advocate for unrestricted access to abortion, Maguire's book argues that the right to an abortion is "solidly grounded in the world's great religions—including Catholicism." He writes that in the past, the Church had held that "sometimes the ending of incipient life is the best that life offers." He also argues that throughout history, "women have been the principal cherishers and caretakers of life. We can trust them with these decisions. This book shows that the world's religions urge us to do so."[21]

In an effort to prove that Catholicism provides the right to abortion to women, Maguire's book first dismisses papal authority on issues of contraception and abortion by writing that "States that do not have any population problem—in one particular case, even no births at all (the Vatican) are doing their best, their utmost, to prevent the world from making sensible decisions regarding family planning."[22] Rejecting papal authority, Maguire argues that "Christianity was born in a world in which contraception and abortion were both known and practiced. The Egyptians, Jews, Greeks, and Romans used a variety of contraceptive methods . . . And, Catholic teaching on contraception and abortion has been anything but consistent."[23] Maguire claims that what most people think of as the Catholic position on abortion actually is quite recent and only dates from the 1930 encyclical, *Casti Conubbii,* of Pope Pius XI. Prior to that time, he claims that Catholic Church teaching on abortion was a "mixed bag." Arguing that the Catholic position on abortion is "pluralistic—with a strong pro-choice tradition," Maguire devotes much of his book to what he believes the Church "really" says about abortion.

Throughout his writings, Maguire dismisses Church teachings on abortion and claims, "neither the pro-choice nor the anti-choice tradition of the Church is more Catholic than the other." Despite the fact that Church teachings have remained unchanged and steadfastly anti-abortion since the earliest days of the founding of the Catholic Church, Maguire maintains that the hierarchical attempt to portray the Catholic position as univocal and unchanging is untrue. And, he adds that "By unearthing this authentic openness in the core of the tradition to choice on abortion and contraception, the status of the anti-choice position is revealed as only one among many Catholic views."[24]

In addition to denigrating official Church teachings on abortion, Maguire also claims that the Bible does not condemn abortion. Counter to Catholic teachings on natural law, Maguire claims that a human being is not being killed in the abortion procedures. In fact, Maguire seems to invoke his own theological magic himself when he claims that God does not infuse a soul into the body of the fetus until the woman consents to the pregnancy. Claiming to draw from the writings of St. Thomas Aquinas, Maguire presents the theory of delayed animation, or delayed ensoulment, as proof that even the most esteemed of medieval theologians allowed abortion. In this respect, Maguire ignores the twentieth-century advances in ultrasound technology that dismiss the medieval concept of delayed animation. While Maguire attempts to make a case for allowing abortion within the Catholic tradition, he goes even further by proposing that the Church not only allows abortion, it celebrates it by rewarding with sainthood those who are pro-choice. Offering no verification for such a statement, Maguire redefines Catholic teachings to support his own abortion advocacy.

This distortion of the truth in the teachings of the Church by academic theologians like Maguire is exactly what *Ex Corde Ecclesiae* was designed to address. If the papal decree were enforced the way the pope had intended it to be enforced, Professor Maguire would never have received the mandatum to teach Catholic theology from his bishop and would have been removed from his teaching position. However, since Maguire's archbishop was, until recently, Rembert Weakland, Maguire continues in good standing in his position as professor of religious ethics at Marquette University, and he continues to teach courses in moral theology there. In an interview on the fallout from *Ex Corde Ecclesiae,* Maguire boldly told a reporter from *The Chronicle of Higher Education* that "I do not intend to change anything."[25]

In addition to a lack of Episcopal oversight, it appears that academic oversight is absent also as Fr. Robert Wild, S. J., president of Marquette, has been unwilling to require Maguire to teach authentic Catholic theology. In fact, when Marquette students, alumni, donors, or concerned Catholics write to the school to complain about Maguire's heretical writings and activities, *First Things* editor, Richard Neuhaus, reports that Fr. Wild sends them a form letter that acknowledges Maguire's theological positions are not "totally consonant with formal Church teachings," yet also acknowledges Maguire's academic freedom and tenure.[26] Fr. Wild's letters also draw an analogy between Maguire and the disciples of Christ, "I also find it useful to recall that even Jesus did not have a perfect group of disciples," and conclude by reassuring those who question Maguire's suitability to teach theology on a Catholic campus by telling them that Maguire teaches no required theology courses, only theology electives for those who elect to enroll in his advanced theology classes.[27]

One of the reasons that Maguire has been so secure in his position and so defiant in his public assertions in spite of his refusal to submit to the conditions of *Ex Corde*, is because the Archbishop Rembert Weakland, leader of the Milwaukee diocese at the time of the implementation of the papal document and Maguire's clerical authority, has refused to enforce the mandatum. Defying the papal requirement that he oversee the teachings of Catholic theologians, the archbishop predicted in 1999 that

Ex Corde would "create a tremendous pastoral disaster for the church." Weakland complained that because of *Ex Corde*, "the tension between the hierarchy and theologians now is the highest I have seen it in my 36 years as a superior in the Catholic Church."[28] And, in response, Weakland refused to implement the provisions of the document.

This was not the first time Archbishop Weakland had defied papal authority. Just a few weeks after Professor Maguire published his insolent letter stating that he would seek neither the mandatum nor ecclesial blessing, Weakland himself made national headlines when it was revealed that he had become involved in a same-sex relationship with a young man twenty years earlier. On May 23, 2002, Paul Marcoux, a former Marquette University student, appeared on ABC's news program, *Good Morning America*, and accused the longtime Milwaukee archbishop of sexual assault. Producing a number of handwritten letters from the archbishop as proof of the sexual relationship, Marcoux also revealed that, in 1998, Weakland paid him a sum of $450,000 to keep their sexual affair quiet. Now, fifty-three years old, Marcoux claims that he had been a theology student at Marquette University in the 1980s when he approached the archbishop for advice on entering the priesthood. It was during this encounter that Marcoux alleges that the abuse took place.[29]

While Weakland denied the assault charges, he acknowledged the relationship and publicly apologized to the members of the Milwaukee diocese, "for the scandal that has occurred because of [my] sinfulness." Claiming, however, that the $450,000 paid to Marcoux was taken from funds that he had "personally earned from articles and lectures over the years that far exceeded that amount," Weakland did not admit to embezzling the money from diocesan finances. This did not stop the US Attorney's office from conducting an investigation into the source of the settlement.[30] The investigation revealed that Weakland had earned only a small portion of the amount he paid to his former lover. The remainder came from Milwaukee parishioners' donations—which Weakland has promised to eventually repay.

The revelations were not a complete surprise to many Catholics throughout the United States. For more than twenty years, orthodox Catholics have criticized Weakland for his heterodox views on sexual morality and reproductive rights. As the Australian journal, *AD2000* noted in 1992:

> Along with Cardinal Bernardin of Chicago, Archbishop Weakland has led the push for a far more distinctively American Church, as independent as possible from Rome. Associated with this push have been Weakland's highly controversial policies and

views on abortion, homosexuality, AIDS education, sex education, clerical pedophilia and feminism. Presumably these developments would make the American Church more American. That it would also be less Catholic is equally clear. Whether it would be Catholic at all remains an open question.[31]

For theologians like Maguire, claiming to want to "Americanize" Catholic colleges is code for reserving the right to redefine Catholic teachings they may not agree with. While most do not state this outright, they use euphemisms like saying that *Ex Corde* is unworkable in American Catholic colleges because American colleges, unlike those elsewhere, are so unique in terms of academic freedom. For example, in an article published in *The Chronicle of Higher Education* in 1999, Fr. James Heft, formerly the Chancellor and professor of faith and culture at the University of Dayton, suggested that *Ex Corde* "should be adapted to the American scene, which recognizes institutional autonomy and academic freedom in higher education." Heft believes that American colleges should be exempt from the demands of *Ex Corde* because these Catholic colleges and universities "are also *ex corde patriae*—from the heart of the nation. And in the American tradition, they have on the whole, benefited from institutional autonomy and academic freedom."[32]

Despite these criticisms, keeping Catholic colleges "Catholic" has been the only goal of *Ex Corde Ecclesiae*. Pope John Paul, like thousands of other Catholics, had become alarmed by the shift on Catholic college campuses from a commitment to Catholic teachings to an embrace of secular values and liberal ideologies. In most cases, dissident theologians have led the movement. Creatively deconstructing Catholic moral teachings to conform to what Notre Dame's Fr. Ralph McInerny calls the "secular zeitgeist," theologians like Notre Dame's (former) chair of theology and religious studies, Richard McBrien, have received a great deal of attention in the secular media and the liberal Catholic press by redefining Catholic teachings on abortion, birth control, homosexuality and gay marriage, and most recently embryonic stem cell research to make them more acceptable to a secular audience.

McBrien has been especially recalcitrant in his response to *Ex Corde*. In a published statement in *The Chronicle of Higher Education*, McBrien's contempt for the bishops was clear:

> The idea of even suggesting any kind of oversight by non-academic operations of a university—Catholic or not—is odious to anybody in an academic institution. I'm not saying we're above criticism, but I want the criticism to come from people with the credentials to criticize. Bishops should be welcome on a Catholic-university campus. Give them tickets to ball games. Let them say Mass, bring them to graduation. Let them sit on the stage. But there should be nothing beyond that. They should have

nothing to say about the internal academic affairs of the university or any faculty member thereof.[33]

Like Maguire, McBrien has had a long history of defying Church teachings. In 1985, the United States bishops, in consultation with the Vatican, declared that the views presented by McBrien in his published encyclopedic work, *Catholicism,* run contrary to "authoritative" Church doctrine. In an unusual statement, the bishops' committee on doctrine issued a warning about the contents of McBrien's book, *Catholicism,* claiming that the insights contained in the book are "difficult to reconcile with authoritative Church doctrine." In particular, the committee cited sections of the book questioning the "virginal conception" of Jesus, the "perpetual virginity" of Mary, and the binding nature of Catholic dogma. The bishops also objected that the book is "not supportive" of Church teaching on such controversial issues as the ordination of women, homosexuality, and artificial contraception.[34]

So concerned about the influence McBrien might have on faithful Catholics, Bishop Robert Finn, the leader of the Kansas City-St. Joseph, Missouri Diocese made it a point as one of his first acts since assuming leadership of the diocese in 2006 to order the editor of the diocesan newspaper to immediately cease publishing columns by McBrien.[35] Still, McBrien retains his tenured position at Notre Dame and is often called upon by the mainstream media when they need a "Catholic expert" to speak on an issue like the Catholic perspective on gay marriage, abortion, the death penalty, or the just war theory.

Although there are many theologians like Maguire and McBrien teaching on Catholic campuses throughout the country, there are still a few academics that support clerical approval of what is taught in theology courses. The Rev. Giles Dimock, chairman of the theology department at Franciscan University of Steubenville supports the mandatum: "Students have a right to the teaching of the church, . . . Many theologians are substituting their own beliefs for the teaching of the church, depriving them of Catholic doctrine." Fr. Dimock maintains, "The bishop, not the theologian, is the successor to the apostles. . . . Scrupulous adherence to orthodoxy is particularly important in introductory courses."[36] Of course, Fr. Dimock is teaching at Franciscan, one of a handful of orthodox Catholic colleges that cannot be viewed as representative of most Catholic colleges.

It is likely that few mainstream Catholic college theology faculty would agree with what they would see as Father Dimock's "privileging" of

Catholic teachings. Most theology faculty members would instead favor a critical approach to Catholic theology that is rooted in the "acceptance of experience as a legitimate source for theological reflection"—and includes what some left-leaning theologians call a "hermeneutics of suspicion to the sources and questions of theology" as "pluralism," as is now the hallmark of progressive Catholic theology. Unlike those with a more traditionalist perspective of theology, most theologians have embraced the Enlightenment's philosophical "turn to the subject." Such a development undermines the notion of a divine, supernatural revelation operating independently of human reason.[37] In contrast to orthodox or conservative Catholic theologians, Pope John Paul II, and Benedict XVI, who argue that Catholic theology has always cautioned against trusting personal experience, liberal theologians argue that revelation and the inspiration of the Holy Spirit can be discerned only from within human experience.[38] These theologians claim that their position is grounded in Vatican II's definition of the Church as the people of God (*Lumen Gentium*) and is consonant with an empowered laity whose experience must be considered along with that of the ordained as the Church moves forward in history.[39]

Such a pluralistic approach to theology points to what liberal theologians view as a need to reflect on lived experience as a source for the renewal and strengthening of the Church. As self-described liberal academic theologians Mary Ann Hinsdale, chair of theology at the College of the Holy Cross, and Theology Professor Emeritus John Boyle, write in the publication, *What's Left? Liberal American Catholics:*

> We can point to the appeal made to the experience of married Christians in the discussion of acceptable ways of preventing pregnancy prior to *Humanae Vitae*, and in the critical way in which the encyclical was received by many lay men and women...In the decades since 1968, other issues of sexual morality, such as abortion and homosexuality, have been dealt with in Church teaching documents, to be met with similar appeals to the experience of Christians in the formation of the believer's conscience.[40]

Such an experiential approach to theology raises theological questions about the status of tradition and authority within the Church. For liberal theologians like Hinsdale, Boyle, and others, the experience of the individual is of primary importance. From this perspective, if an individual woman feels called to the priesthood or called to an abortion, then her call to priestly ordination or the right to terminate a pregnancy should take precedence over any Church teaching that claims that the Catholic Church has no authority to ordain women as priests or allow abortion.

For liberal theologians, "the refusal of those in authority to attend to the experience of Christian believers raises questions about the fundamental fairness of the Church's processes in dealing with disputes over doctrine or moral teachings." Liberal theologians claim that from the "critical theology" perspective, "when the Church ignores the experience of its members, it tends to impoverish the perspectives available to enrich the theological task."[41]

A leading proponent of what many left-leaning theologians have called "Popular Catholicism" is Orlando Espin, a professor of theological and religious studies at the University of San Diego and director of the Center for the Study of Latino/a Catholicism at the university. "Popular," for Espin does not refer to "prevalent," but rather to the religious practices and beliefs that emerge from the people themselves. Espin emphasizes the "contextual nature" of all theological reflection and maintains that theology is always cultural and historical. For Espin, any attempt to de-culturalize the theological and religious expressions of a community is dehumanizing and, thus, "sinful." Rather, Espin maintains that the consequences of this cultural emergence is that elites, or those he calls "the hegemonic group and their allies," have been successful in using the symbols and ideologies of religion to oppress the marginalized. Espin is especially critical of those scholars who privilege the ecclesiastical institution as the witness to true Catholicism, "while the real-life, daily-life religion of most Catholics is regarded as an adulterated version of the institutional norm."[42]

From this starting point, Espin reframes many cultural icons including that of the Virgin Mary—he is critical of the cooptation by the elites of the symbol of the Virgin, because it has led women to "hand on to the next generation some of the worst possible assumptions about gender and social roles and about family and community responsibilities." Espin claims that counter to elite beliefs, "Latino devotion to the Virgin of Guadalupe might not always—in fact, probably seldom—has to do with the historical Mary of Nazareth, the mother of Jesus."[43] Critical of "Mariology," or devotion to Mary of Nazareth, Espin proposes that a pneumatological reading of the Guadalupe story and devotion reveals that for the poor within the Latino/a community, a reframed view of Guadalupe rather than Jesus is the best symbol for grace.[44] Such a reading, for Espin, reveals Our Lady of Guadalupe "as a Mexican representation of the Holy Spirit" and not the Mother of Jesus. This redefinition away from the historical Mary of Nazareth, and toward Guadalupe as a representation of the Holy Spirit legitimizes the divine as understood through feminine categories—a goal that many feminist theologians have had for decades—especially those who continue to lobby for women's ordination. Although Espin claims to be finally paying attention to the marginalized in his reframing and is critical of scholars who disregard the practices and beliefs of the oppressed, he is also critical of those who fail to see the symbol of the Holy Spirit in the Virgin of Guadalupe.[45]

Espin is even more critical of those with devotion to the Virgin: "This religious symbol seems at times to derail the people's solidarity with each other, blinding them to compassion and social responsibilities, condoning domestic violence and the perpetuation of dehumanizing gender and family roles, perpetuating their self image as victim . . . Through popular Catholicism's devotion to the *Virgen* of Guadalupe, Latina mature women have been told that they must endure the abuse, the assaults, and the violence."[46] For Espin, until women see the symbol of the Holy Spirit in Guadalupe instead of the Virgin, they are doomed. In fact, he maintains that such piety can itself be sinful: "The call to freedom and to the struggle for justice that many Catholics have heard from Guadalupe is frequently muted here—the call itself being abused and betrayed. These are experiences of sin, even when cloaked under the religious veil of piety."[47]

This redefinition of the theology of Mary has become increasingly popular on Catholic campuses. Like Espin, Elizabeth Johnson, a Sister of St. Joseph who teaches theology at Fordham, attempts to de-throne the Virgin Mary by maintaining that devotion to the docile and humble Mother of God has inspired violence against women. Inveighing against Mary's humility and her virginity, Johnson believes that devotion to the Virgin Mary gives her an "unearthly asexual exaltation" and demeans other women who are sexually active.[48] Claiming that the patriarchy invented Mary as a way to control women, Johnson demeans what she defines as Mariology and those who have devotion to her.

While such redefinitions can be hurtful to those involved in the devotions to the Virgin Mary, it must be acknowledged that students attending Catholic colleges are unfortunately the real victims of the revisionist approach to Catholic teachings because, although they may learn critical thinking skills and learn about the contextual nature of theological reflection, they often do not develop an awareness of some of the very teachings of the Church they are learning to criticize. Even those theologians who generally support such a critical perspective must admit, as

Thomas Rausch of Loyola Marymount University in Los Angeles does, that students are not always well served by a critical perspective. In fact, Rausch reports that when surveyed by a faculty committee reviewing the theology program at Loyola, students responded that "they had been better instructed in modern and postmodern developments and critiques of the tradition than in the tradition itself."[49] Rausch acknowledges that we must begin to pay attention to the religious and theological illiteracy of many young adult Catholics, yet he also acknowledges—as most academic theologians do—that theology is different from catechesis. This is the real dilemma for theologians teaching on Catholic campuses: How to bring students to an appreciation for the faith, both intellectually and pastorally—or as Rausch asks: "Do they have no responsibility for the religious development of their students?"[50]

For many theologians, the answer is no. And, on many Catholic campuses, the academic deans provide cover for these theologians. Mark Roche, dean of Notre Dame's College of Arts and Sciences, is one example of an academic dean who leads by example in openly defying authoritative teachings on abortion in his 2004 op-ed piece in *The New York Times* entitled "Voting Our Conscience Not Our Religion."[51] Likewise, Nicholas M. Healy, formerly the dean of the College of Arts and Sciences at the University of San Diego has suggested that a "profound change" in Catholic leadership is needed to address what he sees as the "crisis in authority." He writes:

> The crisis of authority in the Roman Catholic Church cannot be resolved by demanding blind obedience to judgments the rationales of which seem lacking in cogency, and by stifling constructively critical theological inquiry. Legitimate church authority cannot work that way anymore, if it ever really could. A more profound change in the leadership practices of the hierarchy is needed of the Roman Catholic Church.[52]

Healy's postmodern view of authority clearly demonstrates what Philip Rieff describes in *Sacred Order/Social Order: My Life Among the Death-works* as "the leveling of all of the verticals in authority."[53] For Rieff, one of the reasons that we have such problems with social order is that moral constraints are now read as social constructions that have no status in being beyond what is given by those who have constructed these constraints.[54] The role of faithfulness and obedience are diminished when the directives are viewed as "lacking in cogency," as Healy has said.

Notre Dame Professor Ralph McInerny is especially hard on theologians who "seem to have forgotten the nature of faith." In an article entitled, "The Romance of Orthodoxy" McInerny reminds theologians that "Christian faith is the acceptance of whatever God has revealed because He has revealed it. For a Catholic, the authoritative interpreter of that revelation is the Church, preeminently the Pope. One cannot pick and choose among the things revealed and sanctioned by church authority, assenting to those one finds palatable and dismissing those one cannot swallow."[55] Picking and choosing among church teachings has a name derived from the Greek verb *haireomai,* meaning "to choose"—the name is heresy.[56]

While there are many examples of what orthodox Catholics might define as heretical teachings on America's Catholic campuses, the Vatican has responded punitively on only a few occasions. Yet these cases are often cited by liberal theologians as evidence of another "Catholic Inquisition." The fact that the Vatican has only acted twice to remove American Catholic theologians from their positions in teaching Catholic theology on Catholic campuses, despite the reality of dozens of dissenting theologians throughout the country, is hardly evidence of a Vatican crackdown on heretical teaching. Rev. Charles Curran was forced to leave a tenured position at Catholic University in Washington in 1986 because he became one of the strongest critics of *Humanae Vitae* in his advocacy of a woman's right to contraception, sterilization, and abortion—and he dissented from official Church teaching on homosexuality and divorce. And, in 2001, Roger Haight was removed from his teaching position at the Weston Jesuit School of Theology in Cambridge, Massachusetts because the Vatican found "serious doctrinal errors" in his 1999 book *Jesus: Symbol of God.*

Roger Haight argued in his book that theology must be done in dialogue with the postmodern world. Like Karl Rahner, who has sought to theologize in conscious dialogue with modernity (even at the cost of cultural accommodation), Haight claimed in his book that in a postmodern culture, with its pluralistic consciousness, one can no longer claim the superiority of Christianity to other religions or that Christ is the centerpiece of God's plan for salvation.[57] Haight's insistence that Catholic theology be in "dialogue" with the modern world led him to deny the divinity of Christ, that the Word was made flesh in Jesus Christ, and that salvation is offered to all through Jesus. Haight also denies that the Son and the Spirit are separate persons within the Trinity, not simply metaphors for actions of the one God, and that the Word of God has existed from all eternity.[58] All of these are heretical within the Catholic Church yet, in the upside-down world of Catholic academic theologians, where dissent is viewed more favorably than conformity to Church teachings,

Haight's book, *Jesus: Symbol of God*, won the top prize in theology from the Catholic Press Association and was reviewed positively in the Jesuit journal *America* by Fordham theologian Elizabeth Johnson.[59]

There are some signs that the writings of American theologians will be under increased scrutiny. In 2007 John Allen, the *National Catholic Reporter* Vatican correspondent, reported that both the Vatican and the US bishops are investigating a book by Fr. Peter Phan, a professor of theology of religion at Georgetown and former president of the Catholic Theological Society of America. Allen reports that the Vatican has described Fr. Phan's 2004 book, *Being Religious Interreligiously*, as "notably confused on a number of points of Catholic doctrine and also contains serious ambiguities."[60] Claiming that there is a "gnostic tenor running through the book," the most serious charges by the Congregation for the Doctrine of the Faith (CDF) are that Phan's book can be read to suggest that "non-Christian religions have a positive role in salvation history in their own right and are not merely preparation for the Christian Gospel; that it makes little sense to try to convert non-Christians to Christianity; that it would be better to avoid terms such as 'unique,' 'absolute,' and 'universal' for the saving role of Jesus Christ; that the Holy Spirit operates in a saving way in non-Christian religions; that the Catholic Church cannot be identified with the church of Christ; and finally, that God's covenant with the Jewish people does not find its completion in Jesus Christ."[61]

The United States Conference of Catholic Bishops concurred with these Vatican observations—especially with concerns over Phan's treatment of "the uniqueness of Jesus Christ and the universality of his salvific mission, the salvific significance of non-Christian religions, and the uniqueness of the church as the universal instrument of salvation."[62] According to Allen, Phan's theological defenders argue that church authorities tend to approach issues of religious diversity from a Western, often European, perspective that perhaps does not do justice to Phan's background as a Vietnamese-American immigrant with deep ties to Asia. However, Allen also points out that "Others say that not everything comes down to differing modes of expression—that there is a rule of faith, a doctrinal bottom line, and however unpleasant it may be, somebody has to enforce it."[63]

This debate over theological pluralism continues on Catholic campuses throughout the country as those who dissent most publicly from Church teachings on moral issues are often given endowed chairs with generous salaries and all the accolades that accompany such high-status positions. In 2006, Georgetown University named a human rights chair for a controversial priest who, until his death in 2007, had been actively supportive of abortion during and after his time as a US congressman. The Robert F. Drinan, S. J. Chair in Human Rights was announced to honor what Georgetown administrators maintain is Fr. Drinan's lifelong commitment to public service. The fact remains that Fr. Drinan was a strong supporter of abortion rights during his time in public office and afterwards as well, providing "cover" for Catholic politicians. For example, at a critical moment in the partial birth abortion debate, Fr. Drinan published articles in the *New York Times* and the *National Catholic Reporter* supporting President Clinton's decision to veto the ban on partial birth abortion and urging members of Congress to sustain that veto.

While a congressman, Drinan was one of the most outspoken Catholic politicians in the country to begin opposing pro-life initiatives and supporting legalized abortion and its public funding. One of a number of liberal Jesuits who helped to convince the Catholic Kennedy family and a generation of Catholic Democratic politicians that Catholic politicians could support liberalized abortion laws yet still remain in good standing within the Catholic Church, Fr. Drinan continued until his death to support a woman's right to choose an abortion.

Critics of Fr. Drinan maintain that "Drinan did worse than set a bad example for Catholic politicians. He enabled them to rationalize support for pro-abortion legislative initiatives, on the ground that they were doing nothing that a Catholic priest in good standing was not able and willing to do."[64] Moreover, Fr. Drinan provided a much imitated model for Catholic politicians who wished to support the pro-abortion movement while claiming to be faithful to Catholic moral teaching. Fr. Drinan left Congress in 1980, yet he continued his tireless support for abortion in his position as president of Americans for Democratic Action when he sent out a fund-raising letter urging "the moral necessity of electing candidates to Congress who favored legal abortion and its public funding."[65] Fr. Thomas Euteneur, president of Human Life International, called the naming of the new chair "deeply disturbing," complaining that the university has established a human rights chair "in the name of a heretical priest who has spent much of his lifetime advocating for the most heinous of human rights violations: abortion."[66]

Despite this well-documented history of Fr. Drinan's pro-abortion advocacy, or quite possibly because of it, Georgetown's Dean T. Alexander

Aleinkoff announced the establishment of the chair in a formal ceremony on the Georgetown campus in which Fr. Drinan was lauded as having made a "lifelong commitment to public service." Dean Aleinkoff added that "few have accomplished as much as Fr. Drinan, and fewer still have done so much to make the world a better place."[67]

The use of endowed chairs in theology on Catholic campuses has actually provided the needed cover to enable faculty members to hire theologians without going through the same kinds of national search hiring protocols that a simple search for an assistant professor might necessitate. At the University of San Diego, current theology faculty members have, on several occasions, invited former colleagues or their own professors from graduate school to fill distinguished chairs at the university. The first person to hold the Distinguished Monsignor John Portman Chair of Systematic Theology in 2001 was retired Archbishop of San Francisco John R. Quinn, whose book on the reform of the papacy calls for decreased papal authority, decentralization, more control granted to bishops, and parishioner involvement in the selection of bishops. In fact, implementing Archbishop Quinn's suggestions would bring the Catholic Church in line with most Protestant denominations and radically weaken the papacy. Yet, he was honored with the endowed chair on the Catholic campus.

Invited to teach undergraduate theology students at the University of San Diego, Quinn has openly criticized in his writings and speeches the Roman Curia for "wanton disregard" of the local Church and "blind, rigid application of Church law," arguing that the Vatican should reopen discussion of such issues as the ordination of women, birth control, and married priests. In May of 1999, the Catholic newspaper *San Francisco Faith* reported that at a meeting of US bishops in Washington, D. C., then-Archbishop Quinn called for rejection of *Ex Corde Ecclesiae*.[68] Although Quinn resigned from his position as archbishop of San Francisco in 1995 at age sixty-six, nine years earlier than the mandatory retirement age of seventy-five, the University of San Diego welcomed the longtime critic of *Ex Corde Ecclesiae* and the papacy itself as the first recipient of the prestigious Portman Chair.

Quinn seemed to set the pattern of inviting dissident theologians to hold the Portman Chair as subsequent chair holders hold similar negative views of papal authority and critical views of Catholic Church teachings on reproductive rights and the role of women in the Church. For example, the 2002 chair holder, Peter Hunerman, professor emeritus of

Catholic theology at the University of Tubingen, believes that barring women from ordination in the Catholic Church is based on "undefensible premises."[69] In 2003, Fr. Bernard Marthaler, OFM, a professor of religion and religious education at Catholic University of America, was invited to hold the Portman Chair. A proponent of the "new catechetics movement" that privileges personal experience over formal Church teachings and dismisses "book-centered catechesis" as filled with what he called "tired customs and trite devotions," Marthaler was one of the eighty-seven original dissenters who joined with Charles Curran in 1968 to protest against the papal encyclical on birth control, *Humanae Vitae.* Yet, unlike Fr. Curran, Marthaler faced no disciplinary action and not only maintained his tenured position at Catholic University, but was also invited to hold the prestigious chair at the University of San Diego for a year.

Following Marthaler, Mary Hines and Thomas Franklin O'Meara, both Rahner scholars "in the spirit of Vatican II," each held the Portman Chair. While Mary Hines questions the sanctified role of the Blessed Virgin Mary—along the same lines as Espin and Johnson, Fr. O'Meara, a retired theology professor from Notre Dame, dismissed what he called the "trappings and autocracy of the Vatican bureaucracy." O'Meara published an article in which he decried the hierarchy of the Church and applauded the fact that "the baroque period in Catholicism is past."[70] And, in a speech at the Newman Theological College, O'Meara lashed out at the Vatican for banning discussion on the ordination of women, suggesting "the ordination of married men to the priesthood and of women to the deaconate is only a matter of time."[71] Dismissing Catholic teachings on women's ordination, O'Meara claims that "it is hard to argue that women should not have public roles because the Holy Spirit doesn't discriminate on the basis of biology."[72]

Most recently, Fr. Peter Phan was invited to present the prestigious Portman Lecture at the University of San Diego in 2008 despite his precarious status as a theologian under investigation by the Vatican and the bishops for his views that Jesus is but one path among many paths to salvation.

Beyond the Portman Chair, visiting professors to the San Diego campus continue the commitment by the faculty of encouraging those with pluralist views of Church teachings to teach undergraduates. Theologian Bernard Cooke, a longtime visiting professor (and former professor and colleague of a San Diego faculty member) is one of the best-known dissenting theologians today. With a national reputation for criticizing Church teachings on priestly celibacy, divorce and remarriage, homosexuality, contraception, and women's ordination, Cooke is a former Jesuit priest who left the priesthood three decades ago to marry and has been critical of the current status of the priesthood ever since. Going well beyond the usual left-wing dissidence on sexual morality and reproductive choice, Cooke has been especially critical of the elevated status of ordained priests over the laity, and in his book, *The Future of the Eucharist*, Cooke claims that although a liturgical leader may preside, "it is the community that celebrates the Eucharist."[73] In a lecture on the San Diego campus, Cooke claimed that "the existence of a socially privileged group (priests) within the Church is not meant to be . . . I hope that in a relatively short time, the inappropriate division between clergy and laity will vanish."[74]

Criticizing the status of priests has characterized Cooke's career for the past thirty years. Claiming that the growing shortage of priests will lead to a "liturgical starvation" for an expanding US Catholic population, Cooke's solution is to empower the laity and allow married priests like him to assume leadership once again. A member of CORPUS, an advocacy organization of former priests lobbies for optional celibacy in the Catholic Church, Cooke is also a board member of Call to Action, a movement of laity demanding women's ordination, an end to priestly celibacy, and a change in the Church's teachings on sexual morality.

Call to Action goes beyond most other dissenting Catholic groups in its combining dissent against Church teaching with new age and Wiccan spirituality. Membership draws heavily from former clergy and feminist nuns seeking to reform what they view as the sinful structure of the patriarchal Church. Recently, the activities of Call to Action were deemed to be "so irreconcilable with a coherent living of the Catholic faith" that the Vatican publicly affirmed an Episcopal decree of excommunication for any member of the dissident organization.[75] Claiming that Call to Action is "totally incompatible with the Catholic faith," and is "causing damage to the Church of Christ," Cardinal Giovanni Battista confirmed that membership in Call to Action causes the member to be automatically excommunicated from the Catholic Church.[76] Despite this, many Catholic theologians teaching on Catholic campuses retain an active membership in Call to Action—openly participating in meetings and conferences.

One of the reasons that theologians have confidently challenged the teaching authority of the Catholic Church is because many theologians like Nicholas Healy, currently at St. John's University, believe that they are already an "alternative" magisterium:

No single authority trumps the others so that one could say that it is the decisive authority on which all the others rest. Certainly the bishops and popes are weighty authorities. They have something of a U. S. Supreme Court or British lords' function in that they are to make the final authoritative judgment in cases of controversy. But only that: their teaching itself is not final in the sense that it halts or inhibits further debate on the same matters. For all their judgments must be interpreted and those interpretations discussed by the other magisterium, that of the theologians . . . [77]

Woven throughout the writings of many Catholic theologians remain questions about papal infallibility—and error. Peter Steinfels argues, "it is possible for popes, despite the guidance of the Holy Spirit, to fall into tragic error . . . many liberal Catholics believe that was probably the case in the 1968 issuance of *Humanae Vitae* and cannot be ruled out in the refusal of ordination to women."[78] So concerned about papal error, Steinfels lists five areas "where an effective church witness would surely demand the continuing contribution of liberal Catholicism—human sexuality, technological control over genes and the mind, relations among world religions, quantum leaps in historical consciousness and cultural pluralism, and a worldwide revolution of individual freedom and democracy."[79]

Still, orthodox Catholics continue to ask whether the judgment of Healy's "alternative magisterium" of the Church as represented by liberal theologians like Richard McBrien, Daniel Maguire, or Bernard Cooke can be trusted to interpret Church teachings for followers. So concerned about such heterodoxy, Tarcisio Cardinal Bertone, the Vatican secretary of state said that dissident theologians are "a more worrisome problem than atheists." In comments published in *L'Avvenire*, the official newspaper of the Italian bishops' conference, Cardinal Bertone said, "Much more worrisome are those inside the Church who work to distort its faith and moral principles, or who oppose the Pope and his design for renewal of the Church."[80] Likewise, John Allen reminds readers of the *National Catholic Reporter* that more than a decade ago, Pope Benedict, Cardinal Joseph Ratzinger head of the Congregation of the Doctrine of the Faith in 2005, described what he saw as the greatest doctrinal threat of the day as a confluence of the "a-religious and practical relativism of Europe and America with Asia's negative theology, producing a profound mutation in core Christian teachings—with Christ seen as simply another spiritual sage comparable with Buddha or Muhammed, and Christianity as one valid religious path among many others."[81]

In September of 2007, at a private Mass with his former doctoral students Pope Benedict warned Roman Catholic theologians against becoming arrogant and forgetting God: "Theologians could know everything about the history of the Scriptures and how to explain them, but know nothing about God."[82] This Vatican response to dissident theologians calls to mind John Paul II's stern rebuke to the Liberation theologians of the eighties—and his letter to the Nicaraguan bishops denouncing the "People's Church" in especially harsh terms. More than two decades ago, Pope John Paul II predicted that "The Church born of the people is a new invention that was both absurd and of perilous character . . . only with difficulty, could it avoid being infiltrated by strangely ideological connotations."[83] As the pope predicted, today's dissidents draw from the same ideology, and implement the same language and methods, of the Liberation theologians of the past. Yet, as the following chapter will show, the Liberationists of today are even more radical in their agenda than those of the past.

Notes

1.   Peter Steinfels. "Liberal Catholicism Reexamined." Included in *Believing Scholars: Catholic Intellectuals*. Edited by James L. Heft, S. M. (New York: Fordham University Press, 2005), 140.
2.   Ibid.
3.   Ibid.
4.   *Ex Corde Ecclesiae*. The Apostolic Constitution of the Supreme Pontiff John Paul II on Catholic Universities. Given in Rome on 15 August, the Solemnity of the Assumption of the Blessed Virgin Mary into Heaven in the year 1990, the twelfth of the Pontificate: http://vatican.va
5.   Ibid.
6.   J. Donald Monan and Edward A. Malloy. "*Ex Corde Ecclesiae* Creates an Impasse." *America*. (January 30, 1999): http://209.35.85.31/articles/excordeecclesiaemonan-malloy/cfm
7.   "New Norms for Catholic Higher Education: Unworkable and Dangerous." *America*. (November 14, 1998): 3-4.
8.   Jon Nilson. "The Impending Death of Catholic Higher Education." *America*. Vol. 184, No. 18. (May 28, 2001.): http://americamagazine.org/content/article.cfm?article_id=927
9.   Ibid.
10.   *Ex Corde Ecclesiae*. "Guidelines Concerning the Academic Mandatum," Article 1, a-b.
11.   *Ex Corde Ecclesiae*. "The Apostolic Constitution of the Supreme Pontiff John Paul II on Catholic Universities." Given in Rome on 15 August, the Solemnity of the Assumption of the Blessed Virgin Mary into Heaven in the year 1990, the twelfth of the Pontificate: http://vatican.va
12.   Beth Mc Murtrie. "Catholic Bishops Offer Revised Guidelines for Carrying out Papal Statement. *The Chronicle of Higher Education* 46. (October 1, 1999): A18.
13.   Ibid.
14.   Ralph McInerny. "Picking and Choosing Church Doctrines." Beliefnet: www.beliefnet.com/story/17/story_1729.html

15. Tim Drake. "Notre Dame to Parents: We Won't Tell." *National Catholic Register*. (July 6-12, 2003).

16. McInerny. "Picking and Choosing Church Doctrines." Beliefnet.

17. Nicholas M. Healy. "By the Working of the Holy Spirit: The Crisis of Authority in the Christian Churches." *Anglican Theological Review*. (Winter 2006).

18. Daniel C. Maguire. "Academic Freedom and the Vatican's Ex Corde Ecclesiae." *Academe*. (May/June 2002).

19. Ibid.

20. Kit Lively. "U. S. Bishops Endorse Papal Statement on Catholic Colleges." *The Chronicle of Higher Education* 43. (November 22, 1996): A8.

21. Daniel C. Maguire. *Sacred Choices: The Right to Contraception and Abortion in Ten World Religions*. (Minneapolis, MN: Fortress Press, 2001).

22. Ibid.

23. Ibid.

24. Ibid.

25. Kit Lively. "Liberal Roman Catholic Theologians Say Vatican Statement Won't Change Their Views." *The Chronicle of Higher Education* 44. (July 10, 1998).

26. Richard Neuhaus. *First Things*. (December 2006): 73.

27. Ibid.

28. McMurtrie. "U. S. Bishops Approve Guidelines to Help Colleges Adhere to Ex Corde."

29. Peter W. Miller. "Archbishop Weakland's Legacy. *Seattle Catholic*. (June 7, 2002).

30. Ibid.

31. Ibid.

32. James L. Heft, S. M. "Have Catholic Colleges Reached an Impasse?" *The Chronicle of Higher Education*. (November 12, 1999).

33. Lively. "U. S. Bishops Endorse Papal Statement on Catholic Colleges."

34. The Editors. "Catholic Bishops Issue Statement on McBrien's Work." *The Angelus*. Volume VIII, Number 8. (August 1985).

35. Dennis Coday. "Extreme Makeover: the Diocese." *National Catholic Reporter*. (May 12, 2006).

36. Lively. "U. S. Bishops Endorse Papal Statement on Catholic Colleges."

37. Mary Ann Hinsdale and John Boyle. "Academic Theology: Why We are Not What We Were." Included in *What's Left: Liberal American Catholics*. Edited by Mary Jo Weaver. (Bloomington, IN: Indiana University Press, 1999), 111.

38. Ibid., 114.

39. Ibid.

40. Ibid.

41. Ibid., 115.

42. Orlando O. Espin. "An Exploration into the Theology of Grace and Sin." Included in *From the Heart of Our People*. Edited by Orlando Espin and Miguel H. Diaz. (Maryknoll, NY: Orbis Books, 1999), 136.

43. Ibid., 138.

44. Ibid., 137-138.

45. Ibid., 137.

46. Ibid., 140.

47. Ibid., 141.

48. Elizabeth Johnson. *Truly Our Sister: A Theology of Mary in the Communion of Saints*. (Edwin Mellen Press. Continuum, 2004).

49.   Thomas P. Rausch. "The Vatican's Quarrel with Roger Haight." *The Christian Century*. (May 3, 2005): 28-31.

50.   Ibid.

51.   Mark W. Roche. "Voting Our Conscience, Not Our Religion." *The New York Times*. (October 11, 2004): www.nytimes.com/2004/10/11/opinion/11roche.html

52.   Nicholas M. Healy. "By the Working of the Holy Spirit: The Crisis of Authority in the Christian Churches." *Anglican Theological Review*. (Winter 2006): http:// findarticles.com/p/articles/mi_qa3818/is_200601/ai_n16066352/print

53.   Philip Rieff. *Sacred Order/Social Order: My Life Among the Deathworks*. (Charlottesville, VA: University of Virginia Press, 2006).

54.   Ibid., xxii.

55.   Ralph McInerny. "Romance of Orthodoxy: Picking and Choosing Church Doctrine." www.beliefnet.com/story/17/story_1729.html

56.   Ibid.

57.   Thomas P. Rausch. "The Vatican's Quarrel with Roger Haight." *The Christian Century*. (May 3, 2005): 28-31.

58.   John Thavis and Cindy Wooden. "Vatican Forbids. U. S. Jesuit to Teach as Catholic Theologian." Catholic News Service. (February 8, 2005).

59.   Elizabeth Johnson, C.S.J., Book Review of *Jesus: Symbol of God* (Orbis, 1999) in *America*. (November 5, 1999).

60.   John L. Allen. "All Things Catholic". *National Catholic Reporter Café*. (September 14, 2007): http://ncrcare.org/node/1334

61.   Ibid.

62.   Ibid.

63.   Ibid.

64.   Robert P. George and William L. Saunders. "The Failure of Catholic Political Leadership." *Crisis*. (2000): www.catholiceducation.org/articles/politics/pg0020. html

65.   Ibid.

66.   Amy Welborn. "Open Book." (October 24, 2006): http://amywelborn.typepad. com/openbook/2006/10/see_the_point_i.html

67.   Ibid.

68.   Anne Knight and Sally Thomsin. "Anti-Papal Love Fest." *San Diego News Notes*. (April 2000).

69.   Peter Hebblethwaite. "Ban on Women Priests is Shaky Conclusion: Noted Theologian sees Scholarly Flaws: Peter Hunermann." *National Catholic Reporter*. (September 2, 1994): http://findarticles.com/p/articles/mi_m1141/is_n38/ai_ 15834092

70.   Cited by Richard Neuhaus in *First Things*.

71.   Ramon Gonzalez. "Married Priests a Given—O'Meara." *Western Catholic Reporter*. (March 19, 2003).

72.   Ibid.

73.   Bernard Cooke. *The Future of the Eucharist*. (Mahwah, NJ: Paulist Press, 1997), 32.

74.   Lecture by Bernard Cooke. May 7, 1998, Reported by *San Diego News Notes*. (June 1998).

75.   "Holy See Upholds Excommunication for Dissident Groups." *The Wanderer*. (December 7, 2006).

76.   "Vatican Confirms Excommunication for U. S. Dissident Group." *Catholic World News*. (December 7, 2006): www.cwnews.com/news/viewstory. cfm?recnum=48072

77. Healy. "By the Working of the Holy Spirit."
78. Steinfels. "Liberal Catholicism Reexamined." 146.
79. Ibid., 147.
80. John Henry Westen. "Cardinal Bertone Says Dissidents More Worrisome Than Atheists." *The Wanderer*. (January 5, 2007).
81. John L. Allen. "All Things Catholic. National Catholic Reporter Café. (September 14, 2007): http://ncrcare.org/node/1334
82. Tom Heneghan. "Pope Warns Theologians of Arrogance." *Reuters*. (September 19, 2007).
83. Malachi Martin. *The Jesuits: The Society of Jesus and the Betrayal of the Roman Catholic Church*. (New York: Simon and Schuster, 1982), 63.

6

Liberation Theology and the Women's Movement

While Peter Steinfels believes that liberal Catholicism is "papal teaching a hundred years too soon," the reality remains that, in many ways, rather than looking to the future of the Church, most Catholic feminists look back to the earliest days of the Catholic Church to find support for issues like women's ordination. Claiming that recently discovered—and allegedly previously hidden biblical texts including the Gospel of Thomas, the Gospel of Mary, and even the Dead Sea Scrolls—"preserve memories of an age when women were far more important in the Jesus movement than later writers would indicate."[1] Catholic feminists believe that it was time when "women were apostles and prophets, leaders and bishops." And, they ask, if that was the case in the first century, how could a similar role be denied to succeeding generations? For a society engaged in an ongoing controversy over women's ordination and feminist revisions of liturgy and scriptural language, this is all highly relevant and, as a result, many Catholic feminists remain angry.

One of the angriest of these feminists is Boston College theologian Mary Daly who, for more than three decades, refused to allow males to enroll in her undergraduate and graduate courses. Author of *The Church and the Second Sex,* a 1968 analysis of what she viewed as the misogyny of the Catholic Church, Daly claimed that her classroom had to be maintained as a male free "space on the boundary of a patriarchal institution."[2] Resisting reprimands in 1974 and again in 1989 from Boston College administrators concerned about her women-only stance, the self-described "radical feminist, lesbian, and post-Christian hag" finally met her match in 1999 when a male student initiated a lawsuit when he was locked out of Daly's courses. "I am caught in a double bind," Daly said in an interview for *National Catholic Reporter*, "Either I go in and teach men who would ruin my classes, or I find a way to negotiate a solution."[3] Critical of Boston College administrative demands that she allow males to enroll in her class, Daly maintains that "one of the hallmarks of a great university is that it allows for diversity of methodology."[4]

Indeed, as the previous chapter pointed out, many left-leaning theologians claim pluralism as the greatest strength of the current state of theology on Catholic campuses. They fail to mention, however, that respect for those with orthodox views is not a part of this theological pluralism. This is especially true for feminist theology, which has embraced some of the most diverse ideologies and methods. While Daly is extreme, her ideological writings mirror those of many feminist theologians. Daly's contempt for men in general, and the Catholic Church in particular, is reflected in her writings that promise to "spin new covens" within what she calls "the shell" of Roman Catholicism. Often photographed holding a battle-ax, which she calls the symbol of her particularly ideological lesbianism, Daly's philosophical motto is "to sin is to be."[5] Of her rejection of the Church, she writes: "My lust was for the Life of the Mind. The simple fact is that the more I studied and explored, the more I was in touch with myself, and going to church became odious."[6] (Daly capitalizes words that are especially meaningful to her although she never capitalizes "catholic" or "church."[7]) As an important part of this diversity, Mary Daly has promoted her own brand of theology.

Daly rejects the Creed as "mythological" and the Trinity as a "model for cloning." She regards the Immaculate Conception as "the ultimate depiction of pre-natal woman battering" and maintains that the incarnation of Mary was "rape by the Patriarchal deity."[8] Daly points to what she argues is the Catholic Church's "androcentric use of language" and charges that "the patriarchal use of language, images, and symbols has structured Christian religious culture and institutions in quite specific ways that limit the God-symbol and stifle the development of the church community."[9] In an effort to redefine the "God-symbol" and expose the patriarchy of the Church, Mary Daly has spent her entire career battling the Catholic Church and attempting to create a new feminist world. Her 1987 book, *Wickedary*, is described as a "parody of patriarchal dictionaries" that she uses to encourage readers to move beyond the misogyny, and her more recent book, *Outercourse*, urges readers to "spiral into leaps of consciousness" and "ecstasies of transgression." In her books, she has claimed that sin is simply "heightened being" and encourages women to learn to embrace the "deliciously ineluctable forces of nature."[10]

A strong proponent of abortion rights, Daly published an article in 1972 in the Catholic journal *Commonweal* arguing that Church opposition to abortion "should be seen within the wider context of the oppression of women in a sexually hierarchical society." Daly viewed the continued prohibition of abortion as part of the "sexual caste system" upon which the Church was founded and warned of a situation in which "open war is declared between feminism in this country and official Roman Catholicism."[11] All of her writings reflect a strong anti-male sentiment that has grown more strident with each of her books.

In fact, in her more recent books, Daly moves beyond attacking the church and claims to long for the day when "men are eliminated from the planet . . . If life is to survive on this planet, there must be a decontamination of the Earth. I think this will be accompanied by an evolutionary process that will result in a drastic reduction of the population of males."[12] In her book, *Pure Lust: Elemental Feminist Philosophy*, she advocates research that might make it possible to create and develop an embryo without need for a male seed, thus creating an ideal, male-free world. And, in an interview for *Cross Currents*, Daly describes the Trinity as a model of cloning because it is "total sameness" with Christ as a "perfect clone . . . they are the same guy masturbating."[13]

Despite her retirement from Boston College, Mary Daly continues to be an important icon for feminist theologians because she was the first to publish a feminist perspective of women's role in theology. *The Church and the Second Sex*, published in 1968, became what some still view as the feminist movement's foundational text. Reissued in 1975 with a "New Feminist Post-Christian Introduction" in which Daly not only repudiated her Catholicism, she also called for an exodus of women from the Church. Her next two books, *Beyond God the Father: Toward a Philosophy of Women's Liberation* and *Gyn/Ecology: the Meta-ethics of Radical Feminism,* furthered her agenda of "uncovering the sexism and misogyny of human history and providing an alternative language for women."[14] It is this "alternative language" that leads to an alternative theology for academic feminist theologians today who laud Daley's "ability to name the outrages perpetuated against women over the centuries."[15]

Although Mary Daly certainly cannot be viewed as representative of all feminist theologians on Catholic campuses today, her theme of a misogynistic Church designed to oppress women is a consistent one that has been adopted by most left-leaning theologians—both male and female. And, while Mary Daly has been influential for today's Catholic feminists, the reality remains that religious feminism is, at its heart, a spin-off from liberation theology—a form of theology which called upon the Church to identify more with the poor and oppressed and to struggle with them for their total liberation. Emerging from "base ecclesial communi-ties among the poor" (or, as the liberation theologians always describe them, "the people of God") and affirmed at the 1968 meeting of the Latin American bishops in Medellin, Colombia, the "theology of liberation" was at first embraced by the bishops who called on the Church to deal with structural conditions that cause human suffering—to try and build a more just, more equitable social order.[16] And, although these early days of liberation theology were welcomed by the Latin American bishops, it did not take long before the theology became distorted in critical ways by dissident liberation theologians like former Franciscan Priest Leonardo Boff, a Brazilian theologian who is viewed by critics as one who shifted the traditional focus of liberation theology away from the political and social structures that create and maintain poverty to structural faults within the church itself.[17]

Still, Leonardo Boff, who was later disciplined by the Vatican because of his heretical writings, is the liberation theologian most frequently cited by feminist theologians critical of Catholic teachings on women's ordina-tion and reproductive choice. One of the leading liberation theologians to have emerged from South America, Boff openly expressed his depen-dence on Marxist ideas when he claimed that "Liberation theology freely borrows from Marxism."[18] Still, it was not Boff's Marxism that drew the attention of the Vatican. Rather, it was his book, *Essays in Militant Ecclesiology,* that concerned Rome because it "distorted old doctrines by reinterpreting them in new contexts." The Office of the Congregation of Christian Doctrine (then headed by Cardinal Ratzinger) accused Boff of employing "ideological perspectives from history, philosophy, soci-ology and politics which were not informed by theology."[19] According to theologian Robert McAfee Brown, Cardinal Ratzinger was "deeply disturbed" by Boff's ecclesiology:

> (Cardinal Ratzinger) first accused Boff of suggesting Jesus did not determine the specific form and structure of the Church, implying that other models besides the Roman Catholic one might be consistent with the gospel. A second charge was that he is cavalier about dogma and revelation.

Boff responded by acknowledging, "dogma is needed to protect against heresy but not in the same way in all times and places." Yet, Boff argues that "it is ultimately the life of the Spirit in the Church that protects faith against encrustation in 'timeless truths' that can only negate spiritual progress." Ratzinger feared that such a doctrine of the spirit would legitimate the ideological whim of the moment.[20]

While it was Boff's ecclesiology that brought the negative attention from the Vatican, the Marxist analysis that permeates liberation theology has held the greatest appeal to feminist critics of the Church. Citing "the expropriation of the religious means of production" (including forgiveness, sacraments, and so forth) as a means by which the clergy deny power to the people, Boff claimed that such excessive concentration of power leads to domination, centralization, marginalization of the faithful, triumphalism, and institutional hubris. Likewise, the feminists have created a theology based on Marxist ideology and praxis, which maintains that the Church's teachings on women's ordination and reproductive rights, including the right to abortion, are tools used to oppress women and are tantamount to an unlawful violation of the rights of women. Like the liberation theologians who believe that the primary intention of Jesus was to liberate the poor and oppressed, feminist theologians believe that the Church has no right to interfere with a woman's right to priestly ordination or a woman's right to choose. To support this right, Catholic feminists often use conventional theological language, but replace its doctrinal content with an emphasis on the "emergent" message of the Holy Spirit working through the "people of God"—a calculated move which has the potential to challenge the validity of the present ecclesial structures of the Church.

Liberation Theology and Reproductive Rights

The rhetoric of liberation theology is at the forefront in the reproductive rights movement among feminists on Catholic campuses. In fact, for the past four decades, feminist anger has focused primarily on the Church's condemnation of contraception and abortion, and its unwillingness to ordain women as priests. While the Catholic position on birth control was not too far removed from the social norm through the fifties, the gulf widened in the sixties as the availability of the birth control pill made effective contraception more widely available and acceptable to the general public.[21] Feminist demands for the right to control their reproductive decisions converged with the public's growing desire to control what was becoming defined as the problem of "overpopulation" in the sixties. Best-selling books like Paul Ehrlich's *The Population Bomb* linked population worries to fears of environmental catastrophe and resource exhaustion.[22]

For population control advocates, and, increasingly, the general public in the sixties and seventies, the Catholic Church was becoming quite literally the primary obstacle to human survival of the planet.[23]

For feminist critics, the official Catholic position indicates how far the Church has fallen behind any kind of social reality, and suggests that the Church sees no role for women except as wives and mothers. In 1970, in an attempt to begin to address this "Catholic obstacle" to reproductive choice and population control, the organization Catholics for a Free Choice originated under the name Catholics for the Elimination of All Restrictive Abortion and Contraceptive Laws. Fr. Joseph O'Rourke, S. J., a Jesuit who left the priesthood in 1974, served as the first president of the pro-abortion organization, yet it was not until Frances Kissling assumed control that the pro-abortion organization gained visibility—and funding from prominent population control organizations.[24] Raised in Flushing, NY, Kissling spent six months as a postulant at the Convent of the Sisters of St. Joseph, after having spent two years as a student at St. John's University. When she left the convent, Kissling says that she "left her faith behind as well."[25] Yet, she continues to call herself "Catholic" claiming that (contrary to Church teachings) "membership is not based simply upon following a certain set of rules and regulations." Following the example of Leonardo Boff and the liberation theologians, Kissling maintains that "The Catholic Church is a Church of the people. My faith is a contract and a covenant that I have with God personally."[26]

As an important part of her strategy, Kissling enlisted prominent Catholic feminists—many of them feminist theologians teaching on Catholic campuses—to build a major media presence in an effort to convince the world that Catholics support abortion. With no actual membership (critics routinely refer to the organization as a "well-funded letterhead," and even Kissling has admitted under pressure that "We're not a membership organization. We have no membership"[27]) Catholics for a Free Choice was created by philanthropic institutions with a pro-abortion bias. Foundations like the Turner Foundation, the Ford Foundation, the David and Lucille Packard Foundation, and the Rockefeller Foundation, as well as Hugh Hefner's Playboy Foundation have all given financial support to the pro-abortion "Catholic" organization.[28]

Frances Kissling has spent millions of dollars trying to convince others that although the Church may seem to teach that abortion is wrong, it is not necessary to pay attention to such teachings. Maintaining that there is no single Catholic stance on abortion (despite the fact that for more than two thousand years, the Church's constant condemnation of abortion has never wavered) the group argues that a number of Catholic theologians as well as Catholic laity oppose the Church's teaching on abortion on legitimate theological grounds. One of their key publications in the earliest days was a pamphlet authored by Marjorie Reiley Maguire and her then husband, former priest and current Marquette theologian, Daniel Maguire entitled *Abortion: A Guide to Making Ethical Choices.* The pamphlet, a precursor to Daniel Maguire's book, *Sacred Choices,* concludes that the "Catholic Church, when considered in its rich diversity, teaches that some abortions can be moral and that conscience is the final arbiter of any abortion decision." They also suggest that "the Catholicism that is taught in many Catholic parishes does not reflect the richness of the Catholic faith."[29]

In his research on Catholics for a Free Choice, historian Thomas E. Woods has found that the primary theological argument advanced by CFFC in favor of abortion as a morally legitimate option involves a principle called probabilism—according to which a person may have recourse to his conscience when a doubtful matter of fact is involved in a moral question. According to Maguire, probabilism also allows that "if you find five or six theologians—known for their prudence and learning—who held the liberal dissenting view, you could follow them in good conscience even if the other ten thousand theologians—including the pope—disagreed."[30] And, one of the most successful strategies that Kissling has employed has been enlisting feminist theologians teaching on Catholic campuses who are only too happy to challenge two thousand years of Catholic teachings on the evils of abortion.

Indeed, on her website Kissling advises women considering abortion to "weigh all the circumstances in your life and your pregnancy and follow your own conscience." To help inform the conscience, she publishes articles by pro-abortion theologians like Xavier University Theology Professor Christine Gudorf (who has since moved to Florida International University) or statements by dissident clergy like Fr. Robert Drinan. Drawing from their theological expertise, Kissling advises women that, "if you carefully examine your conscience and then decide that an abortion is the most moral act you can do at this time, you are not committing a sin. Therefore, you are not excommunicated, and you do not need to tell it in confession, since in your case, abortion is not a sin."[31] *Conscience,* in fact, is the name of the flagship quarterly magazine of Catholics for a Free Choice.

In an effort to convince even more Catholics that abortion can be a moral decision, Kissling has spent millions of foundation-donated dollars advertising her cause—creating the illusion that she has a constituency among grassroots Catholics as well as among pro-choice foundations. Catholic college faculty members and administrators played an especially important role on October 7, 1984 when Kissling placed a full-page advertisement in the *New York Times* asserting that "there is more than one theologically and ethically defensible viewpoint on abortion within Catholicism," and calling for a dialogue among Catholics to acknowledge this "situation of pluralism" in the Church. The ad explicitly asked for the cessation of institutional sanctions against those with dissenting positions on abortion, "Catholics—especially priests, women religious, theologians, and legislators, who publicly dissent from hierarchical statements and explore areas of moral and legal freedom on the abortion question, should not be penalized by their religious superiors, church employers or bishops."[32] Ninety-seven Catholic scholars, religious and social activists—including twenty-four women religious, four priests and brothers, and a large number of lay professors working at Catholic colleges and universities signed *The Times'* ad.[33]

Among the signers of the ad were Joseph Fahey, a professor at Manhattan College; Elisabeth Schussler Fiorenza, then a theology professor at the University of Notre Dame who now teaches at Harvard; and Daniel Maguire of Marquette and his wife Marjorie, who was then working as a Fellow in Ethics and Theology at Catholics for a Free Choice. Other signers included Michael Barnes, a professor at the University of Dayton; Mary Buckley, a professor at St. John's University; Mary Byles, a professor at Maryville College; Daniel DiDominzo, a professor at Marian College; Christine Gudorf, a professor at Xavier University; Paul Knitter, also a professor at Xavier University; Joe Mellon, a professor at the University of Notre Dame; Gerald Pire, a professor at Seton Hall University; Mary Savage, a professor at Albertus Magnus College; Ellen Shanahan, a professor at Rosary College; Jane Via, a professor at the University of San Diego; and Arthur Zannoni, a professor at the University of Notre Dame. A second ad in the *New York Times,* published on March 2, 1986, was, in effect, a show of support for those who had signed the October, 1984 ad and featured more than one thousand signatures, "representing a large percentage of the Catholic feminist constituency," and including hundreds of Catholic feminists teaching on Catholic campuses.[34] According to some of the signatories, there was tremendous pressure placed on both tenured and untenured faculty on many Catholic campuses to sign the ad—yet, such coercion from feminist campus leaders was never identified as such.

One of those who signed the original pro-abortion ad, Notre Dame theologian Elisabeth Schussler Fiorenza, is still an honored guest lecturer on Catholic campuses including most recently, at the University of San Diego, Seton Hall, and St. Louis University. She has moved on from her early days with Catholics for a Free Choice to help unite many of the feminist groups into a coalition called the Women-Church Convergence, "a movement of self-identified women and women-identified men from all denominations whose common goal is to reinterpret the Gospel from the perspective of women's liberation."[35] Led by Catholic theologian Rosemary Ruether, women in the group have created their own life-cycle ceremonies, including rituals to mark an abortion or the union of lesbian couples. In her presentations on Catholic college campuses, Schussler Fiorenza cites her own brand of feminist theology to argue that the Catholic Church has always been "pluralist" when it comes to abortion. She also tells those in attendance at her lectures that she rejects the divinity of Jesus, the true presence of Christ in the Euchararist, and the doctrine of the Trinity among other fundamental beliefs of the Catholic Church. She also wants "God" to be replaced by "Goddess."

Schussler Fiorenza and Kissling are aware that because they call themselves Catholic, they can say things about the Church that the personnel of national abortion organizations like Planned Parenthood cannot. Most recently, Kissling appropriated a popular devotional image to promote abortion among Hispanic Catholics. In a prayer card asking Our Lady of Guadalupe to "keep abortion legal," Kissling uses the figure of the Guadalupe, revered by Hispanics, in an attempt to convince them that abortion can be a sacred choice.

On many occasions, the feminist critique of the Church on reproductive choice has crossed the line into anti-Catholicism. Kissling's own words reveal her revolutionary intention. In a 1989 interview with *Mother Jones* magazine, Kissling remarked, "I spent 20 years looking for a government to overthrow without being thrown in jail—I finally found one in the Catholic Church." And, so she has devoted most of her career to destroying the Church. At a roundtable discussion on population issues at the United Nations sponsored by Catholics for a Free Choice in March of 1999, she described the Catholic Church as "fatally flawed" and said, "I might have had more success in the Episcopalian Church, where it is not quite so bad, but there are so few Episcopalians, it's not worth it."[36] Enlisting theological cover from feminist theologians like Maguire or Gudorf, Kissling's rhetoric goes beyond criticism of Church teachings on sexual morality: "What I am doing is not just dealing with the issue of abortion or reproduction, but with the structure of the Catholic Church . . ."[37]

Faculty hostility to the structure of the Catholic Church, papal authority, and Church teachings on sexual morality and reproductive rights is best summarized in an interview published in the *National Catholic Reporter* with a tenured San Diego theology professor, Pilar Aquino. Released in 2005, following the death of Pope John Paul II, Aquino responded to the pontiff's death by dismissing any contributions he made throughout his tenure as pope and complaining that "large numbers of Catholic scholars and intellectuals show a clear rejection of the outdated, imposed and one-sided thought patterns of the Roman Curia and the Vatican as a whole . . . We feminist Catholic theologians profoundly disagree with the intractable position of official Roman Catholicism regarding reproductive rights and women's human rights."[38]

A long time critic of Pope John Paul II, Aquino declared that his pontificate exhibited "strong signs of theological intolerance and of rigidity in the exercise of power . . . the model of Church promoted by John Paul II was widely characterized by authoritarianism, centralism, conservatism, imperialism, and by mono-culturalism, is consistent with the patterns of dominant male-centered Western European Christianity." Like Kissling's rhetoric, Aquino charged that the pope "fashioned a non-participative Church where the clerical structure and sexist hierarchy had primacy," and claimed "he showed no inclination nor will to discuss issues of the full participation of women in all spheres of the Church's life." And, like Kissling, Aquino longs for a day when the current structure of the Catholic Church is gone: "This Church will survive as a whole only if it has the vision and the strength to become a discipleship of equals."[39]

The contempt for the Church and her leaders expressed by Professor Aquino is shared by many feminist theologians of her generation. Continuing to clamor for an end to what they resent as "clericalism," and a rejection of papal authority in this "discipleship of equals," Aquina's words capture the sentiments of many of her feminist colleagues both on and off campus. Yet, with the exception of Pennsylvania State University Professor Philip Jenkins, few seem to identify such stridency as bigotry or blasphemy. Jenkins believes that the reason for the failure to criticize these feminists is most likely that the Catholic Church offers its critics a "ready-made demon" figure that automatically symbolizes sexism because of its all male hierarchy. The fact that the institution refuses to ordain women appears to some that it is committed to continuing male supremacy. Jenkins believes that the American public takes a negative view of such dogma and orthodoxy. And, as a result, feminist theologians have found that if a conflict over social issues can be framed in terms of a battle between women and the Catholic Church, then feminists have every reason to expect "not just that they will win support, but that they will be seen as representing the social mainstream."[40] As Jenkins writes in his book, *The New Anti-Catholicism*, "Imagine a debate between, on the one hand, women speaking the language of progress, secular values, individual tolerance, and on the other hand, men who are using otherworldly religious rhetoric and whose very clothing seems archaic and foreign. It is very much in the interest of women's groups to portray opposition to their issues as specifically religious and Catholic, and also to present these religious interests in the most obnoxious and oppressive way."[41]

For example, in their *Brief, Liberal, Catholic Defense of Abortion*, Daniel Dombrowski and Robert Deltete, both professors at the Jesuit-led Seattle University, assert that the reasons why the church forbids abortion are based on a "recent" papal attempt to suppress feminine authority and erroneous assumptions about conception and life. Claiming that performing an abortion on a non-sentient fetus is like removing plant life, these Seattle authors believe that pre-sentient beings have no moral standing: "A fetus becomes a human being in the moral sense of the term at the same approximate point when it acquires the ability to survive outside the womb."[42] While some might find their physiology chilling, their theology, not surprisingly, contains the feminist nostalgia for the early Church when abortion was allowed. In fact, moving beyond St. Paul's misogyny, Dombrowski and Deltete blame "Mariology," or devotion to the Virgin Mary, for what they call the Church's "recent" anti-abortion stance. These authors claim that this devotion began when Pope Pius IX defined the Immaculate Conception as a dogma of faith, thus setting the stage for the harsh language on the denial of access to abortion for women. And, they accuse Pius IX of erroneously reasoning that since the Virgin Mary was herself conceived immaculately—that is, without sin—then she must have been a "person" from conception.[43]

Although orthodox Catholic reviewers found the book dishonest since they believe that abortion has always been condemned by the Catholic

Church, many pro-choice advocates lauded the Seattle authors as finally acknowledging the "inconsistency and complexity in Church teachings on abortion." Feminist theologian Mary Doak, formerly a professor at Notre Dame and most recently hired to teach theology at the University of San Diego, described the book as "a fine example of theological and ethical argumentation that would be an excellent pedagogical resource."[44] In fact, Doak recommends that faculty members encourage their undergraduate students to read the book in their theology courses because "it presents a tight argument that should be accessible to undergraduates yet sufficiently sophisticated for graduate students."[45] Likewise, former priest and pro-choice theologian, Anthony Padovano posted a glowing review of the book on the Catholics for a Free Choice website lauding the authors for finally exposing the "fact" that the Catholic Church's "holy crusade against abortion" was calculated to put an end to "permissive sexuality and feminine autonomy."[46]

The Catholic campus politics of abortion escalated during the 2004 presidential elections when Catholic college faculty and administrators throughout the country provided John Kerry, the pro-choice Catholic candidate, with financial support for his candidacy and theological cover for his pro-abortion voting record. Although the documented financial support to the pro-abortion Kerry from faculty on Catholic campuses like Georgetown and Boston College was significant, the far greater contribution to the Kerry campaign came from the theological cover that Catholic faculty members provided, which enabled Kerry to maintain that he could remain a Catholic in good standing and still vote in favor of making abortion available.

In fact, one month before the November 2004 presidential elections, Mark Roche, Dean of the College of Arts and Letters at the University of Notre Dame, published an essay in *The New York Times* encouraging Catholics to vote for Kerry for president. Acknowledging that while Kerry is indeed pro-choice, Roche claims that Kerry is "closer to the Catholic position" on other important issues including the death penalty or access to universal health care.[47] Roche also suggested in his essay that President Bush's decision to use military force in Iraq violated the Catholic doctrine of just war. Yet, Roche failed to mention that the pope never declared the war to be unjust, nor did he forbid Catholics from supporting it or Catholic soldiers from fighting in it.

Roche concludes his essay by ignoring the fact that Catholic teachings on abortion are unequivocal, and instead, he equates abortion as simply one issue within a long list of other issues—including environmentalism. Roche claims that while Catholics may be "dismayed at John Kerry's position on abortion and stem cell research, they should be no less troubled by George W. Bush's stance on the death penalty, health care, the environment and just war," and he advises Catholics to move beyond their concerns about Kerry's abortion stance and "reaffirm their tradition of allegiance to the Democratic Party in 2004."[48]

In his writings, Roche is defying the *Catechism of the Catholic Church,* which clearly states: "Since the first century, the Catholic Church has affirmed the moral evil of every procured abortion. This teaching has not changed and remains unchangeable. Direct abortion, that is to say, abortion willed either as an end or means, is gravely contrary to the moral law."[49] The Church also teaches that those who treat abortion as just one of many issues are misleading others. "Abortion is unique among policy issues because it is not a matter of prudential judgment. From a Catholic perspective, politicians are not making an application of a principle to a specific situation. All instances of abortion are morally wrong." Yet, as Roche has done, some pro-choice Catholics will try to minimize the importance of the abortion issue by citing a long list of issues, with abortion being only one among them. Their method of convincing voters of their "Catholic credentials" is to trade disagreement on this issue with agreement on several others. But, the bishops denounced such a strategy in their 1998 document, *Living the Gospel of Life.*[50]

In some important ways, Roche is simply continuing the Notre Dame tradition of providing the same theological cover to politicians begun in the sixties by Rev. Theodore M. Hesburgh, longtime president of the University of Notre Dame. Like Roche, Fr. Hesburgh attempted to equivocate Catholic moral teachings on abortion by claiming that "while Republicans who were against abortion agreed with only 5% of Catholic teachings, Democrats who were pro-choice were on the Catholic side in 95% of the other issues."[51] According to his biographer, Fr. Hesburgh "wanted the Church to modify its position, urging the Vatican to make no official pronouncement on sexual matters for a period of ten years." While he personally opposed abortion, Hesburgh's biographer suggested that the Notre Dame president refused to ally with the pro-life movement. And, his involvement as chair of the board of the Rockefeller Foundation, a source of strong support for legalized abortion around the world, also compromised his role as a mediator between the Church and the secular culture.[52] And, in 1991, Fr. Hesburgh invited New York's

Governor Mario Cuomo to Notre Dame to offer a noteworthy public defense of his position on abortion. The now-infamous position of being "personally opposed to abortion yet unwilling to deny the right to an abortion to others," was given Fr. Hesburgh's stamp of approval at Notre Dame in 1991. In an article still proudly posted on the Notre Dame website, Fr. Hesburgh described Cuomo's speech as "a brilliant talk on religion and politics," and acknowledged that "there is not a consensus in America for the absolute prohibition of abortion."[53]

In a review of Fr. Hesburgh's role in the pro-choice movement at Notre Dame, Monsignor George Kelly, a founder and, until his death, president emeritus of the Fellowship of Catholic Scholars, criticized the role that Fr. Hesburgh played in providing protection for pro-choice politicians and theologians on Catholic campuses—far beyond Notre Dame. In fact, Monsignor Kelly wrote that that during his years as Notre Dame's president, "Fr. Hesburgh's ecclesiology became steadily more hostile to the hierarchy":

> In 1972 he was a delegate to the International Congress of Catholic Universities, a meeting held on Vatican territory—within mere feet of the office of Pope Paul VI—where he threatened to walk out and take the American delegation with him if Rome dared to impose norms for the conduct of American colleges.[54]

Monsignor Kelly acknowledges that "at times there is a sting to Fr. Hesburgh's rhetoric," and provides an example of that attitude in a recent incident that is not reported in his biography—but is well-known on the Notre Dame campus:

> A prominent Notre Dame official went to Fr. Hesburgh as to a mentor, worrying that the implementation of the Vatican document *Ex Corde Ecclesiae* might bring the American bishops into the governance of the university. The retired president consoled his worried friend, ending his counsel with this message: "What is the worst thing that can happen to us? John Paul II will tell the world that Notre Dame is not a Catholic university. Who will believe him?"[55]

This story has become almost a "legend" at Notre Dame and beyond as Fr. Hesburgh's words are often repeated by faculty and administrators on other Catholic campuses in order to reassure faculty members that compliance with *Ex Corde Ecclesiae* is not necessary. In fact, the Notre Dame faculty obviously took Fr. Hesburgh's reassurance to heart more than a decade later when the faculty senate voted unanimously to ignore the requirements of *Ex Corde Ecclesiae.*

Liberation Theology and Women's Ordination

Reviewing the history of the feminist battles over reproductive rights reveals that many of those fighting the abortion wars have also enlisted in the battle over women's ordination. As early as 1970, National Organization for Women members publicly burned a copy of the Roman missal that prohibited women from serving as lectors in the Catholic Church.[56] And, in 1974, Patricia Fogarty McQuillan, one of the founders of Catholics for a Free Choice, crowned herself pope on the steps of St. Patrick's Cathedral in New York on the first anniversary of the *Roe v Wade* decision. Some of the most visible feminist theologians allied with Catholics for Free Choice, including Catholic theology professors Elisabeth Schussler Fiorenza and Rosemary Ruether, have also been on the front lines protesting Catholic teachings on the priesthood.

Rosemary Ruether, longtime board member of the Catholics for a Free Choice and theology professor at Garrett Theological Seminary in Evanston, Illinois until 2002 when she moved to serve on the faculty of the Graduate Theological Union in Berkeley, has been one of the harshest critics of the Catholic Church's stand on women's ordination. Drawing upon pagan themes in many of her books, Ruether is the author of *Gaia and God: An Ecofeminist Theology of Earth Healing.* Denying most of the teachings of the Catholic Church, Ruether, like Daniel Maguire and Schussler Fiorenza, has developed her own theology. According to Thomas Wood's research on Ruether's writings and lectures:

> Taken as a whole, Ruether's work is a thorough and complete rejection of Catholicism . . . Ruether rejects practically every dogmatic teaching of the Church. She does not believe in the transubstantiation of the bread and wine into the Body and Blood of Christ in the Mass, and she rejects the entire Catholic theology of the priesthood. She even rejects the Church's fundamental contention regarding the immortality of the individual soul—the touchstone on which all forms of Christianity are based.[57]

For Ruether, since there is no individual soul, redemption cannot have the classical significance it has always possessed. She believes that feminist theologians such as herself, "reject the classical notion that the human soul is radically fallen, alienated from God, and unable to reconcile itself with God, in need of an outside mediator."[58] The role of Jesus and his sacrifice for our sins becomes quite differently defined in feminist theology as Ruether believes that "no one person can become the collective human whose actions accomplish a salvation which is then passively applied to everyone else."[59] Since the redemption story, or the Christian belief that Jesus suffered and died for our sins, is the basis of all Christianity, it is difficult to understand how she can continue to remain employed as a "Catholic" theologian. And, although she is not teaching on a Catholic campus, she continues to be an honored guest lecturer on such campuses. In fact, the University of San Diego recently invited

Ruether to hold the prestigious Portman Chair in Theology.

For Ruether, feminist Christianity, rather than the Bible, is the true gospel of Jesus because it involves the dismantling of the patterns of patriarchal Christianity and the reconstruction of a radically different understanding of the key touchstones of Christian theology. She writes: "What happens to Christian feminist theology when Christian symbols are one resource among others, along with Shamanism and Buddhism . . . Multi-religious solidarity and syncretism are not only allowable, they are required."[60] The Catholic Church has never allowed syncretism, yet, this has not stopped Catholic campuses from offering courses and spirituality workshops that blend syncretistic mixtures of elements from various sources including Kabbalah, astrology, as well as Sufi mysticism, Yoga, Buddhism, and numerology.

In an investigation of what she calls the "dark side" of Catholic feminism, journalist Donna Steichen has documented the use of goddess religion and witchcraft on many Catholic campuses—especially within Catholic campus theology departments. In the eighties, Fr. Matthew Fox was the most renowned Catholic apostle of the new mysticism that Steichen claims resembled the old pantheism. Although he is no longer influential in Catholic higher education today, Fox built a national reputation in the eighties as director of the Institute for Culture and Creation Spirituality (ICCS), which he founded at Chicago's Mundelein College but moved in 1983 to Holy Names College in Oakland, California where it was housed for twelve years. Steichen writes that during the days of his influence at Holy Names College, Fox lectured frequently on Catholic campuses on the need for the availability of legal abortion for all women. Fox publicly lauded committed same-sex genital acts as "celebrations of creation" and, according to Steichen, Fox claimed to find the mass "less boring" when it incorporates witchcraft, chants, and dances.[61]

In his book, *Original Blessing*, Fox, like most feminists, looks to the early Church to declare that "no one believed in original sin until Augustine," and he denounced belief in God's transcendence as the ultimate dualism and blamed it for separating God from humanity and reducing religion to a childish state of pleasing or pleading with a God "out there."[62] At a San Francisco conference in 1984, Fox was a panelist at a "Gaia Consciousness Conference and Celebration of the Re-emergent Earth Goddess" held by the California Institute of Integral Studies at the Franklin Street Unitarian Center.

Although Fox eventually fell out of favor with the Catholic left because of his increasingly bizarre theology and in 1996 moved his program in creation spirituality to his own "university" called the University of Creation Spirituality, none of this has prevented theology faculty on Catholic campuses from honoring Fr. Fox with invitations to speak on their campuses throughout the country. Fox was invited to lecture several times at the University of San Diego—and each time he played to the liberation theologians on campus to deny the divine nature of Christ accusing the Church of hiding its head in the sand about population control and, one time, even opposing the canonization of Father Junipero Serra.[63] Eventually even the left-leaning *National Catholic Reporter* described Fox's work as "a combination Doonesbury cartoon theology and Shirley MacLaine spirituality."[64]

Still, Fox's unconventional Catholicism remains on many Catholic campuses, especially in the areas of spirituality, as many of the Holy Names graduates have gone on to create their own unique brand of Catholic/Creation spirituality in their positions in campus ministry or religious education. Most recently, Mount St. Mary's College, a women's college near downtown Los Angeles, hosted a series of six spirituality workshop on the "enneagram—a system based on numerology that promises self-realization by using a symbolic circle with nine numbered, equally spaced points on its circumference and lines connecting several of the points . . . Teachers of the system claim that by use of the enneagram one can explain why people tend to act in particular ways and can prescribe goals for adjustment and development of one's own personality."[65]

In addition to syncretism, polytheism is often an integral part of feminist theology. Rosemary Ruether disclosed her involvement in polytheism in an interview with a reporter for the journal *U. S. Catholic*. Based upon his research, Thomas Woods believes that for Ruether, ordaining women would constitute "an essential first step" in implementing her radical changes in Catholic theology including a rejection of monotheism, a rejection of the notion of sin and the need for redemption, and a rejection of the central role of Christ as a sacrifice for humanity.[66]

Like Ruether, Elisabeth Schussler Fiorenza has edited and contributed to published collections of the writings by feminist theologians who, as she writes, "inquire into the links between feminist spiritualities and diverse feminist struggles on the one hand and the importance of human or divine Chokma/Sophia/Wisdom as their hermeneutical horizon."[67] Filled with jargon and new age syncretistic mixtures, the edited collections focus on religious resources for spirituality and "articulate a spiritual vision

that not only expresses wo/men's struggles to survive and transform relations of domination but also critically identifies religious traditions and
resources for such a discernment of the Spirit-Shekhina-Sophia's working
in different global contexts." Concluding that the contributors to her most
recent edited collection of feminist writings function as "ministers of
Divine Wisdom that have been sent out to the public places of the global
village . . . and invite all of us to eat the bread of Wisdom-Sophia, drink
of her wine and walk in her ways of creative justice."[68]

To support their feminist contentions about a Sophia/Wisdom spirituality—and to help undermine the historical validity of the New Testament
and the divinity of Christ, many feminist scholars and theologians draw
upon the "hidden gospels." In his research on the ways in which feminists
have been "ambitious in using the newly found gospels to reconstruct
the early churches in their own image" Philip Jenkins writes that for
feminists, the "hidden gospels" reveal an early Christianity headed by
a radically egalitarian Jesus who welcomed a proto-feminist movement
that venerated female leaders like Mary Magdalene. Many feminists believe that the privileged role of women in the early Church was annexed
by sinister figures like St. Paul—a "misogynist and homophobe, who
imposed his dark, repressive vision on the emerging Church." And, as
Christian theology became more complex, these same feminists believe
that "the mechanisms of the Church became hierarchical, bureaucratic
and oppressive . . . The main victims of this transformation were women
who lost their positions and prestige within the Church."[69]

Gary Macy, Santa Clara University theologian, and his colleague,
longtime San Diego Visiting Professor Bernard Cooke, have been among
the strongest proponents of this revisionism. Calling Mary Magdalene
the "Apostle to the Apostles" because it was she who first announced the
resurrection of Jesus to the Apostles, Macy argues that it was "not only
the Magdalene, however, but from this we gather that these women (in
Jesus' company) were established in some sense to be apostles above the
apostles."[70] To build his argument that women were ordained for over
1,200 years in the Catholic Church, he has drawn from the published
letters between Heloise and Abelard on the Ordination of Abbesses. According to Macy, these letters demonstrate that Abelard quoted sources
that refer to deaconesses and abbesses as an *ordo*—as ordained.[71]

Macy and Cooke's writings are often cited on the websites of the pro-
women's ordination movements—including Call to Action—and they are
used as "evidence" that in the twelfth century the separation between

the roles of the laity and the minister widened as the power bestowed upon the minister in ordination became seen as absolutely necessary for the efficacy of Christian rituals including, of course, consecrating the Eucharist. Macy and Cook also believe that eventually the "power" came to be reserved to males only at the Council of Trent (1545-1563) when the clerical exclusivity of males was codified.[72]

Much of this revisionism is cited by modern feminist theologians—like Rosemary Ruether who has included "the evidence" in her collection of readings supporting a feminist theology, or an alternative feminist canon. Likewise, Schussler Fiorenza and Aquino drew upon the material in the hidden gospels to advocate a whole new range of approaches that should be applied in feminist research. Characteristic of these approaches is what they call a "hermeneutic of suspicion," based on the presumption that patriarchal texts—including most of the New Testament—would unnecessarily exclude or demean women and the feminine and cannot be trusted. Yet, as Jenkins points out, the "hidden gospels" are themselves contested terrain. In his book, *Hidden Gospels: How the Search for Jesus Lost Its Way*, Jenkins argues that far from being "revolutionary," such attempts to find an alternative Christianity date back at least to the Enlightenment. By employing scholarly and historical methodologies, Jenkins demonstrates that the hidden texts purported to represent pristine Christianity were in fact composed long after the canonical gospels found in the New Testament: "Produced by obscure heretical movements, these texts offer no reliable new information about Jesus or the early church. They have attracted so much media attention chiefly because they seem to support radical, feminist, and post-modern positions in the modern church."[73]

Jenkins also points out that feminists found additional ammunition against a patriarchal Catholic Church from the *Pistis Sophia,* which became available in English in 1896 because "it revealed a tradition in which female disciples and supernatural figures played a vital role." Most of the text takes the form of a dialogue on spiritual mysteries between Jesus and his disciple, Mary Magdalene, whom Jesus addresses as "thou spiritual and light-pure Mary, inheritress of the light," and who is depicted as his primary follower and disciple.[74] Feminists draw upon this earlier exalted view of the Magdalene to provide support in their contention that the democratic spirituality of Jesus became the legalistic authoritarianism and misogyny of the Catholic Church. Jenkins points out that these arguments have an importance far beyond the purely academic—if they were truly part of the "gospels" of the first century, as "the existence of female prophets, presbyters, bishops or apostles in the first centuries would destroy the ideological arguments advanced today to prevent women from being ordained in the Roman Catholic Church."[75]

Co-editor of *In the Power of Wisdom*, the most recent edited collection of feminist writings on "Sophia," Maria Pilar Aquino echoes much of Schussler Fiorenza's feminist jargon when she too describes the edited collection as a "variegated feminist exploration of a Wisdom spirituality of struggle with a critical reflection, gathering in and sifting through the rich intellectual fare and spiritual harvest . . . For feminist movements around the world, the religious traditions of critical Wisdom are those that provide backing for their struggles to achieve the objectives of liberation."[76]

While it is often difficult to decode the feminist jargon in the Sophia/ Wisdom writings by feminist theologians like Aquino and Schussler Fiorina, a careful analysis of their work reveals the familiar language of liberation theology merged with the Gnostic texts. Aquino writes, "this new feminist language is created in order to confront and eliminate the kyriarchal systemic domination characteristic of the current paradigm of global free market capitalism as well as its dehumanizing effects, clearly visible in the spread of injustice, inequality, and social exclusion."[77] Enhancing the language of liberation theology with the Gnostic Sophia writings, Aquino suggests that "for feminist movements around the world, the religious traditions of critical Wisdom are those that provide backing for their struggles to achieve the objectives of liberation."[78] Lest there be any mistake about the liberationist origins of the feminist theology, Schussler Fiorenza writes, "Divine Wisdom does not dwell in kyriarchal institutions or in text but 'among the people,' in quests and struggles for liberation in the midst of a world in which suffering caused by injustice, poverty, inequality and social insecurity abounds."[79]

The continued reliance on the core philosophy of liberation theology on Catholic college campuses like the University of San Diego remains strong. In 2006, Gustavo Gutierrez, known as the "Father of liberation theology," was an honored guest speaker at the first annual lecture of the University of San Diego's Center for the Study of Latino/a Catholicism. Gutierrez, a Peruvian priest, became the earliest spokesman for the movement when he wrote the most notable text for liberation studies, *A Theology of Liberation*—a text that continues to be assigned to hundreds of undergraduate theology students on Catholic campuses each year. According to Gutierrez, theology is "situational" and defines a process not an outcome.[80] This redefinition of theology allows the feminist followers of Gutierrez to intertwine Biblical concepts with Gnostic myths and Marxist ideology and move to empower "the people of God" as equals in the teachings and activities of the Catholic Church—thus opening the door of ordination to women.

It was especially appropriate that Fr. Gutierrez visited the San Diego campus in 2006 because just a few months before his visit, Jane Via, longtime theology professor at the University of San Diego, was illicitly ordained as a Catholic priest on June 24, 2006, aboard a riverboat in Switzerland. In a ceremony that was described by Patricia Fresson, one of three female Catholic bishops who claim to have been secretly ordained by active Roman Catholic bishops, as "both a political and a sacramental action," Via became one of a growing number of American women who have received ordination to the priesthood in recent illicit ceremonies through Roman Catholic Womenpriests.

Womenpriests is a reform movement that claims to have ordained dozens of women priests and deacons. According to Fresson, "The women being ordained are being called by name and sent out, as Mary Magdalene was, to proclaim the good news of Jesus' life, message and Resurrection."[81] While Fresson acknowledges that the ordinations are breaking Church law, she states that "We believe we are breaking an unjust law. I come from South Africa. We learned from Nelson Mandela and others that if a law is unjust, it must be changed."[82]

Via, like most feminist theologians, has been a longtime critic of Church teachings on reproductive rights and a woman's right to ordination in the Church. One of the original signers of the 1984 Catholics for a Free Choice *New York Times* ad protesting the Church's stand on abortion, Via has enjoyed more than two decades of job security at the University of San Diego where she has served as an adjunct professor of theology. And, although her signature on the pro-abortion ad in *The New York Times* did not seem to concern her University of San Diego employers, the publicity surrounding the news of her ordination as a priest helped to end her long-term teaching career at the university in 2006. However, Via took seriously Fresson's invitation to go forth and proclaim the good news as Mary Magdalene did when she co-founded a new Catholic congregation in San Diego, the independent Mary Magdalene the Apostle Catholic Community. Via's decision to call her newly founded Church the Mary Magdalene the Apostle Catholic Community was surely a calculated one as many academic feminist theologians like Via teach that Mary Magdalene is a founding mother of Christianity with a primacy equivalent to that held by Peter in Catholic sources.

"I am a Roman Catholic woman priest," Via told a reporter for the *San Diego Union Tribune*, "We are Catholic, this is our tradition, and we claim it . . . The institution chooses not to recognize us . . . I believe that my ordination is valid. I acknowledge that it's illicit under canon law."[83] And, while San Diego Bishop Robert Brom would not comment publicly on Via, Karl Keating, the head of *Catholic Answers*, a national apologetics organization, stated that, "Not only is she not a Catholic priest, she has incurred automatic ex-communication . . . Our local bishop doesn't need to come out publicly with an announcement to confirm that Jane and whoever else is involved here have removed themselves from the Church."[84]

Still, at Via's first mass, the religion and ethics editor of the *San Diego Union Tribune* reported that "In the packed sanctuary of a rented church in Mission Hills, a balding man in a short-sleeved shirt stepped up to the microphone and said, 'Folks, I want to welcome you to the revolution.'" As Via presided over the ceremony, reporters claimed that her voice "cracked with emotion" as she spoke of her ordination and her plans for her new Church.[85] While the service contained some of the ingredients of the traditional Catholic Mass—including her attempt to consecrate the Eucharist, the Creed was deleted and the Lord's Prayer was replaced with a gender-inclusive prayer that began "Our God of all creation."[86] In the days following Via's Mass, one of the published letters to the editor of the *San Diego Union-Tribune* echoed Macy's writings to argue that, "There were women priests and deacons in the early centuries of the church, only to be relegated to the sidelines by a man-made canon that states only baptized males can be ordained . . . It is time to rethink ancient church law. We, the laity are the Church. "[87]

This published letter points to the real problem of much revisionist feminist teaching in theology on Catholic campuses. While Mary Daly at Boston College, Jane Via, or Pilar Aquino at the University of San Diego may claim to simply be exercising their academic freedom in providing a "diverse" theological perspective for students, the problem is that there remains very little diversity in these theology programs. The real victims of such pluralism are the undergraduate students, many of whom have little background in Catholic theology before their arrival on a Catholic campus, who are exposed to some of the most heretical teachings about the Catholic Church without ever hearing an orthodox position. While attempts have been made on some Catholic campuses to integrate a minor or major in "Catholic Studies" so that students might have an opportunity to learn the truth about the history and the teachings of the Catholic Church, theology professors routinely block approval for such courses.

At the University of San Diego, it took one professor three years to win approval to offer a single Catholic studies course on Catholic culture in the United States. Theology professor complaints about the proposed course focused on the lack of attention to "diverse" perspectives as reflected in the Catholic studies professor's proposed lecture topics and choice of texts. Complaining that the proposed course reflected a "blind acceptance" of the Magistereum, and a "Eurocentric" perspective in which "women's voices were silenced," the curriculum committee's refusal to approve the course until the professor added the politically correct themes and texts not only delayed the scheduling of the course for several years, but the lengthy delay and humiliating process for the Catholic studies professor sent a chilling message to any faculty member who wanted to offer an alternative perspective to the liberal orthodoxy that has been allowed to prevail.

In 2001, just four years before he was elected to the papacy, Cardinal Ratzinger wrote: "The problem central to our time is the emptying of the historic figure of Jesus Christ. An impoverished Jesus cannot be the sole Savior and Mediator." Many feminist theologians have denied the divinity of Christ and have declared that Jesus is simply "our brother." Feminists, like Mary Himes and Elizabeth Johnson, have pronounced Mary of Nazareth a girl just like any other girl, and Rosemary Ruether and Elizabeth Schussler Fiorenza have pronounced God as female. And feminist theologian Orlando Espin conflates Our Lady of Guadalupe with the Holy Spirit to posit a female God.

All of this has damaged not just the Catholic Church—it has damaged Christianity itself. As Philip Rieff writes in his *Life Among the Deathworks*, "The Death of God the father will not lead to the birth of God the mother, nor to another twelve or more sacred messengers . . . The mother-as-god movement will be smothered in its own feminist animus."[88] The vacuum that was created by deposing the male God has spawned alternative theoretical systems on Catholic campuses on Catholic campuses. The syncretism of the New Age/Wisdom feminist spirituality and the growing strength of the Marxist Liberationist theology and its feminist and gay successors have constructed what Rieff calls a "psychosis about the established commanding truths in sacred order." Rieff warns that "commanding truths will not be mocked, except to the destruction of everything sacred."[89] As the following chapter on the gay liberation movement on Catholic campuses will show, the desire for a utopia that can never come has driven sacred and social order farther and farther apart.

Notes

1.   Philip Jenkins. *The Hidden Gospels: How the Search for Jesus Lost Its Way.* (New York: Oxford University Press, 2001), 124.
2.   Scott Heller and Alison Schneider. "Boston College Feminist Fights Order to Allow Men in her Class," *The Chronicle of Higher Education* 45, (March 5, 1999): A50.
3.   Pamela Schaeffer. "Law Firm Forces Mary Daly's Hand." *National Catholic Reporter.* (March 5, 1999).
4.   Ibid.
5.   Jeannette Batz. "Smuggle Back What's Lost." *National Catholic Reporter*, "Smuggle Back What's Lost." (May 31, 1996): http://findarticles.com/p/articles/mi_m1141?is_n31_v32?pnum=3&opg=18363123
6.   Mary Daly. *Outercourse: The Bedazzling Voyage.* (San Francisco, CA: Harper Collins, 1992), 60.
7.   Stephen Hand. "The Witch of Boston College." (January 2005): www.tcrnews2.com/marydaly.html
8.   Mary Daly. *Gyn/Ecology: The Metaethics of Radical Feminism.* (Boston, MA: Beacon Press), 75.
9.   Mary Ann Hinsdale and John Boyle. *What's Left: Liberal American Catholics.* Edited by Mary Jo Weaver. (Bloomington, IN: Indiana University Press, 1999), 120.
10.   Mary Daly. *Outercourse.* 292.
11.   Philip Jenkins. *The New Anti-Catholicism.* (New York: Oxford University Press, 2003), 73.
12.   Susan Bridle. "No Man's Land: An Interview with Mary Daly." http://www.wie.org/j16/daly.asp?pf=1
13.   Catherine Madsen. "The Thin Thread of Conversation: An Interview with Mary Daly. *Cross Currents.* www.crosscurrents.org/madsenf00.htm
14.   Susan A. Ross. "Catholic Women Theologians of the Left" Included in *What's Left: Liberal American Catholics.* Edited by Mary Jo Weaver. (Bloomington, IN: Indiana University Press, 1999), 20.
15.   Ibid.
16.   Alan Clark. "Rome Silences the Critics." *New International.* (January 1986): www.newint.org/issue155/rome.htm
17.   Ibid.
18.   Eamonn Keane. *A Generation Betrayed.* (Long Island City, NY: Hatherleigh Press, 2002).
19.   Robert McAfee Brown. "Leonardo Boff: Theologian for All Christians." www.religion-online.org/showarticle.asp?title=1405
20.   Ibid.
21.   Jenkins. *The New Anti-Catholicism.* 71.

22.   Ibid., 72.

23.   Paul Ehrlich. *The Population Bomb*. (New York: Ballantine Books, 1968).

24.   Thomas E. Woods, Jr. *War on the Faith: How Catholics for a Free Choice Seeks to Undermine the Catholic Church.* (New York: International Organizations Research Group, 2001), 5.

25.   Ibid.

26.   Ibid., 29.

27.   Ibid., 14.

28.   Kathryn Jean Lopez. "Aborting the Church: Frances Kissling and Catholics for a Free Choice." *Crisis.* (April 1, 2002).

29.   Marjorie Reily Maguire and Daniel Maguire. *Abortion: A Guide to Making Ethical Decisions, Catholics for a Free Choices.* (September 1983).

30.   Daniel Maguire. "Where There's Doubt, There's Freedom." *Conscience.* (Spring/ Summer 1993): 15. Cited by Woods, Jr. *War on the Faith.* 9.

31.   Frances Kissling. "You are Not Alone: Information for Young Catholic Women about the Abortion Decision." Catholics for a Free Choice. www.catholicsforchoice.org/topic/abortion/documents/2000youarenotalone_000.pdf

32.   Rosemary Reuther. "Catholics and Abortion: Authority vs Dissent." *Christian Century.* (October 3, 1985): 859-62.

33.   "A Diversity of Opinions Regarding Abortion Exists Among Committed Catholics: A Catholic Statement on Pluralism and Abortion." *The New York Times..* (October 7, 1984): Section 4.

34.   Woods. *War on the Faith.* 7.

35.   Reuther. "Catholics and Abortion." 859-62.

36.   Anne Hendershott. *The Politics of Abortion.* (New York: Encounter Books, 2006), 98.

37.   Woods. *War on the Faith.* 13.

38.   Arthur Jones. "Interview with Maria Pilar Aquino." Included in "No Time for Glorifying and Exalting: Two Perspectives." *National Catholic Reporter.* (April 14, 2005).

39.   Ibid.

40.   Jenkins. *The New Anti-Catholicism.* 70.

41.   Ibid.

42.   Daniel Dombowski and Robert Deltete. *A Brief, Liberal, Catholic Defense of Abortion.* (Urbana, IL: University of Illinois Press, 2000), 24.

43.   Ibid., 15.

44.   Mary Doak. Book Review of *A Brief, Liberal Catholic Defense of Abortion* by Daniel Dombrowski and Robert Deltete. Review published in *American Journal of Theology and Philosophy.* Vol 22, No. 3. (September 2001): 293.

45.   Ibid.

46.   Anthony Padovano. Review of *A Brief, Liberal, Catholic Defense of Abortion*, in *Conscience.* (Summer 2000): www.catholicsforchoice.org/conscience/archived/dissentingview.htm

47.   Mark W. Roche. "Voting Our Conscience, Not Our Religion." *The New York Times*, (October 11, 2004).

48.   Ibid.

49.   *Catechism of the Catholic Church.* 2271.

50.   Deal W. Hudson. "How to Vote Catholic." *Crisis.* (October 2006).

51.   William McGurn. "Life of the Party." Speech presented at the Bob Casey Lecture in the Catholic Archdiocese of Denver. Text of the speech published in *National Review Online.* (October 28, 2004). See also "Notre Dame Alumnus Regrets Misrepresentation of Catholic Teachings by Some University Officials." www.

catholicnewsagency.com
52. Michael O'Brien. *Hesburgh: A Biography.* (Washington, DC: Catholic University Press, 1998).
53. Rev. Theodore M. Hesburgh. "Hesburgh on Cuomo." Published in the archives: *The Story of Notre Dame.* (September 30, 1991). First published by Universal Press Syndicate. Later included in the archives: http://archives.nd.edu/episodes/visotrs/cuomo/hesburgh.html
54. Monsignor George Kelly. "A Man of Influence." (November 20, 2001): www.cwnews.com/news/viewstor.cfm?recnum=20761
55. Ibid.
56. Toni Carabillo, Judith Meuli, and June Bundy Csida. *Feminist Chronicles, 1953-1993.* (Los Angeles, CA: Women's Graphics, 1993). Cited in Jenkins. *The New Anti-Catholicism,* 77.
57. Woods. *War on the Faithm.* 16.
58. Rosemary Radford Ruether. "Created Second, Sinned First: Women, Redemption and the Challenge of Christian Feminist Theology." *Conscience,* Published by Catholics for a Free Choice. (Spring 1997) 3-6.
59. Ibid. Also, Woods. *War on the Faith.* 16.
60. Ruether. "Created Second, Sinned First." 3-6.
61. Donna Steichen. *Ungodly Rage: The Hidden Face of Catholic Feminism.* (San Francisco, CA: Ignatius Press, 1992), 220.
62. Ibid.
63. Ibid., 225.
64. "Silencing Fox a Fruitless Exercise." Editorial. *National Catholic Reporter.* (October 21, 1988): 10.
65. "Does This Sound Catholic to You?" *California Catholic Daily.* (January 19, 2007).
66. Woods. *War on the Faith.* 18.
67. Elisabeth Schussler Fiorenza. *In the Power of Wisdom.* Edited by Maria Pilar Aquino and Elisabeth Schussler Fiorenza. (London: SCM Press, 2000), 7-10.
68. Ibid., 10.
69. Jenkins. *The New Anti-Catholicism.* 87.
70. Gary Macy. "Heloise, Abelard and the Ordination of Abbesses." *Journal of Ecclesiastical History.* Vol 57, No. 1. (January 2006): 16-18.
71. "Macy: Women priests until the 12th Century." Churchwatch. Call to Action. (January-February 2001): www.cta-usa.org/watch01-01/macy.htm
72. Ibid.
73. Jenkins. *The Hidden Gospels.* front book flap.
74. Ibid., 127.
75. Ibid., 131.
76. Maria Pilar Aquino. "Towards a New World in the Power of Wisdom." Included in *In the Power of Wisdom.* Edited by Maria Pilar Aquino and Elisabeth Schussler Fiorenza. (London: SCM Press, 2000), 130.
77. Ibid., 129.
78. Ibid., 130.
79. Ibid.
80. James F. Wilson. "Liberation Theology: Is There a Future For it?" (Fort McNair, Washington, DC: Industrial College of the Armed Forces, 1993).
81. Ann Rodgers. "Twelve Women Ordained as Catholic Priests." Religion News Service. www.beliefnet,com/story/196/story_19680_1.html

82. Ibid.
83. Sandi Dolbee. "Ordination Puts Woman, Backers at Odds with the Catholic Church." *San Diego Union Tribune.* (August 5, 2006).
84. Ibid.
85. Ibid.
86. Stanford Espedal. "God of the Unclean: A Visit to San Diego's Womanpriest Mass." *San Diego News Notes.* (November/December 2006).
87. "Letters to the Editor." *San Diego Union-Tribune.* (August 10, 2006).
88. Philip Rieff. *Sacred Order, Social Order: My Life Among the Deathworks.* (Charlottesville: University of Virginia Press, 2006), 97.
89. Ibid., 194.

7

Blurring the Boundaries

DePaul University, which proudly calls itself "the nation's largest Catholic university," achieved yet another distinction in 2006 when it was named one of the "Top 100 Best Campuses" in the United States for gay, lesbian, bisexual, and transgendered students. Citing DePaul's October "Queer Kiss-In," as well as its yearly "Coming Out Ball," its "Springtime Drag Fest," and its support services for students "transitioning from male to female, or female to male," the university has long been known, as the editors of the *Advocate College Guide for Lesbian, Gay, Bisexual and Transgendered Students* write, as an "extremely progressive campus for LGBT issues." The campus developed a Safe Zone program to highlight the many allies across campus. In addition, there are a number of gay, lesbian, bisexual, and transgendered student groups at DePaul, including Pride, T-Global, and Spectrum. The counseling center has support groups, and the university ministry organizes training for peer ministers on gay and lesbian issues and concerns. There are course offerings focusing on gay and lesbian topics and, as recently as 2005, a core group of faculty developed a minor in LGBT studies.[1]

It is clear that DePaul is on the front lines in the battle for rights for gays and lesbians, and although many Catholic campuses have gay and lesbian themed social activities, support groups, and course offerings, DePaul is the first Catholic university in the country to offer the lesbian, gay, bisexual, transgendered, and queer studies minor. Open to all undergraduate students, the academic minor builds upon courses that had already existed including, for example, "Creating Change: Contemporary LGBT Politics," and "Deconstructing the Diva."[2] Achieving status as a minor indicates a strong commitment from DePaul's administration and board to provide the funds to hire new faculty and reassign current faculty time to teach courses on gay and lesbian issues.

As a result of DePaul's encouraging environment for gay and lesbian students, one gay student contributor to the *Advocate LGBT Guide* declared that DePaul has become "a gay mecca," while another said, "We have Boystown right around the corner—what more could you want?" And a third student shared poignantly: "I have always been proud to be a Catholic. My gay identity always kept my faith in question and conflicted with what I was taught to believe. I have found peace with who I am at DePaul University—It's okay to be gay."[3]

Indeed, this student's comment reveals what the LGBTQ program is really all about—supporting gay, lesbian, and bisexual students. Drawing upon DePaul's Vincentian Catholicism and its "commitment to serving marginalized and oppressed groups through service to the community," the university builds on its Catholic commitment to social justice, which places an emphasis on the human dignity and value of each individual person's life to support the gay and lesbian advocacy activities. *The Advocate* states, "Quite simply, the campus embraces a progressive Catholic ideology that openly accepts LGBT students."[4]

While DePaul's goal of inclusion and acceptance of all persons regardless of sexual orientation is laudable because it is indeed in keeping with Catholic teachings on the dignity of all human beings, there are problems with the ways in which this progressive Catholic ideology has been implemented that have met with the greatest resistance from those concerned about Catholic colleges and universities. Although the Catholic Church affirms the humanity of those with same sex attraction, Catholic teachings distinguish between engaging in homosexual acts, and having a homosexual inclination. While the Church teaches that the former is always objectively sinful, the later is not. And as a result of its unwillingness to accept the goodness of homosexual acts, the Church has become a symbol not only of repression, but also of hypocrisy, as it is accused of harboring within itself a strong homoerotic culture and a large number of gay priests.[5]

Church teachings on homosexuality are clear. For more than two thousand years the Catholic Church has taught that homosexual acts are "contrary to the natural law . . . Under no circumstances can they be approved."[6] These teachings of the Catholic Church were reinforced at the 2006 meetings of the United States Conference of Catholic Bishops when the bishops issued an even stronger and more specific statement, which held that although homosexual men and women who are Catholic should be welcomed into parish communities, treated kindly, and helped to live chastely in accordance with Catholic teachings, the statement cautioned that "Catholics who are gay and lesbian, should not publicly come out as such . . . Special care ought to be taken to ensure that those carrying out the ministry of the Church not use their position of leadership to advocate positions or behaviors not in keeping with the teachings of the Church . . . They must not belong to groups that oppose Church teachings."[7]

The bishops may have had Catholic campuses like DePaul in mind when they issued a 2006 document on ministry to homosexuals—a statement produced by the US Bishops' Committee on Doctrine to help the bishops evaluate programs directed at gay ministry to ensure their conformity with Catholic doctrine. The document stated, "Persons who experience same-sex attraction, yet are living in accord with Church teachings, should be encouraged to take an active role in the life of the faith community." However, the Bishops maintain that the Church has a right and a duty to deny roles of service to those whose behavior violates her teaching because such service may seem to condone an immoral lifestyle and may even be an occasion of scandal."[8]

These teachings appear to have been ignored at DePaul, which continues to celebrate "coming out" and gay sexual relationships through such activities as the "Queer Kiss-In." Held on October 11, 2006, as part of "Coming Out Week" at DePaul, the "Kiss-In" was sponsored by the gay and lesbian support groups on campus. DePaul's student newspaper, *The DePaulia*, reported that more than fifty students participated in the very public same-sex "Kiss-In." The purpose of this unique approach was described by DePaul student leaders as intending "to raise awareness of queer relationships and tackle the issues of subtle homophobia seen on campus." And, while that may be true, the student newspaper cited interviews with the students who created the kiss-in to conclude that a more important purpose of the activity was to show people on campus (the event was held in the middle of the campus student center, the main student activity building for DePaul) that "homosexual relationships are not uncommon—and to show people that they are normal." While the "Kiss-In" was billed as providing the opportunity to plant "platonic kisses on the cheeks," the session itself was described by at least one student observer as a "full-blown make-out fest with lustful groping."[9] Robin Wolf, president of Spectrum, the gay and lesbian support group at DePaul, claimed that "We are trying to challenge people's perceptions as to what is normal . . . The more you see it, the more normalized it becomes."[10]

Held each October at DePaul, "Coming Out Week" in 2006 featured a revisionist performance of the play, *Peter Pan,* highlighting the same-sex orientation of the cast members. In April of each year, DePaul celebrates "Spectrum Pride Week," which culminates in a drag show that has become so outrageous that even the pro-gay secular publication, *The Advocate,* acknowledges that one should "be prepared to be shocked" by the cross-dressing participants.[11] Throughout it all, and, contrary to the requirements of *Ex Corde Ecclesiae*, DePaul University president, the Rev. Dennis H. Holtschneider, a Vincentian priest, has publicly joined Fr. Jenkins at Notre Dame to say that he would not interfere with these decisions.[12]

To be fair, DePaul is far from the only Catholic campus that supports gay and lesbian clubs on campus. According to a Duquesne University survey in 2006, there are currently forty-six Catholic campuses with gay support clubs. By 2008, a survey published in LifeSiteNews.com revealed that ninety-six Catholic colleges and universities hosted gay support clubs.[13] Twenty-four of the twenty-eight member institutions of the Association of Jesuit Universities and Colleges currently have gay and lesbian clubs.[14] Likewise, DePaul is not the only campus to celebrate "coming out" weeks, gay awareness months, or days of silence for gays and lesbians. Notre Dame celebrated Gay, Lesbian, Bisexual, and Questioning Awareness Week in 2006 by constructing a large "closet" in the center of campus and encouraging students to "come out" and proclaim their sexual preference. During Coming Out Week, Notre Dame student activists used student association funds to distribute orange T-shirts that read, "Gay? Fine by me," sponsor a showing of *Brokeback Mountain* as part of the Gay Film Festival, and invite Bradley Bogaert to speak about his struggles as a gay man. An article in the *New York Times* with the headline, "At Religious Universities, Disputes over Faith and Academic Freedom" was strategically placed alongside a photo of Notre Dame's new president, Fr. John Jenkins, and a photo of four Notre Dame students wearing the orange "Gay? Fine by Me" T-shirts.[15]

Like Notre Dame, Gay Awareness Month at the University of San Diego encourages students to show support for gays and lesbians by wearing PRIDE T-shirts with the USD crucifix logo imprinted on them—implying the support of the university and the Church itself. Encouraged to celebrate the accomplishments of "famous gay historical figures" from Socrates to Shakespeare, students view exhibits of the contributions of gays throughout history in the student center. Advertising the gay and lesbian themed events a few years ago, there was a twelve-foot banner placed on the outside of Serra Hall, an academic building in the heart of the campus which read: "Stop Heterosexism." The San Diego campus has also hosted James Dale, the former Eagle Scout who has done tremendous damage to the Boy Scouts because of the scouting organization's unwillingness to allow openly gay men to serve as troop leaders; lesbian comedian Margaret Cho; as well as Betty DeGeneres, the mother of celebrity-lesbian Ellen DeGeneres; and the mother of Matthew Shepard, the young gay icon who was brutally murdered in Laramie, Wyoming.

Beyond Gay Awareness Month, the University of San Diego has managed to couple advocacy for the gay and lesbian community with support for people of color during African American History Month by inviting African American gay and lesbian speakers to campus. A few years ago, former Black Panther and longtime Communist Angela Davis was invited to campus to talk about the ways in which her lesbian identity and African American heritage have shaped her political ideology. Likewise, Sabrina Sojourner, the first open lesbian to be elected to Congress as the US representative from the District of Columbia, gave a lecture on campus that tied her perceived oppression as a woman of color to her oppression as a lesbian. Attendance is always strong at these lectures as students are often required to attend these lectures as part of a class assignment, or they are given extra class credit simply for their presence.

Indeed, it is difficult to avoid participating in these types of activities as the re-education of students begins as soon as they arrive on campus. At the start of the 2006 school year, the University of San Diego offered a walking tour of Hillcrest, San Diego's gay community as one of several orientation activities for incoming first-year students. The event was advertised as "a walking tour with a history of the area, a restaurant and business guide as well as an open discussion of the Gay, Lesbian, Bisexual, Transgendered and Queer community that lives there."[16]

Beyond these optional activities, there is often pressure placed on students to visibly show their support for the gay and lesbian community on campus. In fact, during the first day of San Diego's freshman orientation a few years ago, incoming students received "welcome packs" containing pink "gay pride" triangles to display in their dormitory rooms that proclaim the students' room to be an "Open Zone" for gay, lesbian, bisexual, and transgendered students. During the university's orientation week, upper-division students functioning as orientation leaders and role models for the first-year students are instructed to proudly display the pink triangles on their orientation-team folders and encourage freshmen students to display their triangles also.

Likewise, for faculty members, there is tremendous pressure to conform. A few years ago, a non-tenured adjunct San Diego faculty member paid a high price for his reluctance to post the symbolic pink triangle on his office wall. The popular part-time faculty member had taught at the university for several years. He was a strong presence in the classroom, with the highest student evaluations in his department, yet he was not offered a contract to teach again. No explanation was given for this abrupt decision, but those familiar with the case believe that the reason was his unwillingness to display the obligatory pink triangle proclaiming his office "An Open Zone for Gay, Lesbian, Bisexual and Transgendered Persons." When asked to post the symbol in the office space he shared with other part-time instructors, he responded in writing that he would do so if requested, but that, "if the space were mine, I would not post such a sign." This response was widely circulated on campus as an example of a violation of one of the most important campus norms—support for the gay community. The part of his response that probably sealed his fate was his assertion that "any institution, especially a Catholic institution, marginalizes itself with such vapid symbolism." One senior professor publicly denounced him as a "homophobe" at an American Association of University Professors faculty meeting for even questioning the appropriateness of displaying the pink triangle. Most of those in attendance failed to appreciate the irony of such a violation of a professor's academic freedom at an AAUP faculty meeting.

Beyond extra-curricular initiatives like what has now become the "sacred symbol" of the triangle and university sponsored and organized "walking tours" of the gay community for first-year students during orientation week, the University of San Diego offers several gay and lesbian themed courses. A few years ago, an inter-disciplinary theology/sociology course, entitled "Gay and Lesbian Voices," brought negative attention because several of the students enrolled in the course complained to administrators about the content of the course—and brought their concerns to the chair of the sociology department and to the dean of the College of Arts and Sciences. A parent of one of the students enrolled in the course requested a refund of the tuition for the course after his daughter was required to participate in a graphic classroom presentation and discussion on the value of using sexual aids for gays and lesbians. A representative from a San Diego shop that catered to the LGBT community had been invited to the class to instruct students on the value of such aids for gay men and lesbian women.

Students were initially attracted to the course because enrollment in the cross-listed theology/sociology course would fulfill one of the three general education theology course requirements students must complete before graduation. For some students, the catalogue description of the course on the history of the gay and lesbian social movement sounded like a more attractive option than the usual theology course offerings on the Old Testament or the Sacraments. But, after a number of complaints from students and their parents, the dean of the college instituted a policy that allowed students to drop the course with a full refund even after the deadline for withdrawal had passed.

This course, like many of the LGBT initiatives on the San Diego campus and on other similar Catholic campuses, has been supported by general academic funds supplemented by generous donations from foundations with interests in bringing diversity or pluralism to the Catholic Church. The "Rainbow Visibility Project" at the University of San Diego began in September of 1999 as a result of the Rainbow Visibility Grant funded by the James Irvine Foundation (one of the biggest donors to Planned Parenthood) through San Diego's Cultural Competencies Project. Rainbow Visibility was designed to be a comprehensive plan to "raise the collective awareness of the university community to lesbian, gay, bisexual and transgender culture and history."[17]

The Rainbow Visibility Project had five components. First, a conference was organized to launch what the organizers called "the campaign" with Betty DeGeneres. Once the conference was completed, the grant provided funds to assist faculty in revising their existing courses to incorporate "significant attention to sexual orientation in their course content, pedagogy and interactions with students." Participating faculty received substantial stipends for attending curriculum development workshops where they not only learned about gay and lesbian history, they also learned how to integrate gay and lesbian themes into their existing courses in sociology, theology, psychology, history, and the sciences or to create new courses that explore gay and lesbian issues. At the conclusion of the curriculum workshops, faculty were encouraged (with yet another stipend) to revise their syllabi to include gay and lesbian books, films, and topics for discussion for students. Once the syllabi were revised and the course scheduled, faculty received still another stipend—giving faculty a strong financial incentive to create courses that integrate and highlight gay and lesbian issues. The faculty has risen to the challenge—a number of gay and lesbian themed courses have been designed including, most recently, a school of education designed a course that helps future teachers introduce gay and lesbian themed books for elementary school children.

One component of the Irvine Grant underwrote the creation of a PRIDE Resource Library through the purchase of books and audiovisual materials exploring sexual orientation. And, another funded a university colloquium, which gathered ten representatives from the faculty, staff, student, and administrative communities on campus for monthly dinner meetings throughout a full academic year. At the conclusion of the year, participants in the colloquium voted to encourage the board of trustees to revise the non-discrimination policy on campus to include sexual orientation as a protected group along with race, gender, and age.

The final, and perhaps most important component of the Irvine Rainbow Visibility Grant used funds to support the Rainbow Educators—a team of students, faculty, staff, administrators, and alumni who are trained to provide presentations to students in dorms and classrooms and lead workshops on sexual orientation as a form of diversity.[18] The Rainbow Educators learn to respond to questions that students might have about Catholic teachings and homosexuality. But, in contradiction to Catholic Church teaching that states that homosexual inclination and acts are disordered, the Rainbow Educators website (and presentations) answers the question, "What Does the Bible Say about Homosexuality?" as follows:

> In the past, many have claimed that the Bible's message about homosexuality is un-equivocally negative. Contemporary Bible scholars, however, raise questions about the matter and suggest that biblical texts must be read in their historical and cultural contexts. Read this way, biblical authors do not appear to address issues of lifelong sexual orientation or adult, loving homosexual relationship as we understand them today.[19]

From the initial award of the Irvine Grant in 1999, the goal of the grant has been "full inclusion of gay and lesbian students, staff and faculty." And, although inclusion is a noble goal in terms of working to ensure that persons of homosexual orientation are not discriminated against, campus activists have redefined Church teachings on homosexuality in an effort to affirm gay and lesbian sexual behavior. The advocacy component of the grant is revealed in subsequent grant applications for additional funding from other foundations to support the campus gay and lesbian initiatives. In an application for funding from the Strauss Foundation, the San Diego grant writer showed clearly the advocacy aspect of the earlier grants when he claimed that "each component of the grant aims to create meaningful and long-lasting changes in the attitude of the USD community toward gays and lesbians." As one grant writer claimed, "Rainbow Visibility's objective is to be the spark that moves USD beyond tolerance and toward inclusion of its own gay community."[20]

Now that the Irvine Grant has become institutionalized on campus, and Rainbow Educators and other gay and lesbian initiatives on campus are supported by campus funds, attention to these issues is integrated into many areas of university life. For example, the 2007 Hate Crimes Awareness Week devoted little time to issues of race or ethnicity and, instead, showed students *The Laramie Project*, the iconic film about Matthew Shepard, the gay victim of a brutal murder, and invited Shane Windmeyer, the gay author of *Advocate College Guide for Lesbian, Gay, Bisexual and Transgendered Students*, to be the keynote speaker for the week.[21] Rather than focusing on hate crimes, Windmeyer's speech focused on the positive aspects of his own coming out as a gay man to his fraternity brothers. Claiming that his coming out experience was "one of the most rewarding undergraduate experiences," Windmeyer told the student audience that his coming out was the inspiration for his books—including *Out on Fraternity Row: Personal Accounts of Being Gay in a College Fraternity, Secret Sisters: Stories of Being Lesbian and Bisexual in a College Sorority,* and his most recent release, *Brotherhood: Gay Life in College Fraternities.*[22]

Likewise, at a recent San Diego Faculty and Curriculum Development Workshop, Brent Scarpo was invited to present an interactive session that was advertised as an opportunity to help faculty and staff "learn to examine how student self-hatred contributes to sabotaging their college careers." And, while this innocuous description sounds like it would apply to all students, the reality is that Scarpo is an openly gay motivational speaker who integrates information about his own "coming out" into his presentations. He is best known as the creator and presenter of his first interactive program, "Coming Out—The Never Ending Story." On his website, Scarpo promises that through his seminars, participants will learn that "coming out can be the best experience in your life!"[23]

Sometimes such advocacy and integration of gay and lesbian issues has created controversy on campus. In 2004, Jessica Lawless, a Los Angeles based self-described "Queer artist," claimed to have been censored on the University of San Diego campus when a portion of her artwork was not included in a campus art exhibit called "The Open Show." Lawless had been invited to display her art by undergraduate student, Jaime Egan, social issues director for the associated students. But, because of complaints from other students and staff on the Catholic campus, Lawless was asked not to exhibit her most suggestive piece—the one entitled "Blue Things That I Love," because it contained a picture of a sexual aid tied with a blue trimmed baseball sock. In an interview for *Zenger's Newsmagazine* and posted on the internet, Egan decried what she called the university's "censorship" and claimed to have invited Lawless because "As a bisexual woman on this campus, I'm used to being silenced and having my identity denied, and I thought this would push my agenda in a less frightening way than a speaker or a debate . . . I saw Jessica's pieces and saw the dildos as a statement about gender as a social construct, not sexual."[24]

In response to what Lawless and Egan saw as censorship, a forum was held on campus to "provide an opportunity for Lawless to argue for the legitimacy of exhibiting her work."[25] The two-hour meeting provided the participants an opportunity to describe the campus as "homophobic" for failing to exhibit the lesbian art. And, at the conclusion of the meeting, undergraduate students were served slices of cake that had been decorated with the same image of the blue-ribbon tied sexual aid that matched the artist's censored artwork.[26]

Indeed, students are the primary target of gay advocacy on Catholic campuses. And, it appears that the advocacy has been effective. A survey of students at the College of the Holy Cross conducted in spring, 2004, found that 72 percent support gay marriage. And a Cardinal Newman-sponsored report on students at thirty-eight Catholic colleges and universities nationwide found that students' support for legalizing gay marriage increased from 55 percent to 71 percent between their first and fourth year on a Catholic campus. The report from the Cardinal Newman Society concluded that "far from strengthening adherence to Catholic doctrine, attending one of these Catholic institutions, including Gonzaga, John Carroll, Loyola Marymount and the University of Notre Dame, makes a student more likely to approve of legalizing same sex marriage."[27]

Recalcitrant students are encouraged to become more accepting of gay and lesbian relationships. Sometimes coercion is involved. In early May of 2005, Tim Lopez, a senior philosophy major at Santa Clara University and president of the Santa Clara pro-life organization, wrote a letter to the editor of the student newspaper in protest of the annual drag show and addressed the problem of homosexual propaganda on campus. Subsequent to his letter's publication, Lopez became a target of hatred on campus. A University of Santa Clara professor of religious studies wrote a letter to the editor of the paper denouncing Lopez and dismissing his views on the immorality of homosexual relationships. In describing the events surrounding the response to his letter, Lopez alleges that a Santa Clara administrator attempted to interfere with his right to speak with a bishop, and recalls that a mass email was sent out to over two hundred people identifying Lopez and those who share his views as "inciting fear and violence on campus." In his defense, Lopez has written that "I am a devout Catholic and never would I promote hatred against those with same sex attractions." Lopez maintains that "Santa Clara is disseminating material only in regard to living the homosexual lifestyle . . . If I was a Catholic student with same sex attraction, I would only be amidst material and information encouraging me to be active in my attractions. And this, I believe, is an injustice to those who do suffer same-sex attraction."[28]

Following the events of 2005, Lopez attempted to create a campus chapter of Courage—a national organization that helps those with same-sex attraction live chaste lives. But, with little support from faculty and administrators on campus, such attempts to provide an opposing voice by students most often end in failure and ridicule. Currently, despite attempts to provide services to Catholic colleges and universities, Courage has not been invited to participate on any Catholic campuses. Ever the optimist Fr. John Harvey, founder and current director of Courage, remains hopeful that Catholic campuses will someday allow chapters on campus in the same way they allow gay and lesbian clubs that support the homosexual lifestyle.[29]

In the meantime, as a commitment to social justice, students on Catholic campuses are encouraged to bring their advocacy to the greater community and beyond. In fact, many Catholic colleges have become springboards of advocacy for the legalization of same-sex marriage, as well as changes in Church policy to allow gay adoption, and lobbying Congress and the Supreme Court for gays in the military. Many Catholic college students learn advocacy techniques on their Catholic campuses that they implement to make changes on a national level. Kara Suffredini; a graduate of Boston College Law School and now the legislative attorney for the National Gay and Lesbian Task Force, which advocates same sex marriage and strives "to build political power for the Lesbian, Gay,

Bisexual and Transgendered community"; told an alumni gathering of the Lambda Law Students that "I want to begin by saying that everything I know about queer activism, I learned at Boston College Law School. Put that in your admissions brochure."[30]

Suffredini most likely appreciates the fact that, for more than twenty years, Boston College Law School has barred military recruiters as a matter of institutional policy. In fact, the very origins of the Forum for Academic and Institutional Rights (FAIR) and its lawsuit against the military for its reluctance to allow openly gay soldiers to serve grew out of Boston College's pro-gay rights advocacy. Beginning in the early 1980s, Boston Law School's policy banned job recruiters that "discriminate" based on sexual orientation. Since the military continues to bar gay men and lesbian women from serving, recruiters were banned from the Boston campus. For years, the Boston College Law School argued that its decision to ban military recruiters from campus was "an expression of Jesuit, Catholic principles and values."[31] Barring the military was viewed as yet another example of the Jesuit commitment to social justice.

As a result, military recruiters were not given equal access to Boston College students until 2002 when the federal government implemented the Solomon Amendment—a federal law barring taxpayer funds to universities that restrict military recruiters' access to students in opposition of the military's ban on openly homosexual soldiers. Threatening to withhold $40 million in taxpayer funds from Boston College, administrators reluctantly allowed military recruiters on campus. However, in an attempt to overturn the Solomon Amendment, Boston College Law School professors joined other professors from Catholic colleges to bring a lawsuit against the federal government. Professor Kent Greenfield, a faculty member at Boston College School of Law, was the lead plaintiff in *Rumsfeld v. Forum for Academic and Institutional Rights* (FAIR). FAIR members included representatives of the law faculties of four Catholic universities including DePaul, Fordham, Georgetown, and the University of San Francisco. Georgetown hosts FAIR's website, and professors from Georgetown and Boston College sit on FAIR's Board of Directors. Joining FAIR as a plaintiff in the lawsuit included the Society of American Law Teachers, which joined the lawsuit in 2003 under the leadership of Michael Rooke-Ley, a professor at the Catholic Seattle University School of Law. Greenfield chairs the Society of American Law Teacher's Committee on Homosexual Issues, and professors from Boston College, Seattle, Catholic University of America, St. Louis University, and Loyola

University of New Orleans sit on the society's board of governors.[32]

Although the US Supreme Court unanimously rejected the bid by law schools and faculties to bar US military recruiters from campuses in protest against the military's ban on openly homosexual soldiers, professors from Catholic campuses were lauded by the gay community for their work on behalf of gays and lesbians who desire to serve in the military. Dean of Seattle University School of Law Kellye Testy, who argued for the rights of gay and lesbians to serve in the military, and Boston College Law Professor and former Law School Dean James Rogers, who was a leader in the opposition to the Solomon Amendment, won the National Lesbian and Gay Law Association's Allies for Justice Award "for their work on behalf of justice for the gay and lesbian community."[33]

As working for social justice continues to be broadly redefined on Catholic campuses, students rarely hear authentic Church teachings about homosexuality. Several Catholic theologians from Catholic campuses are involved in the debate over gay marriage—and most often they oppose the Church. Fr. Bryan Massingale, an associate professor of moral theology at Marquette University, published an essay in *The Catholic Herald* in which he advised Wisconsin voters to vote "no" on the pro-marriage amendment. In direct contradiction to the position of Wisconsin's Catholic bishops, Massingale wrote that the pro-marriage amendment, read in its entirety, poses a dilemma for many faithful people: "The amendment upholds certain beliefs about the uniqueness of marriage, but it does so at a cost, namely potentially damaging impacts upon the welfare of individuals and their children."[34] A week before the election, *The Milwaukee Journal Sentinel* chose to publish Fr. Massingale's sentiments on the front page rather than the statement of the Wisconsin Catholic bishops.[35]

With such sentiments, students may never hear authentic Church teachings. In fact, when Boston College administrators decided to cancel an AIDS benefit dance sponsored by the college's LGBT leadership council because it "promoted a lifestyle that is in conflict with Church teachings," the student newspaper dismissively responded that "Boston College should follow Jesuit values, not Catholic doctrine."[36] Students seem to have little idea that Jesuit values are supposed to reflect Catholic values and teachings. But it is not their fault. The fault lies within the faculty and the administration—many of whom function as gay and lesbian advocates on campus and beyond.

The Jesuit University of San Francisco's Lesbian, Gay Bisexual, Transgendered, and Queer Caucus recently co-sponsored a conference with the university's Lane Center for Catholic Studies and Social Thought entitled: "Is it Ethical to be Catholic? Queer Perspectives." Fr. James Alison, one of the speakers at the conference, and author of the book that provided the inspiration for the theme of the conference, is a London based theologian and self-described gay priest who maintains that Pope Benedict's 2007 encyclical *Deus Caritas Est* "leaves room for us (homosexuals)." Fr. Alison suggests that "we read it as an invitation for us to work out what the rich elements and gifts of same sex love can be. How we are to set creating a Catholic culture of same-sex love."[37] Catholic newspapers reported that during the question and answer period, Alison responded that the Catholic Church would eventually have to acknowledge the validity of homosexuality and homosexual relationships.[38]

Following Fr. Alison's presentation was a presentation by a University of San Francisco student who, describing herself as a "representative of USF's queer student body," criticized the Catholic education she received before coming to the University of San Francisco as "abnormally ethics-obsessed."[39] She criticized her elementary school religion teachers for "stressing the importance of the pope's supreme power." And, she recalled that it was not until she arrived at the Jesuit university that she came out as a lesbian and feminist—and began to realize that the pope's power had become what she called "destructive and detractory."[40]

Students can understandably become confused about the Church's teachings on gay and lesbian relationships when they are exposed to gay and lesbian faculty and administrators publicly involved in these relationships. St. Michaels College, established in 1904 by the Society of Saint Edmond, a French Order of Catholic priests, appointed an openly-gay "partnered" man as dean of the college in 2005. Professor Jeffrey Trumbower, who formerly chaired the theology and religious studies department at St. Michaels College, had been on the faculty for sixteen years before he was appointed dean. According to news reports, Trumbower met his partner in Vermont and has been in a long-term, committed relationship.[41]

Likewise, the University of San Francisco recently appointed Fr. Donal Godfrey, as the new director of the university ministry. A longtime advocate for the gay community in San Francisco, Godfrey was quoted in an article published in *This is London* as describing homosexuality as "simply another gift from God."[42] Godfrey became a kind of celebrity in London in 2007 when he celebrated what the BBC described as a "gay Mass" from San Francisco that was broadcast by the BBC. Godfrey said he was "delighted that the BBC was exploring how gay people fit into the perspective of the Christian narrative...Being gay is not special, it is simply another gift from God who created us as rainbow people."[43] The homilist for the BBC broadcasted mass was Fr. James Allison, the self-described gay priest and theologian, and author of "Is it Ethical to be Catholic? Queer Perspectives."

Recently, Catholic college faculty and staff members received help in their commitment to advocating for gays and lesbians on their campuses in 2005 when Santa Clara University hosted "Out There," the first public gathering of gay and lesbian professors from Catholic colleges. Described by *The Chronicle* as providing an opportunity for faculty members "to compare notes on their struggles and successes," the conference celebrated some of the most recent successes for gays and lesbians, which included the implementation of the gay studies minor at DePaul and the inclusion of "domestic partners" in the health-care plan at Georgetown.[44] *The Chronicle of Higher Education* pointed out that "gay and lesbian professors have become increasingly visible on Catholic campuses, speaking out on issues like domestic partnership benefits and recognition of gay student groups."[45] Professor Jacqueline Taylor, a professor of Communication at DePaul, lauded her university for its willingness to provide her lesbian partner the same access as a spouse to the university gym, and other DePaul faculty members "praised the university for creating a welcoming atmosphere."[46]

The 2005 "Out There" conference session topics included "What's Love Got to Do with It?" and "Coming Out Issues in a Catholic College Setting."[47] Among the more than forty Catholic colleges represented at the conference were faculty from Santa Clara, University of San Francisco, Georgetown, Loyola Marymount, Gonzaga, Fordham, DePaul, Boston College, College of the Holy Cross, LaSalle, Notre Dame, Our Lady of the Lake in Texas, Caldwell College, St. Joseph's University in Philadelphia, and Marquette.

Rev. Thomas Brennan, an assistant professor of English at St. Joseph's University in Philadelphia and an openly gay priest, attended the conference and confided to participants that he knew from the time he was twelve or thirteen that he was gay. In an interview published in *The Chronicle of Higher Education,* Fr. Brennan claimed that his frustration with the Catholic Church's treatment of gay and lesbian people has grown in the past decade, as he has seen the unnecessary pain and difficulty it causes people.[48] Fr. Brennan said that he "usually lets students in his classes know that he is gay."[49] And, although many of the participants of "Out There" commended their Catholic colleges and universities for the supportive environment the campuses have provided for gays and lesbians, there were some in attendance who complained about a continued oppression for gay and lesbian faculty members.

By 2007, "Out There" was held at DePaul, and had become so institutionalized or "mainstream" that participants were welcomed by Fr. Dennis Holtschneider, president of DePaul, and Chuck Suchar, DePaul's dean of liberal arts and sciences. And, a keynote address was provided by Fr. Michael Garanzini, SJ, president of Loyola University of Chicago. While one of the sessions was entitled "Not Advocating for Homosexuality: Negotiating Advocacy on Catholic Campuses," many of the sessions appeared to contradict such denials of advocacy. One participant from Our Lady of the Lake University presented a paper entitled "Lesbian Roman Catholic Theology: Choosing Respect, Rejecting Closets, Reclaiming Cunt," another from St. Catherine/Dominican University's presented the provocatively titled "Queer Teens Between the Sheets: GLBT Characters and Stories in Young Adult Literature."[50] Several of the sessions contained the same themes of oppression on Catholic campuses—yet others seemed to celebrate a new "queer community" on their campuses.

Despite this, Notre Dame professors Rev. David Garrick and Mark Jordan claim to have resigned from their faculty positions in the late nineties to protest Notre Dame's unwillingness to "support gay and lesbian students." Fr. Garrick, an assistant professor of communications and theatre, said that he resigned to protest Notre Dame's treatment of gay and lesbian students, and Jordan resigned in 1999 because of what he described as a "culture of silence and fear surrounding gay and lesbian issues at Notre Dame."[51] According to Jordan, the author of *The Invention of Sodomy in Christian Theology* and *The Silence of Sodom: Homosexuality in Modern Catholicism,* the election of one he calls the "homophobic Cardinal Ratzinger" to the papacy "made him sick to his stomach."[52] Jordan said that he "was seeing students and faculty members who had been severely harmed by the homophobic atmosphere, to the point of despair." In an interview for *The Chronicle*, Jordan said that his own "coming out" played a role in how he viewed teaching at the university: "Toward the end, I felt like I was being crushed . . . I felt I had to get out in order to be a teacher and scholar." In 1999, Jordan resigned when Notre Dame refused to officially recognize the gay student group on the campus. Now teaching religious studies at Emory, Jordan said his departure was intended as a statement but it was more than that, "It was also self-protection . . . Do I really want to be part of this machine? What are the intellectual and psychological consequences?"[53]

In response to Jordan's resignation, Notre Dame acknowledged in a written statement that it had been "slow to meet the needs of gay and lesbian members of our community, but that it has worked in recent years to create a more inclusive environment."[54] It is possible that Notre Dame's "coming out" closet, its "Gay? Fine By Me" T-shirts, and its willingness to produce *The Vagina Monologues* and the Queer Film Festival in 2005 and again in 2006 may have had something to do with the administration's desire to be viewed as having created a "more inclusive environment" for gays and lesbians following Jordan's allegations.

Catholic college presidents, like Fr. Jenkins, have learned that it takes tremendous courage to confront a campus culture that has come to reflect the same secular values as the mainstream culture. As the media has become more sympathetic to gay causes, it becomes ever more difficult to publicly support Catholic teachings on homosexuality. Yet, these same college presidents seem to have no problem defying the Vatican. In 1992, Cardinal Pio Laghi, then the prefect of the Vatican Congregation for Catholic Education, opposed the formation of gay support clubs on Catholic campuses by stating that "At a Catholic university, support can be given only to homosexual persons morally, ascetically and spiritually . . . The University's responsibilities toward homosexual persons, doctrinally and pastorally should find their expression in courses in Catholic theology."[55] Despite this directive, many faculty members and administrators seem to believe that the Church will eventually have to reconcile herself and come to terms with modern society's current acceptance of homosexuality as natural and normal. Just as DePaul's "Queer Kiss-In" was described by organizers as a way to show how "normal" homosexuality is, a growing number of Catholic campuses continue to battle those who persist in reminding them of the Church's teachings on homosexuality.

When the Vatican released a new instruction barring active homosexuals from seminaries in 2005, the protests were strongest from faculty at Catholic colleges. A student editorial in *The Georgetown Voice* entitled "Something Queer Afoot in the Vatican" argued that "the fact that homosexual behavior is still considered sinful by the Church is sad in and of itself . . . Progressive Catholics can only hope that this foolish ban will be left behind." Omitting any reference to the theological or natural law origins of Catholic Church teachings, the Georgetown editorial called on Georgetown to protest the new instruction's "willful bigotry."[56]

The current pope has a long history of addressing the problem of what he presciently saw as the growing pro-homosexual culture within the Church itself. In 1986, Cardinal Ratzinger recognized that homosexual activists intended to use the Catholic Church and her institutions (including her colleges and universities) to promote the gay agenda. Ratzinger predicted that those within the Church would seek to legitimate homosexual relationships by creating confusion regarding the Church's position on homosexuality and then to use that confusion to their own advantage. Warning that "increasing numbers of people today, even within the Church are bringing enormous pressure to bear on the Church to accept the homosexual condition as though it were not disordered and to condone homosexual activity," Cardinal Ratzinger was simply reflecting more than two thousand years of Catholic teachings.[57] It is not just Catholics who have regarded homosexuality in this way. Philip Jenkins, Penn State historian, writes, "Homosexuality as such may be a modern construct, but through the long Christian centuries, no church or Christian tradition prior to modern times regarded homosexual acts as other than sinful."[58]

It is difficult to deny that many Catholic campuses have surrendered to the secularists on normalizing both abortion and homosexuality. But, it must also be acknowledged that many of them have not been well served by their Episcopal leaders. It is no coincidence that those Catholic colleges and universities located in the dioceses led by the weakest bishops—like those of Seattle's Archbishop Raymond Hunthausen or Milwaukee's Archbishop Rembert Weakland; both long champions of feminism and gay rights—have suffered the greatest losses of identity and provide a sad reminder that the first law of sociology is that the rot starts at the top.[59]

The following chapter will look closely at this lack of leadership—and will introduce some of the emerging Episcopal leaders like St. Louis' Archbishop Raymond Leo Burke, Ft. Wayne-South Bend's Bishop John M. D'Arcy, and Bishop William Lori of the Bridgeport, Connecticut Diocese who are among a courageous cohort of bishops dedicated to helping Catholic colleges regain their commitment to a Catholic identity.

Notes

1. Shane L. Windmeyer. *The Advocate College Guide for LGBT Students*. (New York: Alyson Books, 2006), 71.
2. Kate McGovern. "Nation's Largest Catholic College Begins Gay Studies Program." *The Tower*. (February 10, 2006): www.cuatower.com
3. Windmeyer. *The Advocate College Guide for LGBT Students,* 71.
4. Ibid., 72.
5. Philip Jenkins. *The New Anti-Catholicism*. (New York: Oxford University Press, 2003), 93.
6. Catechism of the Catholic Church. #2357-2359; See also Catholic Bishops, Human Sexuality 1990. #55-56.
7. Paul Likoudis. "U. S. Bishops Direct Attention to Unity and Reconciliation." *The Wanderer*. (November 23, 2006): A-1, A-7.
8. Ibid.
9. Thoms F. Roeser. "Chicago Catholics Wait for Vatican, Archdiocese to React." *The Wanderer*, (November 2, 2006).
10. Ibid.
11. Windmeyer. *The Advocate College Guide for LGBT Students*, 72.
12. Kate McGovern. "Nation's Largest Catholic College Begins Gay Studies Program." *The Tower*. (February 10, 2006): www.cuatower.com
13. www.lifesitenews.com/ldn/2008/mar/8032701.html: Michael Baggott (author). "Survey Finds Pro-Homosexual Clubs at 96 Catholic Universities in the United States."
14. Duquesne University Survey of Homosexual Clubs on Catholic Campuses. Catholic Campuses with gay, lesbian, bi-sexual, and transgender support clubs include: Albertus Magnus, Alverno, Assumption, Avila, Barry, Boston, Canisius, Cardinal Stritch, Holy Cross, Creighton, DePaul, Duquesne, Edgewood, Fairfield, Fordham, Georgetown, Gonzaga, Iona, John Carroll, LaSalle, Loyola of Maryland, Loyola Marymount, Loyola of Chicago, Loyola of New Orleans, Marquette, Marywood, Mercyhurst, Merrimack, New York Medical Colege, St. Edward's, St. Joseph's (CT), St. Louis, St. Martin's, St. Michael's, Salve Regina, Santa Clara, Seattle, Stonehill, Dayton, Notre Dame, San Diego, San Francisco, St. Thomas (MN), Villanova, Wheeling Jesuit, and Xavier. See also quote from Rev. Charles L. Currie, president of Association of Jesuit Universities and Colleges, included in Neela Banerjee. "At Religious Universities, Disputes Over Faith and Academic Freedom. *New York Times*. (February 18, 2006).
15. Neela Banerjee, "At Religious Universities, Disputes Over Faith and Academic Freedom." *New York Times*. (February 18, 2006).
16. Torero Days: Discover San Diego. "Freshman Orientation at the University of San Diego. September." (2006): www.sandiego.edu/orientation/
17. Rainbow Educators Program History. USD United Front Multicultural Center: Rainbow Educators. www.sandiego.edu/unitedfront/re/
18. Ibid.
19. Ibid.
20. Grant Proposal to the Donald A. Srauss Scholarship Foundation. "Rainbow Visibility—Gay Awareness and Understanding." www.straussfoundation.org/new-proposals-2001/25.html
21. Windmeyer. *The Advocate College Guide for LGBT Students*.
22. Shane Windmeyer. "Out and Greek: Being Gay, Lesbian, Bisexual in a College Fraternity." http://www.lambda10.org/outgreek/

23.   Brento Scarpo. Speaking Programs: "Coming Out—the Never Ending Story." http://www.brentscarpo.com/speaking_programs.htm
24.   Mark Gabrish. *Conlan/Zenger's Newsmagazine*. (March 17, 2004): http://sandiego. indymedia.org/en/2004/04/103827.shtml
25.   Ibid.
26.   Ibid.
27.   Letter from Patrick Reilly, Cardinal Newman Society. 2006.
28.   Letter from Timothy Lopez to Matt Abbott. Published in "Santa Clara Student Speaks Out." www.renewamerica.us/columns/abbott/050624
29.   Personal communication with Fr. Harvey, founder and director of Courage, New York, NY.
30.   Kara Suffredini. Speech at the 2005 annual alumni dinner of the Lambda Law Students Association. Cited by Patrick J. Reilly, Cardinal Newman Society. 2006.
31.   Cited by Admiral Jeremiah Denton, on behalf of the Cardinal Newman Society. March 2006.
32.   Patrick J. Reilly, "Supreme Court Rebuffs Catholic Law School Professors' Activism for Homosexual Soldiers." Cardinal Newman Society. March 7, 2006. www. cardinalnewmansociety.org
33.   Ibid.
34.   Paul Likoudis. "Debate Over Gay Marriage Exposes Rifts in Church." *The Wanderer*. (November 9, 2006): A-1.
35.   Ibid.
36.   Patrick J. Reilly, "Action Alert: Homosexuality on Catholic Campuses." Winter 2006.
37.   James Allison. "Is it Ethical to be Catholic? Queer Perspectives." Presentation at a discussion hosted by the University of San Francisco "Communities in Conversation Project" and held in Most Holy Redeemer Parish, February 12, 2006. Alison Transcript from the presentation.
38.   "A Catholic Culture of Same Sex Love." *California Catholic Daily*. (April 28, 2007): www.calcatholic.com
39.   Henderson. "Is it Ethical to be Catholic? Queer Perspectives." Presentation at a discussion hosted by the University of San Francisco "Communities in Conversation Project" and held in Most Holy Redeemer Parish. February 12, 2006. Henderson Transcript from the Presentation.
40.   Henderson. "Is it Ethical to be Catholic? Queer Perspectives." Presentation at a discussion hosted by the University of San Francisco "Communities in Conversation Project" and held in Most Holy Redeemer Parish. February 12, 2006. Henderson Transcript from the Presentation.
41.   Matt Abbott. "Gay Unitarian Named Dean of Catholic College." May 25, 2005. www.catholic.org
42.   "BBC to Broadcast Gay Mass from San Francisco." April 27, 2007. This is London. http://www.thisislondon.co.uk/news/article
43.   Ibid.
44.   Thomas Bartlett. "Coming Out of the Catholic Closet." *The Chronicle of Higher Education* 52. (December 9, 2005): A-8.
45.   Ibid.
46.   Ibid.
47.   Ibid.
48.   Ibid.
49.   Ibid.
50.   "Out There" Conference Schedule. DePaul University. October 2007.

51.   Bartlett. "Coming Out of the Catholic Closet."
52.   Michael S. Rose. Benedict XVI: The Man Who Was Ratzinger. (Dallas, TX: Spence Publishing, 2005), 86.
53.   Bartlett. "Coming Out of the Catholic Closet."
54.   Ibid.
55.   Fr. John Harvey, O. S. F. S. Letter on Behalf of the Cardinal Newman Society. Winter 2006.
56.   Ibid.
57.   Congregation for the Doctrine of the Faith. "The Pastoral Care of Homosexuals." October 1, 1986.
58.   Jenkins. *The New Anti-Catholicism,* 94.
59.   Philip Rieff. *Sacred Order/Social Order: My Life Among the Deathworks.* (Charlottesville: University of Virginia Press, 2006).

8

Still Looking for Leadership

The death of Fr. Robert Drinan, S. J. at the end of the same month he presided over the 2007 inaugural Mass at Washington's Trinity University for Nancy Pelosi, the new US speaker of the House, presented a dilemma for many Catholics. For liberal Catholics, Fr. Drinan's passing was an occasion for nostalgia for the hopeful days that surrounded the changes brought by Vatican II. One of a number of progressive Jesuits teaching on Catholic campuses who helped to convince a generation of Catholic politicians—including the Catholic Kennedy family—in the sixties, that they could support liberalized abortion laws yet still remain in good standing within the Catholic Church, Fr. Drinan provided a much imitated model for Catholic politicians and academics who wished to support the pro-abortion movement while claiming to be faithful to Catholic moral teaching. In a long forgotten meeting at the Kennedy Compound in Hyannisport, on a hot July day in 1964, the Kennedy family and their advisers and allies were coached by Fr. Drinan, then dean of the Boston College Law School, and a contingent of leading theologians and Catholic college professors including Jesuits Fr. Charles Curran and Fr. Giles Milhaven, to accept and promote abortion with a "clear conscience."[1]

Yet, for orthodox Catholics, Fr. Drinan's death was a requiem for a sad time for the Church, for the country, and for Catholic higher education. It was a time when Catholic theologians and priests like Fr. Drinan enabled Catholic politicians and voters to rationalize support for pro-abortion legislative initiatives. Pro-life Catholics sadly recall that while serving as an elected Democratic representative from Massachusetts from 1970 until 1980, Fr. Drinan could be counted on to provide some extreme pro-choice votes supporting legalized abortion and its public funding and opposing pro-life initiatives. In fact, Drinan was the first member of the Massachusetts congressional delegation to publicly support the legalization of abortion—even before Senator Edward Kennedy. At a time when a new generation of Catholic legislators began to assume power in the Democratic Party in the 1970s, Drinan led some of the most powerful, including Massachusetts lawmakers Tip O'Neill and Ted Kennedy to conform to the culture in supporting abortion rather than their Catholic faith.[2]

When he left Congress in 1980, Drinan continued his tireless support for abortion in his position as president of Americans for Democratic Action when he sent out a fund-raising letter urging "the moral necessity of electing candidates to Congress who favored legal abortion and its public funding." And, in the midst of the partial birth abortion debate during the Clinton Administration, Fr. Drinan published articles in the *New York Times* and the *National Catholic Reporter* supporting Clinton's decision to veto the ban on partial birth abortion and urging members of Congress to sustain that veto.[3]

And, while Fr. Drinan's pro-choice activities angered orthodox Catholics, what perplexed them the most was the fact that he remained a priest in good standing and with full faculties enabling him to administer the sacraments and to preside over the Trinity University Mass for a pro-choice politician like Nancy Pelosi. Pelosi is a Catholic politician who has been endorsed repeatedly by the National Abortion Rights Action League and supported the interests of Planned Parenthood 100 percent of the time in 2006. Since first being elected to the House of Representatives from San Francisco in 1987, Pelosi has been counted on to provide extreme support for abortion. Most recently, she has voted in favor of embryonic stem-cell research, against a ban on partial birth abortion, against the restriction of the interstate transport of minors to get abortions, and against making it a crime to harm a fetus during another crime.

Orthodox Catholics know that Church teachings on life have been unambiguous, mandating that life must be protected with the utmost care from the moment of conception—and describing abortion as an abominable crime against natural law. And, they know that those who persist in supporting abortion through their legislative actions or their lobbying efforts are committing a serious sin. Yet, despite the clarity of these teachings, Fr. Drinan remained part of a cohort of Catholic theologians, philosophers, and academic advocates who have committed themselves to debunking catechetical teachings on abortion. And sadly, like Fr. Drinan, many of these pro-choice advocates continue to teach on Catholic college campuses—and appear to remain in "good standing" with the Church.

Indeed, it was not a coincidence that the Catholic Trinity University was chosen as the site of Nancy Pelosi's inaugural Mass. Pelosi and her aides correctly predicted that Archbishop Donald Wuerl, Washington's Episcopal leader, would be reluctant to criticize a Catholic college decision to allow a Mass for a pro-abortion politician. The Pelosi team was confident that they would find a congenial community for pro-choice views on a Catholic campus. Pelosi most likely knew that most administrators and faculty members at Catholic colleges have long ago stopped supporting Catholic teachings on what she would call "reproductive rights" or gay marriage. Her own daughter, Alexandra Pelosi, a graduate of San Francisco's Convent of the Sacred Heart High School and Loyola Marymount University in Los Angeles, claimed in an interview for *The San Francisco Chronicle* that throughout her Catholic education, she was never taught that abortion was sinful: "I don't remember ever being told that gay was wrong. They never told us there was anything wrong with abortion . . . In my family, we have a hundred years of Catholic school experience, and none of us ever heard that homosexuality was a sin." Echoing her mother, Alexandra Pelosi said that after all of her years of Catholic education through high school and college she had learned that, "they were just choices."[4]

Responding to orthodox Catholic concerns about Nancy Pelosi's abortion advocacy, Alexandra Pelosi said, "My mother, throughout her entire life, has been faithful to the Church, even though the Church has not been faithful to her because of her politics."[5] Yet, despite Alexandra Pelosi's concerns about an unsupportive Church for her mother, neither Pelosi nor Fr. Drinan had anything to fear from the Catholic archbishop in the District of Columbia. They must have known that Archbishop Wuerl would choose to be silent in response to the choice of sites for the inaugural Mass—despite the Pelosi and Drinan's defiance of Catholic teachings on abortion. While *First Things* editor, Fr. Richard Neuhaus, criticized the archbishop's decision to allow Fr. Drinan to celebrate the mass for the pro-choice Pelosi, Archbishop Wuerl's only response was that "Fr. Drinan has full faculties" as a priest in the diocese—meaning that he is authorized to celebrate the sacraments.[6] Besides, it was most likely that Archbishop Wuerl was reluctant to interfere with a Trinity University decision to welcome the Pelosi Mass.

Indeed, this is the real problem. Many Catholic bishops have been reluctant to confront the continued anti-Catholicism on their own Catholic campuses. Archbishop Wuerl must have known that, during the fall semester of 2006, Georgetown University announced the creation of the Robert F. Drinan, S. J. Chair in Human Rights to honor what Georgetown administrators claimed was "Fr. Drinan's lifelong commitment to public service." Despite a well-documented history of Fr. Drinan's pro-abortion advocacy, or more likely, because of it, Georgetown's Dean Alexander Aleinkoff announced the establishment of the endowed chair in a formal ceremony on the Georgetown campus in which Fr. Drinan was lauded as having made a "lifelong commitment to public service." Not surprisingly, in the leadership void that has been left on Catholic campuses since the seventies, the announcement to honor Fr. Drinan was greeted with silence from the archbishop.

A celebration of Fr. Drinan's life was held in February of 2007 at funeral masses at Georgetown University and Boston College. At Georgetown, Senator Edward Kennedy eulogized the priest who had provided political cover for him on abortion for more than three decades, and Nancy Pelosi praised what she called Fr. Drinan's "expansive view of the gospel." She knew that the Georgetown community would understand exactly what she meant by that. And, once again, in defiance of Canon 915 of the Code of Canon Law—which stipulates that the bishops confront those like Nancy Pelosi and Fr. Drinan who vote in support of abortion—Archbishop Wuerl remained silent.

There are a number of bishops like Archbishop Wuerl who continue to defy Canon 915 and allow politicians like Ted Kennedy and Nancy Pelosi to publicly misrepresent the Church's stand on abortion, yet still appear to be in full communion with the Church by receiving the Eucharist. But, during the 2004 presidential campaign, the Democratic Party's candidate, Senator John Kerry, became what *Catholic Insight* labeled the "lightning rod in the storm" because he not only defended a woman's right to abort her unborn child—even in the latest stages of her pregnancy—but also promised support for assisted suicide, embryonic stem-cell research, and same-sex marriage. And while Kerry was certainly the most visible of the pro-choice politicians and, therefore, the most problematic for the Catholic bishops, many other pro-choice Catholic members of Congress also posed problems. The American Life League counted 71 Catholic members of Congress (out of 150) as reliable pro-abortion voters and an additional 415 pro-abortion Catholics in state legislatures. These Catholic politicians favor legislation that their Church says they have a "clear and grave obligation to oppose."[7] Many of these same politicians are honored on Catholic campuses as recipients of honorary degrees or lucrative lecturing contracts.

But, in 2004, the situation with elected officials began to come to a head as many orthodox Catholics began to make unprecedented demands on their bishops to pay attention to the pro-choice politicians within their own dioceses. The first to speak out publicly about whether a pro-choice politician was eligible to receive Communion within the Catholic Church was Archbishop Raymond Burke of St. Louis, who wrote that if Senator Kerry were to present himself for Communion, he would offer a blessing but not the Host.[8] Kerry responded by attempting to portray himself as "under siege" by a paternalistic and autocratic Catholic Church. Meanwhile, the media—and faculty on Catholic campuses—portrayed bishops like Burke as oppressive misogynists. The archbishop acknowledged, "speaking the truth was intimidating because we live, as our Holy Father says, in a culture of death where people want to convince us that everything should be convenient and comfortable. They don't like to hear a voice which says this isn't right. Being outspoken on the truth will bring persecution. Bishops will be persecuted, and also priests and lay people."[9]

And, although courageous bishops like Archbishop Burke have been vilified, the far more common response from Catholic campuses has been simply to ignore the Episcopal leaders. In fact, when Notre Dame's presiding bishop, John M. D'Arcy of Indiana's Fort Wayne-South Bend Diocese, issued a statement denouncing the annual Notre Dame Queer Film Festival in 2007 as "an abuse of academic freedom," Matthew Storin, a Notre Dame spokesman, responded that although the university has "great affection and respect for Bishop D'Arcy," the faculty and administrators "disagree with his interpretation of academic freedom." Storin issued a press release asserting, "we would prefer that our students encounter the secular American culture, with all its faults, in the context of their Catholic education rather than attempting to cloister them till the time they graduate, only then to confront reality."[10]

This dismissive response to Bishop D'Arcy reduced the role of the bishop to that of a single voice among many voices responding to a controversial Notre Dame decision. Ignoring the dignity of the office of the bishop, the theological underpinnings of his critique, and his fiduciary responsibility under *Ex Corde Ecclesiae* as bishop of the diocese in which Notre Dame resides, the university rejected the bishop's concerns—while still claiming to have "great affection and respect" for the archbishop.

Most importantly, Notre Dame's spokesman failed to mention that it is unlikely that students are offered the opportunity to debate about Catholic teachings on homosexuality in the context of their Catholic education. Notre Dame's Queer Film Festival has included a presentation of films by gay and lesbian filmmakers, with panel discussions, including those supporting gay marriage. None of these panels directly addressed the natural law underpinnings of Catholic teachings on gay marriage. Rather than inviting speakers who might support Catholic teachings, Notre Dame invited speakers and presenters who have historically criticized Catholic teachings on homosexuality. Sr. Jeannine Grammick, a nun who was suspended from her gay ministry by the Vatican because of her dissident views on the nature of homosexual acts, was an honored guest at Notre Dame's festival in 2005. Defying a Vatican directive to discontinue speaking out on the "goodness" of homosexual acts, Sr. Grammick remains a member in good standing of the School Sisters of Notre Dame and was quoted in an article posted on *LifeSite* that she is "beginning to believe that the greatest sin for lesbians and gay people is to want to be straight."[11]

Another invited guest on Notre Dame's campus was Terrence McNally, author of *Corpus Christi*, an anti-Catholic play in which Jesus and his disciples are depicted as active homosexuals who suffer persecution at the hands of the "priests" of the Church. In the McNally play, Jesus is a flamboyant and promiscuous homosexual who angrily strikes a priest who dares to present authentic Catholic teachings on homosexuality. McNally's Judas betrays Jesus with the cry, "Sold to the fag haters in the priests' robes." At his trial, Pilate asks Jesus, "Art thou a queer, then?" And, in the end, Jesus is crucified "for his queerness" not for his teachings. Philip Jenkins writes of the McNally play that "it does not take too much imagination to appreciate that the reference to the evil priests" in the play is meant to apply as much to modern day Catholic "homophobic" clergy as to the servants of the ancient Jewish Temple.[12] Yet, instead of the Notre Dame faculty and administration condemning *Corpus Christi* as anti-Catholic hate speech, they are critical of those who have attempted to stop the production on campus—including their own bishop.

Still, there were some Notre Dame students who have had the courage to respond. Rebecca Austen, a Notre Dame law student who attended the Queer Film Festival was quoted in an article in the *National Catholic Register* as saying that "No matter how much they want to deny it, the event was celebrating homosexuality . . . The film was an obvious attack on the Catholic Church. Everyone was saying that the Church has to change its doctrine . . . The University is misled in thinking that this is just a festival showing what a certain genre of film is and exposing it to students . . . Those who run the festival have a specific agenda, which is to accept a certain lifestyle and gay marriage. There is hatred being expressed toward the Church in this festival."[13]

And in yet another, this time a more public attempt to contribute to the conversation at Notre Dame, Bishop D'Arcy wrote an editorial for the *South Bend Tribune* in which he accused Notre Dame of presenting violations of chastity as virtues: "The University has violated the rights of the Church, of students and of parents . . . What about the rights of the Church to have its teachings properly presented? What about the rights of parents of those students at Notre Dame who find the contents of this seminar offensive?"[14] Again, Bishop D'Arcy's concerns were ignored.

Although he showed tremendous courage in the face of an increasingly hostile campus, Bishop D'Arcy's letter of concern about the on-campus activities and invited speakers at Notre Dame was simply an implementation of an important decision by the US Conference of Catholic Bishops in June of 2004. After several decades of scandal over speakers and activities on Catholic campuses, the Bishops Conference, in a near-unanimous vote, approved the statement, "Catholics in Political Life." The statement included the following mandate for Catholic colleges:

> The Catholic community and Catholic institutions should not honor those who act in defiance of our fundamental and moral principles. They should not be given awards, honors or platforms which would suggest support for their actions.[15]

It is likely that this document was influenced by the Cardinal Newman Society's ongoing protest against inappropriate commencement speakers and honorees at Catholic colleges and universities. Since 1998, the Cardinal Newman Society has organized protests, including facilitating letter writing campaigns to Catholic bishops and Catholic college presidents, in an effort to end what they see as the "scandalous" behavior of honoring dissidents on Catholic campuses. In fact, just weeks prior to the bishops' June meeting in 2004, the Cardinal Newman Society released their special report, "The Culture of Death on Catholic Campuses: A Five Year Review," documenting nearly two hundred incidents of speakers and honorees who have vocally opposed Catholic teachings on abortion, euthanasia, and contraception. In December of 2003, the Cardinal Newman Society sent a letter to each of the US bishops urging them to consider diocesan policies banning inappropriate speakers and honorees at Catholic institutions. An excerpt of the Cardinal Newman letter to the bishops is as follows:

> While sanctions against pro-abortion politicians are welcome, we urge you to imple-
> ment diocesan policies that forbid all public advocates of legal abortion—regardless
> of whether they are Catholics or politicians—from speaking at Catholic facilities or
> receiving Catholic honors . . . This can be more easily enforced on Church-owned
> property, but it can also set an expectation for legally independent colleges and other
> Catholic services and organizations—useful when determining their right to use the
> label Catholic in the case of colleges and universities, according to the guidelines
> established by *Ex Corde Ecclesiae*.[16]

Although the bishops responded in their June 2004 meeting to issue the strong statement blocking inappropriate speakers, many bishops chose to ignore it. Bishop Edward Kmiec of the Diocese of Buffalo, New York refused to block an honored appearance at Canisius College by pro-choice New York Senator Hillary Rodham Clinton. Claiming to have voiced his "displeasure" to college officials, Bishop Kmiec said he would "reluctantly" allow the event to proceed in order to "maintain channels of communication with Senator Clinton and others who hold her views."[17] Likewise, the bishop of Washington, DC refused to comment upon a visit by Supreme Court Justice Sandra Day O'Connor to Georgetown University in which she attacked pro-life lawmakers who sided with Terri Schiavo's parents in their efforts to prevent their daughter's euthanasia death. O'Connor, who has sided with the abortion rights justices in the partial-birth abortion case before the Supreme Court, claimed a congressional effort to have federal courts review the Schiavo case was a first step towards a dictatorship.[18]

The Rev. James L. Heft formerly of the University of Dayton, claimed in an interview for the *Baltimore Sun* that, "it is not entirely clear who should be barred from honors."[19] And, while there may be some speakers whose stands on life issues are ambiguous, the overwhelming majority of honorees on Catholic campuses are forthcoming in their pro-choice perspectives.

Some of those identified by the Cardinal Newman Society include former Representative Patricia Schroeder, a pro-choice leader during her twenty-four years in Congress, who was the main presenter at a Women's Conference sponsored by the Gannon Center for Women and Leadership at Loyola University of Chicago. Representative Maxine Waters, an abortion rights advocate in Congress, delivered the keynote address to the National Black Law Students Association's Western Regional Convention—which was hosted by Seattle University School of Law. And, pro-choice fundraiser Ellen Malcolm gave a lecture at St. Michael's College. Malcolm is the founder and director of Emily's List, which raises funds to elect pro-abortion women to federal and state offices.[20]

At the University of San Diego, a frequent honored guest at the University's Peace and Justice Center is Anne Hoiberg, director of the Women's Equity Council of the United National Association. Hoiberg, a pro-abortion advocate in the United Nations, used her opportunity to speak at the Catholic college to reiterate statements she has made in speeches elsewhere, to make it clear how much she resented what she called "the Bush administration's packing the U. S. United Nations delegation with ultra-Right personnel, many of them activists with anti-abortion or so-called pro-family organizations, whose positions and activities undermined the efforts of just about everyone else involved in the commission." In her role on the United Nations Commission on Women, Hoiberg decried the inclusion of pro-life women on the Commission by saying that "These women were incredible as to what they didn't like, they didn't like the U. N., they didn't like reproductive choice, they didn't like the separation of church and state, homosexuals or most anything related to international treaties."[21] Despite this, the University of San Diego honored the abortion proponent Hoiberg a second time two years later.

In 2006 the University of San Diego invited Elisabeth Rehn, former United Nations under-secretary general and former defense minister of Finland to speak at the Peace and Justice Center. An advocate for the "comprehensive approach to sexual and reproductive health and rights," Rehn has written and lectured frequently about the need for the availability of abortion to all women through her work on the United National Population Division. In her writings, Rehn presents an especially passionate plea for "full reproductive rights" including abortion for all women at the notorious International Conference on Population and Development in Cairo, Egypt in 1994.[22] Yet, the administration at the Catholic University of San Diego found Rehn an appropriate honoree for the Joan B. Kroc Distinguished Lecture Series for undergraduate and graduate students.[23]

Likewise, in May of 2006, William F. Schulz, executive director of Amnesty International, and a member of the board of Planned Parenthood Federation of American, as well as the boards of People for the American Way and Americans United for the Separation of Church and State, was invited to the San Diego campus as part of the Kroc Distinguished Lecture Series. In a lecture entitled "Tainted Legacy: 9/11 and the Ruin of Human Rights," Schulz, an ordained Unitarian Universalist Minister, decried the military intervention in Iraq alleging human rights abuses by the United States government and its military.[24] As usual, there was no one to rebut Schulz's claims.

During the 2007 fall semester, the University of San Diego honored Kenneth Roth, executive director of Human Rights Watch, by inviting him to present the inaugural lecture in the Distinguished Speakers' Series for the year. A longtime abortion advocate, Kenneth Roth has published several articles decrying women's lack of access to abortion in places like Mexico, Argentina, and Nicaragua; Human Rights Watch has drawn upon funds provided from the Ford and the Rockefeller Foundations to help bring full reproductive rights to women in these countries. Most recently, Human Rights Watch allied with the Catholics for a Free Choice to lobby for abortion in Nicaragua by issuing a report claiming that the complete ban on abortion in Nicaragua has caused "human rights abuses." In an article published on the Human Rights Watch website, Roth argues that "Pregnant rape victims (in Mexico) are essentially assaulted twice, first by the perpetrators who raped them, and then by officials who ignore them, insult them and deny them a legal abortion."[25] As executive director, Roth has sided against the Catholic Church by acting as a signatory to an amicus brief to the Supreme Judicial Court in Massachusetts, urging it to affirm the legality of same-sex marriage.[26] Many of Roth's published positions are opposed to Catholic teachings, yet he was allowed to speak at the university without rebuttal or response from the Catholic leadership.

Later in the semester Andrea Smith, co-founder of Incite! Women of Color Against Violence (a pro-choice national feminist activist organization), was invited to deliver the prestigious Labovitz Lecture at the University of San Diego Annual Social Issues Conference. Decrying the fact that American Indian women who receive health services through a federal agency such as Indian Health Services, do not have the same access to abortion services as other women, the Pro-Choice Public Education Projects lists Andrea Smith (along with Planned Parenthood founder, Margaret Sanger) as one of a "few trailblazers of the reproductive rights movement."

Likewise, Loyola University of Chicago hosted a lecture by Judith Arcana, an abortion activist and officially recognized a "reproductive health" student club led by an activist for pro-abortion organizations—including the National Abortion and Reproductive Rights Action League. Specifically addressing the value of abortion during her lecture, Arcana stated that the procedure should be "compassionate, caring and graceful."[27] And, as the Cardinal Newman Society pointed out, rather than simply allowing the lecture because of a flawed concept of academic freedom for women's studies faculty, a Loyola spokesman justified Arcana's lecture as reflecting the university's Jesuit mission to "form the whole person" by inviting those who have opposing views to the Catholic Church. Loyola's dean of students granted official recognition to College Advocates for Reproductive Education, which purportedly aims to educate students about reproductive options. The club's president, Katie Kramer, announced that she was an intern at the National Abortion and Reproductive Rights Action League and has attended NARAL's Campus Organizers Training Conference. She described herself in *Facebook* as "committed to protecting reproductive freedom" and has been active on the pro-choice policy scene since attending a Catholic high school in Minnesota. The club's first public activity was distributing condoms to Loyola students adjacent to the Catholic university's front gate, followed by an article in the campus newspaper in which Kramer explained how she, as a Catholic, could be pro-choice.[28]

According to the Cardinal Newman Society, twenty Catholic colleges chose commencement speakers in 2005 who are public advocates of abortion rights, stem-cell research, physician-assisted suicide, homosexual marriage, or women's ordination—yet only three bishops took public action. The Cardinal Newman Society protested Alverno College, which honored the pro-choice Lt. Governor Barbara Lawton; Cabrini College, which honored pro-choice journalist Helen Thomas; Cardinal Stritch University, which honored pro-choice author Jacquelyn Mitchard; Dominican University, which honored pro-choice California Secretary for Education Richard Riordan; and Edgewood College, which honored pro-choice Wisconsin Court of Appeals Judge Paul Higginbotham.

In addition to these 2005 honors, Loyola College honored a former New York City mayor, the pro-choice Rudolph Giuliani; Loyola Marymount University Law School honored pro-choice California Attorney General Bill Lockyer; Loyola University of New Orleans Law School honored pro-choice US Senator Mary Landrieu and Louisiana Lt. Governor Mitchell Landrieu; Loyola University of Chicago honored biotech embryonic stem-cell researcher Leroy Hood; Marquette University honored pro-choice journalist Cokie Roberts; Regis College honored Sara Lawrence Lightfoot, Chairwoman of the notoriously pro-abortion John D. and Catherine T. MacArthur Foundation; and St. Bonaventure University honored the pro-choice US Representative Amory Houghton.

A frequent offender, St. Joseph's College in Connecticut, honored Sr. Theresa Kane, former president of the Leadership Conference of Women Religious in 2005—an organization that has voiced public support for abortion. Likewise, St. Xavier University in Illinois honored theologian Sr. Margaret Farley, an outspoken dissenter from Catholic teaching on sexual morality and human life, who also argues that Catholic teachings allows cloning and destruction of human embryos in stem-cell research as well as homosexual relations. The Cardinal Newman Society also protested Seattle University, which honored the former Washington Governor Gary Locke, who opposed the ban on partial-birth abortion and parental notification in the case of minors seeking abortion. As governor, Locke directed the Public Employee Benefits Board to provide benefits to same-sex partners of state employees and defended a state law that denies scholarships to college students majoring in theological studies—a law deemed "discriminatory" by the US Conference of Bishops. Villanova University came under protest from the Cardinal Newman Society when it announced an honorary degree to be presented to the president of Ireland, Mary McAleese—who, although pro-life, is an outspoken critic of infallible papal teachings on the priesthood.[29]

In 2006, the second year following the US bishops statement on "Catholics in Political Life," the Cardinal Newman Society protested an additional twenty-four Catholic colleges and universities for hosting or honoring advocates of abortion rights, stem-cell research, physician-assisted suicide, gay marriage, and women's ordination. Yet again, the majority of bishops remained silent. In several cases, the commencement honorees are the same individuals from prior years' protests.

Repeat offenders include Notre Dame, which honored Ireland's President Mary McAleese and dissident theologian Sr. Elizabeth Johnson, who was honored at St. Joseph's College in Connecticut. Both had been honored at Villanova in 2005. Pro-choice medical reporter Timothy Johnson was honored at Anna Maria College in 2006 and at the College of the Holy Cross in 2000, the pro-abortion Senator Charles Schumer was honored in 2006 at Iona College and had been previously been honored at St. Thomas Aquinas College in 2004. Fordham University hosted the MSNBC "Hardball" host, Chris Matthews, for the second time despite his pro-choice statements and the controversy that surrounded his appearance at the College of the Holy Cross a few years earlier.

In addition to the repeat offenders, Xavier University hosted pro-abortion US Senator and 2008 presidential hopeful Barack Obama. Loyola

Marymount University hosted the pro-choice Los Angeles Mayor Antonio Villaraigosa. Loyola of Chicago hosted Senator Christine Radogno and Marygrove College honored US Representative John Dingell. Marymount University honored pro-choice advocate General Colin Powell. In addition, the Cardinal Newman Society protested the College of St. Mary in Omaha, the College of St. Rose, Felician College, the New York Medical College, the Ohio Dominican University, St. Leo University, Trocaire College, the University of St. Francis in Joliet, Illinois, and Villa Maria College in Buffalo.[30]

At Boston College, theology professors and other faculty members protested commencement honors given to Secretary of State Condoleezza Rice—but not because of her support for abortion rights, rather, because she was involved in the planning for the Iraq War.[31] And, St. Joseph's College in Philadelphia protested then-Senator Rick Santorum because of his support for Catholic teachings on abortion, embryonic stem-cell research, and gay marriage.

Despite the increased number of Catholic colleges hosting pro-abortion speakers for commencement ceremonies or other campus honors since the US bishops issued their "Catholics in Political Life" statement, only a handful of bishops have publicly reprimanded these colleges. In 2005 Cardinal William Keeler of Baltimore and Archbishop Alfred Hughes of New Orleans publicly boycotted local commencement ceremonies honoring pro-abortion politicians. In a letter to Loyola's president, Cardinal Keeler said he refused to participate in an event honoring Rudolph Giuliani, a public advocate of abortion rights and probable Republican candidate for US president in 2008. Keeler reminded the Loyola president of the "consequences that spring from an invitation having been extended to Giuliani to receive an honorary degree at Loyola." Keeler later explained that his actions were a direct consequence of the bishops' June 2004 ban on such honors.[32]

In addition to Cardinal Keeler, Archbishop Alfred Hughes of New Orleans publicly chastised Loyola University of New Orleans for honoring pro-abortion US Senator Mary Landrieu and Louisiana Lt. Governor Mitchell Landrieu—who have both voted for abortion rights. Hughes refused to attend Loyola's commencement ceremonies as planned. In a statement, Archbishop Hughes said, "I have reluctantly decided not to participate in any commencement exercises of Loyola University, lest my presence confuse the faithful and give the impression that it is appropriate to include in an honor anyone who dissents publicly from Church teachings." Like Cardinal Keeler, Archbishop Hughes cited the bishops' June 2004 ban on scandalous honors as a reason for his concern.[33]

In at least one case, the concerns of a bishop caused a Catholic college to rescind an invitation to honor to a pro-choice politician. In 2005, Bishop James Moynihan of Syracuse advised Sister Marianne Monahan, the president of St. Elizabeth College of Nursing, of his concerns about her decision to honor pro-choice Congressman Sherwood Boehlert as a commencement speaker. According to the Cardinal Newman Society, when Bishop Moynihan informed of the Diocese of Syracuse policy against pro-abortion politicians speaking at Catholic institutions, St. Elizabeth's president "immediately" called Boehlert and informed him days before the commencement that he would not be allowed to speak.[34]

In a controversial commencement case in 2005, Marymount Manhattan College responded to the Cardinal Newman Society's protest of the college's invitation to pro-abortion Senator Hillary Clinton to give its commencement address and receive an honorary degree by publicly declaring itself nonsectarian. While it was reported in some outlets that Cardinal Edward Egan had declared Marymount Manhattan "no longer Catholic" and removed it from the Official Catholic Directory because of the Clinton honor, the reality is that Marymount declared itself nonsectarian. In fact, Marymount Manhattan President Judson Shaver lashed out at the Cardinal Newman Society in his baccalaureate address to the graduating seniors and their families—noting that the "Internet buzzed with criticism and my email box overflowed with complaints from fundamentalists." He proceeded to characterize Catholic colleges that espouse religious teachings as a "sort of non-college where indoctrination would be the goal."[35] And, President Shaver used the commencement as an opportunity to distance the university from such sectarianism—and celebrate its secular status.

Regardless of whether the bishop or the school itself chose to remove Marymount Manhattan from the Catholic Directory, the result is that it is the fourth Catholic college since the release of *Ex Corde Ecclesiae* to be declared "no longer Catholic." The Cardinal Newman Society reported that Bishop Matthew Clark of Rochester, New York no longer recognizes Nazareth College and St. John Fisher College as Catholic. Proceeds from the 2004 performance of *The Vagina Monologues* at St. John Fisher went to Planned Parenthood, and Nazareth's 2004 performance of *The Vagina Monologues* was co-sponsored by the college's campus ministry.

In 2003, Marist College in Poughkeepsie, New York was identified as "no longer Catholic" by the bishop of the Archdiocese of New York following a Cardinal Newman protest of Marist's commencement speaker, the pro-abortion New York Attorney General Eliot Spitzer.[36] Eliot Spitzer was an especially inappropriate choice to speak at a Catholic college as he attempted to block anti-abortion crisis pregnancy centers from implementing ultrasound technology in their own facilities a few years ago. Spitzer issued thirty-four subpoenas to the pro-life centers throughout the state of New York "suspected of deceiving women about their services or practicing medicine without a license."[37] One of the subversive activities that these pro-life centers were allegedly engaged in was simply providing pregnancy counseling coupled with ultrasound imaging to expectant mothers. Working closely with Family Planning Advocates of New York state, an umbrella group that includes seventy-eight family planning clinics and abortion facilities including fifteen operated by Planned Parenthood, Spitzer claimed to be probing complaints that the groups "lure women with the promise of reproductive health services, only to present them with anti-abortion messages." Spitzer issued subpoenas demanding that the centers provide his office with copies of all advertisements, website addresses, services provided, names of staff members, training materials, and blank forms and records.[38] This was clearly harassment of the pro-life agencies, yet, Marist thought Spitzer was a suitable recipient of an honorary degree from a Catholic college.

For orthodox Catholics who might have expected more from their bishops, it is disappointing that so few bishops have publicly spoken out against the pro-abortion or dissident speakers honored on their own campuses—despite their near-unanimous vote in favor of the 2005 "Catholics in Political Life" document. To be fair, there have been a few additional bishops who canceled planned appearances at commencement ceremonies in the past to protest abortion rights advocates—even before they voted on the 2004 document on Catholics in Political Life. In 2003, Bishop James Timlin of Scranton, Pennsylvania announced that he would not attend the University of Scranton's commencement because he "would not be willing to share the stage with a public abortion rights advocate."[39] Likewise, Bishop Daniel Reilly of Worcester, Massachusetts announced that he would not attend the Commencement at the College of the Holy Cross because of their invitation to television talk-show host, Chris Matthews. Bishop Reilly stated, "Holy Cross will confer an honorary degree on a Catholic person who publicly espouses the view that in some cases people have the right to terminate a life in the womb. I cannot let my presence imply support for anything less than the protection of all life at all its stages."[40] And, in 2003, Auxiliary Bishop John Dougherty of Scranton refused to attend College Misericordia's commencement because of concerns about the pro-choice stance of speakers, journalists Cokie and Steven Roberts.[41]

While a growing number of bishops are beginning to pay attention to their June 2004 statement on the suitability of pro-choice honorees on Catholic campuses, most Catholic college presidents have continued their recalcitrance. Like Marymount Manhattan's president who spoke out angrily against the Cardinal Newman Society's "interference," the Rev. Paul Locatelli, president of Santa Clara University, the hosting site for the "Out-There" conference for gay and lesbian leaders on Catholic campuses, called the society a "self-appointed group of vigilantes" and added that "If John Henry Newman were alive, he would ask them to remove his name."[42] Even the usually staid *Chronicle of Higher Education* attempted to diminish the status of the Cardinal Newman Society in an article which dismissively described the society's offices as "a storefront in a run-down strip mall, next to an embroidery shop and a beauty salon called 'Hair I Am.'"[43]

So threatened by the influence of the Cardinal Newman Society, Anthony J. Cernera, president of Sacred Heart University in Connecticut, used the occasion of the 2000 "Examining the Catholic Intellectual Tradition" Conference on his campus to attack the society as an organization that "does not speak for Catholic higher education." Cernera decried the fact that the society was allowed to "define what it means to be Catholic for the rest of us" and angrily dismissed the society's influence on Catholic higher education.[44]

Likewise, Monica Hellwig, who until her death in 2006, was the president of the Association of Catholic Colleges and Universities, angrily dismissed the work of the Cardinal Newman Society, arguing that her association was in a much "better position" to help Catholic colleges define their identity than the Cardinal Newman Society. This is unlikely. A feminist theologian, Hellwig has been a strong proponent of the theologian's role in questioning Church teachings.[45] Hellwig has gone so far as to state that *Humanae Vitae* was Pope Paul VI's "personal opinion." She has also dissented from official Catholic teachings on the divinity of Jesus Christ. In fact, in her book, *The Role of the Theologian in Today's Church*, Hellwig provides a revisionist account of many Catholic doctrines including that of the Resurrection. A presenter at the annual meeting for members of the now-excommunicated dissident organization, Call to Action, Hellwig's book, *Understanding Catholicism*, "rethinks" the meaning of the Eucharist—describing it as a "symbol" rather than the true presence.[46]

A frequent and bitter critic of the Vatican, Hellwig's obituary published in the *Washington Post* lauded her as a "theologian who defended Catholic intellectualism against a Vatican crackdown," and was remembered as one who "spoke forthrightly against efforts by the Vatican officials who think they can shape the world over here and they can't."[47] Throughout her leadership of the Catholic college organization, Hellwig dismissed the authority of the bishops claiming that "the major problem the hierarchy faces may be that Catholics simply don't believe in Hell and eternal punishment the way they used to . . . the American laity, especially the college-educated, is well aware that the hierarchy doesn't have many sanctions against them . . . It's harder to frighten them."[48]

Hellwig maintained a dismissive attitude toward the authority of the Vatican as well as the bishops. Yet despite this, or more likely because of this, Hellwig was often called upon by the left wing of the conference of bishops to function as the "expert" on the implementation of *Ex Corde Ecclesiae* on Catholic campuses. It is difficult to understand why so many of the more liberal-leaning Catholic bishops continued to respond to the problems on Catholic campuses and in their own Churches by enlisting the assistance of those who openly defy Catholic teachings—unless these bishops themselves reject papal authority.

In some important ways, the rejection of the authority of the Vatican by liberal bishops like Archbishop Weakland or Michigan's Bishop Gumbleton, who have openly defied the Vatican, or others like Archbishop Wuerl or Bishop Kmiec, who continue to fail to enforce the bishops' own policies on honoring public advocates of abortion, embryonic stem-cell research, euthanasia, or gay marriage must be considered a contributory factor to the loss of Catholic identity on Catholic campuses. Just as liberal bishops have continued to disregard the tenets of *Ex Corde Ecclesiae*, Catholic college faculty and administrators have rejected the authority of the bishops on their own campuses. Pope John Paul II predicted this in 1987 when he reminded the American bishops that "when they fail to uphold the legitimate decisions of the Holy See, they undermine their own authority."[49]

In many ways, the fallout surrounding the clergy abuse crisis of 2001 and 2002 further diminished the authority of the bishops when reports surfaced that some of the bishops themselves were involved both in the sexual abuse of minors and in the cover-up. Throughout the country, plaintiffs brought suits against the Church—bankrupting the Spokane, Portland, and Orange County Dioceses. In 2005, the Associated Press reported that the costs to the Church through 2005 have totaled more than $1 billion for abuse cases that date back decades. The Diocese of Orange, California settled ninety abuse claims for $100 million in 2004. The Diocese of Covington, Kentucky settled its abuse cases for $120 million. The bankrupt Diocese of Portland, Oregon faced claims topping $500 million and the Archdiocese of Los Angeles will most likely settle cases for at least $500 million and perhaps as much as $1.5 billion.[50]

In Boston, where the scandal first erupted, the diocese reached an $85 million settlement with 552 people in 2003. The Boston settlement reflected, in part, the actions of Fr. John Geoghan, a self-identified gay priest who was accused of more than one hundred cases of molestation that occurred during the thirty years he served in the Boston area. Equally disturbing, it has been alleged that Cardinal Bernard Law, the archbishop of Boston, was aware of Geoghan's deviant history—yet he reassigned him after "treatment" to other parishes where he continued to abuse.

In the midst of the Boston settlements, Anthony O'Connell resigned as bishop of Palm Beach after he admitted to molesting a male student when he was rector of a seminary in Missouri. Worse, the victim had asked the Palm Beach bishop for help after being abused by another diocesan priest, and O'Connell himself had been sent to Palm Beach after the previous bishop left because he too had abused young boys. A few years later, reports surfaced of Archbishop Weakland's payment to a young man who claimed to have been sexually assaulted by the archbishop.

And, although the number of abusive bishops remained low throughout the clergy abuse crisis, there is evidence that in a misguided attempt to rehabilitate priests like Boston's serial abuser, the bishops participated in the abuse by transferring priests from parish to treatment centers and then back again to parishes—where they continued the cycle of abuse. As a result, public perceptions of the "pedophile priest" and a complicit Catholic Church promoted a moral panic. Indeed, the "sins of a few" became exaggerated and extended to what the media continued to call the "sins of the Fathers"—portraying the bishops as weak and the priests as deviant.

While the claims of sexual abuse by priests and the cover-up by some bishops continued to climb throughout 2002 and 2003, a moral panic emerged in which the "threat" posed by priests was greatly exaggerated, and the perceived lack of attention to the problem by bishops was deplored. While research by social scientist Philip Jenkins revealed no evidence that Catholic or other celibate clergy are any more likely to be involved in abuse than clergy of any other denomination, there were powerful cultural reasons that combined to promote the panic surrounding what erroneously became known as "the pedophile priest crisis." For more than three decades, the liberal activist wing of the Church—especially on Catholic college campuses—has been engaged in a battle with the Catholic hierarchy over issues including sexual morality, academic freedom, priestly celibacy, divorce and remarriage, reproductive freedom, and the role and status of women in the Church.

Feminist dissidents within the church have had a powerful incentive to exaggerate the claims of abuse by priests. Following the disclosures in Boston, Lisa Sowle Cahill, professor of theology at Boston College, wrote that the "pedophile scandal exposes the weaknesses of a virtually all male decision making structure." Some have called for "solutions," which most often involve major reform of aspects of traditional Catholicism—notably the elimination of priestly celibacy or the ordination of women. An article in the *Seattle Times* carried the headline: "Pope Deplores Pedophilia, But Won't Lift Priests' Celibacy."[51] Once seen as the foundation of spiritual commitment and a sacrifice that a young seminarian makes in his quest for holiness, celibacy is now viewed as a form of deviance in an age of sexual liberation—a "cause" of pedophilia.

And, although there were indeed priests who have molested very young children, it must be acknowledged that contrary to the media's favorite alliterative term, "pedophile priest," the reality is that other than isolated cases, like Geoghan, the research by the John Jay College revealed that between 80 and 90 percent of the cases of priestly sexual abuse involved self-identified homosexual priests who have been sexually active with post-pubescent young males—adolescents, not children.[52] While homosexual activities by priests with teenage boys are immoral and in some cases criminal, depending upon the age of consent, these cases are not examples of pedophilia or child molestation. Yet, fearful of appearing homophobic, the media were reluctant to report this tie to homosexuality—and focused instead on the pedophile priest angle, dismissing any tie to the gay subculture that had grown within some seminaries and on Catholic campuses throughout the country.

However, there were some courageous priests who were willing to confront the growing problem of homosexuality within the priesthood—even before the Boston scandal broke in 2001. In an essay entitled, "The Gay

Priest Problem" published in the *Catholic World Report* in 2000, Jesuit priest Fr. Paul Shaughnessy described what he called "the ugly and indisputable facts: a disproportionately high percentage of priests is gay; a disproportionately high percentage of gay priests routinely engages in gay sexual activity; the sexual activity is frequently ignored, tolerated, and sometimes abetted by bishops and superiors."[53]

As far back as 1986, Richard Sipe pointed out that the data were already emerging on the alarming increase in AIDS cases within the Catholic clergy. The Pulitzer Prize winning journalist Jacqui Banaszynski reported in a February 1987 *St. Paul Pioneer Press* article that "the incidence of AIDS among Catholic priests is almost four times higher than among the general population."[54] In 2000, a *Kansas City Star* expose revealed that "hundreds of Catholic priests across the United States have died of AIDS related illnesses and hundreds more are living with HIV, the virus that causes the disease, and concluded that priests have an annualized AIDS related death rate of about 4 per 10,000—four times that of the general population's rate of roughly 1 per 10,000 and about double the death rate of the adult male population." Other statistics and experts suggest that those estimates are too conservative. The *Kansas City Star* reported that Joseph Barone, a New Jersey psychiatrist and AIDS expert, puts the number of US priests who have died at one thousand nearly eleven times the rate of the general population. Barone directed an AIDS ministry from 1983 to 1993 for American seminarians and priests at North American College in Rome and, while in Rome, he set up an underground AIDS testing program. Over seven years, he tested dozens of seminarians and found that one in twelve tested HIV positive. By the time Barone left Rome, he had treated about eighty priests with AIDS. Most were gay and contracted the disease through sexual activity.[55]

One of the first priests with AIDS to attract national attention was the Rev. Michael Peterson who died in 1987 at age forty-four. Peterson was a priest of the Archdiocese of Washington and founder of St. Luke Institute, a psychiatric hospital in Maryland for Catholic priests and religious order men—a place where priests often were sent for treatment after they were accused of sexual molestation.[56] It became known as a place for gay priests with "problems."

Shaughnessy also drew attention to the fact that certain orders and institutions were noticeably more affected than others—this is especially true for the Jesuits. Of seven novices ordained in the Missouri Province of the Jesuit order in 1967 and 1968, for instance, Shaughnessy reported that "three have died of AIDS, and a fourth is an openly gay priest now working as an artist in New York." He further noted that gay priests themselves "routinely gloat about the fact that gay bars in big cities have special 'clergy nights,' that gay resorts have set-asides for Catholic priests, and that in certain places the diocesan apparatus is controlled entirely by gays."

In an article on the clergy abuse scandal published in the *Weekly Standard* entitled "The Elephant in the Sacristy," Mary Eberstadt pointed out that a disproportionate percentage of the abusive priests attended Boston's St. John's seminary in the late 1950s and 1960s. She writes, "Regardless of why, the numbers are staggering, especially for certain classes."[57] The class of 1960 contained at least five men involved in sexual abuse allegations. That is out of a class of approximately seventy-seven graduates. Experts put the incidence of the sexual abuse of youth in the general population at around 1 percent. For the St. John's graduates ordained in 1960, the figure appears to approach seven times the national average for men. There were six men accused of sexual abuse from the class of 1968. Since this class had only fifty members, much smaller than those that had passed through St. John's a decade earlier, the incidence of alleged sexual abuse in the class rises to about 12 percent—or twelve times the national average for men.[58]

Eberstadt noted, "Shaughnessy sounded a prescient note in daring to question what he called the dogma that the preponderance of male victims of clerical sexual abuse is entirely unrelated to priestly homosexuality."[59] In addition to Fr. Shaughnessy, Michael Rose's bestselling book, *Goodbye, Good Men,* charged that what he called the "lavenderization" of American seminaries has driven vocations down because a gay subculture has grown so powerful within the seminary system, especially in those seminaries located in large urban areas with large numbers of gay priests—many of them teaching on Catholic campuses.

Echoing Rose's concerns, seminary rector Fr. Donald Cozzens wrote in *The Changing Face of the Priesthood* that the increasing presence of homosexuals in the priesthood caused particular problems for straight seminarians and not for the usual reasons of "homophobia." With an endorsement for his book from Fr. Theodore Hesburgh, the former president of Notre Dame—certainly not a conservative—Fr. Cozzens' book pointed out that "the need gay priests have for friendship with other gay men, and their shaping of a social life largely comprised of other homosexually oriented men, has created a gay subculture in most of the larger U. S.

dioceses. A similar subculture has occurred in many of our seminaries."[60] Cozzens described the consequences of what he called the "gaying" of the priesthood, these included: "the reordering of what had been masculine social life along feminized lines drawn by gossip, favoritism, and cliques and the consequent deterrence of some unknown number of actual and potential heterosexual seminarians." Not infrequently, Cozzens explained, "the sexual contacts and romantic unions among gay seminarians create intense and complicated webs of intrigue and jealousy leading to considerable inner conflict. Here the sexually ambiguous seminarian drawn into the gay subculture is particularly at risk."[61]

Likewise, *Dallas Morning News* reporter Rod Dreher published an article in 2002 that claimed he was advised by a number of reliable sources, including psychiatrist Richard Sipe, that there is a "network of gay priests who support each other, sometimes through sinister ways—blackmailing bishops and others who threaten their activities."[62] Dreher maintains that gay priests in control of seminaries and chanceries used their power to persecute orthodox heterosexual priests and seminarians.

Sadly, much of the support for what Fr. Andrew Greeley called "the lavender mafia" came from gay faculty, many of them former or current gay priests and their allies teaching on Catholic campuses. Michael Rose identifies many of these individuals by name in *Goodbye, Good Men*. And while his book has been criticized as "anecdotal" and "polemical," the fact that many of his conclusions have been verified elsewhere indicates that the growing number of sexually-active homosexually-oriented priests has degraded the culture of the seminaries and the chanceries so drastically that it has most likely deterred significant numbers of orthodox Catholic men from seriously considering becoming priests.[63]

In the wake of the clergy abuse crisis, many bishops reached out to faculty and administrators on Catholic colleges for advice on how to respond. Unfortunately, the Church was poorly served once again. Instead of looking at the role homosexual priests played in the crisis, Fr. William Leahy, Jesuit president of Boston College, suggested discussions about permitting priests to marry and ordaining women in order to "ensure an adequate number of priests for the church."[64] Likewise, laicized priest Thomas Groome, a Boston College theologian and longtime critic of Church teachings on women's ordination, was quoted by a *Boston Globe* reporter as promoting "reform" in the Church after the crisis—maintaining that all options are "going to be on the table."[65] This is not surprising because Groome admits in his own writings to having been "inspired" by pro-choice dissident theologian Elizabeth Schussler Fiorenza and has long pushed for reform of the priesthood—allowing for married priests and women's ordination, and claiming that the male-only ministerial priesthood is not of divine origin.[66]

In addition to Groome and Leahy, the bishops enlisted Monica Hellwig as one of several "prominent Catholics" to provide consultation and advice on how to respond to the clergy abuse crisis during a "private conference" held in Washington, DC in 2003. Hosted by Cardinal McCarrick and convened by former Boston College trustee Geoffrey Boisi, the gathering of well-known dissident Catholics was called "The Church in America: The Way Forward in the 21st Century." In an attempt to help the Church move beyond the humiliation and devastation of the sex abuse scandal, Hellwig joined journalist and longtime critic of Church teachings Peggy Steinfels, as well as John Sweeny, the Catholic president of the AFL-CIO and an open supporter of abortion; Kathleen Kennedy Townsend, former Lieutenant Governor of Maryland and a self-described "pro-choice Catholic"; and Mary Jo Bane, a pro-choice professor of public policy at Harvard. And, although the goal of "moving on" was a laudable one, the bishops never made clear how inviting dissident theologians could ever help strengthen the Church in the future. None of the participants have been known to support the Magisterium.[67] And, more importantly, none of the participants were willing to confront the role homosexuality played in the clergy abuse crisis. There were no orthodox voices allowed at the conference, leading at least one critic to conclude, "I think it's safe to say that the real criterion for involvement was not prominence or influence in the Catholic Church but rather, sympathy with dissenting points of view."[68]

Although some of the bishops may have been sympathetic to the dissident voices, the Vatican has paid much more attention to what most people knew was the real contributor to the clergy abuse crisis. Ignoring the demands for female priests, married priests, or non-celibate priests, the Vatican called for inspections of Catholic seminaries in the United States in 2002.[69] And, while most observers viewed the inspections as the first step toward tightening admission standards to bar self-identified homosexuals from studying for the priesthood, the usual Catholic college dissident faculty decried the assault on gays as a way to cover up the Episcopal errors that led to the sex abuse scandal.[70] Still, at the end of November 2005, the Vatican's Congregation for Catholic Education issued an "Instruction Concerning the Criteria of Vocational Discernment

Regarding Persons with Homosexual Tendencies." Approved by Pope Benedict XVI, the instruction is intended to give bishops and seminary rectors guidance in the admission and evaluation of seminary applicants and candidates for holy orders.

While many of those teaching on Catholic campuses were outraged with what they called the "new" teachings on the suitability of homosexuals for the priesthood, the reality is that the document simply reiterates what has been the consistent teaching of the Church: Homosexual acts are gravely sinful and homosexual tendencies and desires are objectively and intrinsically disordered. It explains that one of the central goals of priestly formation is to develop affective maturity that enables a man to relate correctly to men and women and to develop a true sense of spiritual fatherhood. It declares that it is necessary to state clearly that the Church cannot admit to the seminary or holy orders those who practice homosexuality, present deep-seated homosexual tendencies, or support the so-called gay culture.[71]

In an effort to demonstrate that the Vatican was responding directly to the clergy abuse scandal, the instruction barring homosexuals from the seminary states that it addresses questions made "more urgent by the current situation." Orthodox priest and frequent contributor to EWTN Rev. Benedict Groeschel believes that the instruction was prompted by the rise of the gay movement and its destructive impact on the priesthood and seminary life. The document specifically mentions participation in the "gay culture" as a disqualifying factor for seminary admission and Fr. Groeschel takes this as an important sign: "The real problem is the gay scene or gay culture. This is a culture contrary to the New Testament, to Judaism and most other major religions . . . It has no place whatsoever in a seminary. Just as kleptomaniacs, liars, and compulsives do not belong in seminary, those who grotesquely advertise their confused sexuality do not belong there either."[72]

All of these teachings have been explicit for nearly fifty years. Kenneth D. Whitehead points out in an article published in the *Fellowship of Catholic Scholars Quarterly* that "a 1961 document from the Holy See on selecting candidates for the priesthood expressly excluded homosexuals in a single sentence using language reflective of that time: 'Those affected by the perverse inclination to homosexuality or pederasty should be excluded from religious vows or ordination.'"[73] Had these teachings been followed since 1961, the majority of the abuse cases, the 81 percent of abuse cases involving priests and young males, might have been prevented. Two subsequent Vatican documents reiterated these teachings about the unsuitability of gays in the priesthood—one issued in 1985 and the other in 2002. The 2002 document stated clearly, "A homosexual person or one with a homosexual tendency is not fit to receive the sacrament of holy orders."[74]

The 2002 document caused an uproar on Catholic campuses at the time it was issued because at the same time the Vatican was reiterating teachings on the "perverse inclination" to homosexuality, Notre Dame was preparing to construct its "Coming-Out Closet" and celebrate its first Queer Film Festival—and DePaul was staging its "Queer Kiss-In" and beginning the foundation for the creation of its minor in queer studies. Acceding to the prevalent perceptions of homosexuals as simply pursuing alternative lifestyles, Catholic colleges and universities simply ignored the teachings. It appears that many of the bishops and seminary rectors did the same.

In a 2002 interview for the *San Francisco Chronicle*, the Rev. Joseph Daoust, president of the Jesuit School of Theology in Berkeley criticized "conservatives" who claimed that the clergy abuse scandal was about homosexuality—and asserted that the clergy abuse crisis is about "keeping proper boundaries and dealing with the people with a sexual disease."[75] Claiming that "any mature well-developed person should be welcome, no matter how God made them," Daoust neglected to mention the memo his San Francisco Bay Area seminary allegedly received from national Jesuit leaders advising his seminarians to "avoid (gay) bars that are notorious for one reason or another, bars that are used for cruising and pick ups . . . Think of the reputation of your community, of the Society and the Church."[76]

Beyond the Jesuits, Cardinal Theodore McCarrick, then the Episcopal leader of Washington, DC said in 2002, "the key question is not a candidate's sexual orientation, but whether he is ready, willing and able to live in perpetual celibacy.[77] This, despite the fact that a survey carried out by McCarrick's own Catholic University of America just the year before, found that 41 percent of US priests said that a gay subculture "clearly" or "probably" existed in seminaries where they studied and 55 percent said the same for their parishes or religious institutes.[78]

Once the 2005 instruction was released, one of the most widely reported of the bishops' reactions to the document was the statement from the Bishop William S. Skylstad of Spokane, Washington and then, the president of the US Conference of Catholic Bishops, Bishop Skylstad (and ironically, head of a diocese that was itself bankrupted by sex abuse claims) wrote in his diocesan newspaper that "there are many wonderful and excellent priests in the Church who have a gay orientation, are chaste and celibate, and are very effective ministers of the Gospel . . . Witch-hunts and gay bashing have no place in the Church."[79] Bishop Skylstad's suggestion was that homosexuality, whatever else it might be, was not a bar to the priesthood in the opinion of the president of the Conference of Bishops. Likewise, the newly appointed archbishop of San Francisco, George H. Niederauer, concurred with Bishop Skylstad's view that homosexuals were "perfectly capable of being good priests."[80]

However, unlike in the past, when bishops were reluctant to publicly contradict each other, there were a few courageous bishops who spoke out against Bishop Skylstad's position. Bishop John M. D'Arcy, the presiding bishop of the Fort Wayne-South Bend, Indiana diocese (the diocese that oversees the University of Notre Dame) was quoted in the press as saying that Bishop Skylstad's position was "simply wrong." Kenneth Whitehead points out that "In Bishop D'Arcy's opinion, the new Instruction does bar anyone whose sexual orientation is toward one's own sex—and it is permanent . . . Not everyone is called to be a priest." Bishop D'Arcy supported the Vatican's instruction to "exclude men practicing homosexuality or possessing deep seated homosexual tendencies or supporting the so-called gay culture."[81]

Likewise, Cardinal Anthony Bevilacqua of Philadelphia has long accepted the traditional ban on homosexual seminarians. At St. Charles Borromeo Seminary, homosexual candidates, even ones who say they are celibate, are never considered appropriate for admission to the seminary. Bevilacqua explains his policy on the grounds that homosexuals cannot make the sacrifice that is proper to the priesthood, namely to give up the "moral good" of family and children for the good of the Church. Homosexuals can only give up the "moral evil" of homosexual acts: "He is giving up what the Church considers an abomination."[82]

And, while there are additional bishops and seminary directors who support the Vatican's instruction regarding persons with homosexual tendencies, the overwhelming response from Catholic campuses and many others within the Church's official structures revealed more concern about hurting the feelings of homosexuals than concerns about the threat to Catholic moral teachings—and the authority of the bishops and the Holy Father. Indeed, the bishops' continued refusal to obey yet another instruction from the Vatican is yet another reminder of Pope John Paul

II's words in 1987 when he warned the Bishops that when they fail to uphold the legitimate decisions of the Holy See, they undermine their own authority.

While the issue of homosexuality has taken on a life of its own on Catholic campuses and within seminaries and parish rectories and it is, of course, an important issue to address, the reality remains that it is simply a symptom of a much bigger problem. The real problem is the failure to recognize that there are indeed rules—and a natural law basis for such rules—that for centuries have led to sacred orders or what Philip Rieff calls "interdicts." Following Durkheim, Rieff points out that the challenge to social order is the growing inability of the culture to translate sacred order into social order. In the past, the faithful knew that their identity as Catholics came from what Rieff calls the "vertical axis in authority." Believers looked to authority figures like priests and bishops for guidance as they used to be willing to do the hard work of translating sacred order—helping others to understand the scriptural and natural law basis for the interdicts. Without this willingness to use their teaching authority, there is little direction offered to believers.

This is especially true on Catholic campuses where students and a few beleaguered faculty members are still seeking ways to stop the slide to secularism and the death of the Catholic culture on their campuses. And there are signs that they are beginning to get some help. In an interview published in *The Wanderer*, Rev. Raymond Burke, archbishop of St. Louis, shared an optimistic view for a renewed appreciation for the sacred—a richer appreciation for the presence of Christ in the sacraments. Still, Archbishop Burke acknowledged that this new appreciation will not come easily to Catholic campuses as he lamented the lack of implementation of *Ex Corde Ecclesiae*:

> It's a great challenge and I personally am deeply grieved that the apostolic constitution, in my judgment, has not been applied as it needs to be in this country. And I have felt this myself now being in a city with more than one Catholic university, and I intend to address the issue. The Holy Father has given us that teaching in the discipline to serve the Catholic universities by calling them to their Catholic identity and that is what we have to do.[83]

Pointing to the Land O'Lakes Statement as the cause for the decline in Catholic higher education, and saying that "so much was undone by that statement," Archbishop Burke cites a misplaced striving for status as a major contributor to the problem: "There's a mentality entered into the universities by which those people who dedicated their lives to Catholic education believe that they could not be an excellent university and at the same time be faithful to the Church's teaching and discipline. That is a fundamental error."[84]

The following chapter will introduce a growing number of Catholic universities that have demonstrated, as Archbishop Burke pointed out, that a Catholic college or university can indeed achieve excellence while remaining faithful to the Church.

Notes

1. Paul Likoudis. "Who Should be Denied Communion?" *The Wanderer*. (May 13, 2004); see also Paul Likoudis. "Fr. Robert Drinan Dies in D. C. at 86." *The Wanderer*. (February 8, 2007).
2. Likoudis. "Fr. Robert Drinan Dies in D. C. at 86."
3. Robert George and William Saunders. "The Future of Catholic Political Leadership." *Crisis*. 18. (April 2000): 17-22.
4. The editors. "How Catholic Education Failed Alexandra Pelosi." *California Catholic Daily*. (January 26, 2007): www.calcatholic.com/news/newsarticle. aspx?id=41c5087a-e372-4e08-a263-2eb23a2648bc
5. Ibid.
6. John Henry Westen. "First Things' Fr. Neuhaus Criticizes Archbishop Wuerl on Pro-Abortion Politicians Fiasco. LifeSite News. (January 25, 2007): www.lifesite. net/ldn/2007/jan/07012501.html
7. Alphonse deValk. "Politics, Abortion and the Church, Part II." *Catholic Insight*. (July 1, 2004).
8. Alphonse deValk. "John Kerry, the American Election and Catholic Bishops." *Catholic Insight*. (June 1, 2004).
9. The editors. "St. Louis Archbishop Warns of Upcoming Persecution over Abortion and Homosexuality." LifeSite. (February 9, 2005): www.lifesitenews.com
10. Felicia Lee. "Bishop Protests Notre Dame Films." *New York Times*. (February 12, 2007).
11. "Formerly Catholic Notre Dame Runs Second Annual Queer Film Fest." LifeSite News. (February 14, 2005): www.liesite.net/ldn/2005/feb/05021406.html
12. Philip Jenkins. *The New Anti-Catholicism*. (New York: Oxford University Press, 2003), 107.
13. Tim Drake. "Bishop Finds Notre Dame Events Revolting." *National Catholic Register*. (2005): www.staycatholic.com/bishops_finds_notre_dame_events_re-volting.htm
14. Bishop John D'Arcy. "Notre Dame Queer Film Festival." *South Bend Tribune*. (February 10, 2005).
15. "Loyola College of MD to Honor Pro-Abortion Giuliani Despite College's Catholic Mission." *Cardinal Newman Society News Alert*. (May 16, 2005).
16. Patrick Reilly. "Letter to the Bishops." (December 9, 2003): Published in *Cardinal Newman Society News Alert*. (May 16, 2005).
17. Carolyn Thompson. "Clinton Invitation Draws Protest from Anti-Abortion Groups." Associated Press. *Newsday*. (January 28, 2005): www.newsday.com
18. Steven Ertelt. "Ex-Supreme Court Justice O'Connor Bashes Pro-Life Advocates on Terri Schiavo. Lifenews.com. (March 13, 2006): www.lifenews.com
19. Janice D.Arcy. "Cardinal Says New Policy Led to Loyola Boycott." *Baltimore Sun*. (May 20, 2005): www.baltimoresun.com
20. The editors. *Newsflash. Cardinal Newman Society Mission*. (March-April-May, 2005).

21. Mark Gabrish Conlan. "Anne Hoiberg Maintains Faith in the United Nations." *Zenger's Newsmagazine.* (May 20, 2003): www.sandiego.indymedia.org/en/2003/05/6296.shtml

22. Elisabeth Rehn. "Statement of Finland." Presented at the International Conference on Population and Development in Cairo, Egypt. September 5-13, 1994.Published by the "United Nations Population Information Network." United Nations Population Division, Department of Economic and Social Affairs.

23. Joan B. Kroc Distinguished Lecture Series. University of San Diego. San Diego, CA, October 18, 2006.

24. William F. Schulz. PhD. "Tainted Legacy: 9/11 and the Ruin of Human Rights." Joan B. Kroc Distinguished Lecture Series. Delivered on the 9th of March 2006, at the Joan B. Kroc Institute for Peace and Justice. University of San Diego. Edited by Emiko Noma. http://peace.sandiego.edu/programs/lectureshtml

25. Kenneth Roth. "Mexico: Rape Victims Denied Legal Abortion." www.hrw.org/english/docs/2006/02/23/mexico12712.htm

26. Brief of Amici Curiae. International Human Rights Organizations and Law Professors. Commonwealth of Massachusetts Supreme Judicial Court. SJC No. 09163. www.hrw.org/pub/amicusbriefs/civil_marriage.pdf

27. Cardinal Newman Society. "Abortion Scandal at Loyola Chicago." *Cardinal Newman Society Mission.* (Winter 2006-07).

28. Ibid.

29. Cardinal Newman Society. "Cardinal Newman Society Exposes Commencement Scandals." *Cardinal Newman Society Mission.* (June-July 2005).

30. Cardinal Newman Society. "Commencement Speaker Monitoring." (Summer 2006): www.cardinalnewmansociety.org/cns/projects/commencement.

31. Ibid.

32. Cardinal Newman Society. "Keeler, Hughes Boycott Honors." *Cardinal Newman Society Mission.* (June-July 2005).

33. Ibid.

34. Cardinal Newman Society. "St. Elizabeth College Drops Pro-Abortion Commencement Speaker." *Cardinal Newman Society Mission.* (June-July 2005).

35. Cardinal Newman Society. "Marymount Manhattan College No Longer Catholic." *Cardinal Newman Society Mission.* (June-July 2005).

36. Ibid.

37. Anne Hendershott. *The Politics of Abortion.* (New York: Encounter Books, 2006), 125.

38. Ibid.

39. "Bishops Back Out of Commencement Ceremonies." Association of Students at Catholic Colleges. (May 22, 2003): www.catholiccollegestudents.org/releases.html

40. Ibid.

41. Ibid.

42. Thomas Bartlett. "Bully Pulpit: Patrick Reilly uses his Cardinal Newman Society to denounce Catholic Colleges." *The Chronicle of Higher Education* 52. (June 30, 2006): A-6.

43. Ibid.

44. Anthony J. Cernera. Opening Remarks at the "Examining the Catholic Intellectual Tradition." Conference at Sacred Heart University. November 10-12, 2000.

45. Cited in Donna Steichen. Ungodly Rage: The Hidden Face of Catholic Feminism. (San Francisco, CA: Ignatius Press, 1991), 12.

46. Elizabeth Roney Drennan. "Paulists' RENEW 2000 is Just a Front for Call to Action." *The Wanderer.* (September 24, 1998).
47. Patricia Sullivan. "Georgetown University Theologian, Catholic Activist Monika Hellwig Dies." *Washington Post.* (October 6, 2005): www.washingtonpost.com/wp-dyn/content/article/2005/10/05/AR2005100502300.html
48. Ibid.
49. Cited by Kenneth D. Whitehead. "Homosexuality: Is the Catholic Church Guilty of Discrimination?" *Fellowship of Catholic Scholars Quarterly.* (Spring 2006): 16.
50. Ken Kusmer. "Church Abuse Scandal Will cost $3 Billion. *Washington Post.* (July 10, 2005): www.washington.com
51. "Pope Deplores Pedophilia, But Won't Lift Priests' Celibacy." *Seattle Times.* (June 27, 1999), 15.
52. Laurie Goodstein. "Gay Men Ponder Impact of Proposal by Vatican." *The New York Times.* (September 23, 2005): www.nytimes.com/2005/09/23/national/23priests.html
53. Mary Eberstadt. "The Elephant in the Sacristy." *The Weekly Standard.* Volume 007, Issue 39. (June 17, 2002): www.weeklystandard.com/content/public/articles/000/000/001/344fscdzu.asp
54. A. W. Richard Sipe. "Perilous Choice to Ignore AIDS Issue." *National Catholic Reporter.* (March 31, 2000).
55. Judy Thomas. "Cathoic Priests are Dying of AIDS, often in Silence." *The Kansas City Star.* (January 29, 2000): www.kansascity.com; See also www.bibletopics.com/biblestudy/74.htm
56. Ibid.
57. Eberstadt. "The Elephant in the Sacristy."
58. Ibid.
59. Ibid.
60. Ibid.
61. Ibid.
62. Rod Dreher. "Andrew Sullivan's Gay Problem." National Review Online. (March 13, 2002): www.nationalreview.com/drejer/dreher-archive.asp
63. Michael Rose. *Goodbye, Good Men.* (Washington, DC: Regnery Books, 2003).
64. Scot Lehigh. "B C is Leading the Way on Church Reform." *The Boston Globe.* (June 19, 2002).
65. Ibid.
66. Thomas H. Groome. "Bringing Life to Faith and Faith to Life." *Compass: A Review of Topical Theology.* (Spring, 2006): Vol 40, No. 3.
67. Deal Hudson. "The Dissenters' Secret Meeting." *Catholicity.* (2002): www.catholicity.com/commentary/hudson/secretmeeting.html
68. Ibid.
69. Don Lattin. "Bay Area Priests Fear Crackdown on Gay Seminarians." *The San Francisco Chronicle.* (May 14, 2002): A-1, A-15.
70. Rev. Robert Johansen. "Homosexuality and the Seminaries." *Crisis.* (February/March 2006): 42.
71. Ibid. 42.
72. Ibid. 45-46.
73. Kenneth D. Whitehead. "Homosexuality: Is the Church Guilty of Discrimination?" *Fellowship of Catholic Scholars Quarterly.* (Spring 2006): 14.
74. Ibid.
75. Lattin. "Bay Area Priests Fear Crackdown on Gay Seminarians." A-15.

76. George Neumayr. "Bay Area Seminaries Will Continue to Accept Homosexuals." *San Francisco Faith*. (July/August 2002): www.sffaith.com/ed/articles/2002/0702gn.htm

77. Daniel Williams and Alan Cooperman. "Vatican Contemplates a Ban on Gay Priests." *Washington Post*. (October 11, 2002): A-32.

78. Ibid.

79. Whitehead. "Homosexuality: Is the Church Guilty of Discrimination?"

80. Ibid., 16.

81. Ibid., 15.

82. Neumayr. "Bay Area Seminaries Will Continue to Accept Homosexuals."

83. Christopher Manion. "Upholding Catholicism in Colleges and Politics." *The Wanderer*. (September 2007).

84. Ibid.

9

Making a New Start

In 2005, yet another ranking system for colleges was added to the growing number of listings of the "best" colleges published each year in places like *U. S. News and World Report* or *The Princeton Review*. This list was different though because it identified the "top ten" college campuses where students and faculty with conservative views are welcome. Published by the national Young America's Foundation, this ranking system reassures conservative students and their parents that if you attend any of these schools, "you are going to get a solid education."[1] This was especially good news for traditional Catholic families seeking a welcoming environment for their views because three of the top ten colleges cited were orthodox Catholic colleges—including Christendom College, Franciscan University of Steubenville, and Thomas Aquinas College—all dedicated to academic excellence while maintaining their fidelity to the Magisterium.

Indeed, despite the fact that many Catholic colleges have lost their way, Catholic colleges like Christendom, Franciscan, and Thomas Aquinas continue to flourish while remaining committed to their Catholic identity. And, in spite of concerns within the secularizing Catholic colleges about a loss of status by remaining faithful to Catholic teachings, these more traditional colleges have been recognized for their academic excellence by some of the most prestigious listings of colleges and universities. In fact, for the sixth year, Franciscan was placed in the elite "Top Tier" in *U. S. News and World Report's 2007 Guide to America's Best Colleges*. This top-tier ranking indicates that Franciscan University achieved superior scores on eleven "indicators of excellence" used by *U. S. News* to assess the overall quality of a university education. In addition to the high ranking among Midwest universities, Franciscan University ranked in the top 10 percent of all 557 colleges surveyed in terms of its average graduation rate. According to the *U. S. News and World Report*, an exceptional graduation rate indicates "the better a school is apt to be at offering the classes and services students need to succeed."

In 2006, Franciscan welcomed 600 new freshmen and transfer students with an average GPA of 3.62 (significantly higher than the national average of 3.3) and an average ACT score of 24.9 (over 3 points higher than the national average of 21.1). Franciscan students come from all fifty states including Hawaii and Alaska, as well as a wide range of countries including New Zealand, Togo, Hong Kong, India, and the Netherlands.[2] The top five states represented by incoming students are Ohio, California, Virginia, New York, and Pennsylvania—all attracted to an exceptional university located on the outskirts of an old river town whose central area is derisively described in a 1996 article published in the liberal *National Catholic Reporter* as "marked by crumbling brown mansions, potholed streets, dejected-looking citizens, a continuous traffic jam of pickup trucks and a profusion of sulphurlike odors wafting across the river from the few remaining steel mills in neighboring Wierton, West Virginia."[3] In spite of this, a growing number of excellent students are drawn to the university because of Franciscan's promise of fidelity to its Catholic mission—continuing what Franciscan's president, Fr. Terence Henry, described as a "Franciscan vision of academic excellence, engaging campus culture and a commitment to Jesus Christ and the Catholic Church."[4]

The Franciscan University commitment to the Magisterium of the Catholic Church is reflected in the vision and mission statements of all three of the Catholic colleges cited. Christendom College, a Catholic college located in Virginia's Shenandoah Valley, was founded in 1977 by a group of Catholic laymen concerned about the wayward direction of Catholic higher education. These founders asserted clearly in the vision statement of the college that "the only rightful purpose of education is to learn the truth and to live by it. The purpose of Catholic education is therefore to learn and to live by the truth revealed by Our Lord and Savior Jesus Christ, the Way, the Truth and the Life."[5] Christendom's founders maintain, "Only an education which integrates the truths of the Catholic faith throughout the curriculum is a fully Catholic education."[6] Yet, despite its stated devotion to authentic Catholic teachings, Christendom is listed in the "Best Liberal Arts Colleges" section of the *2007 U. S. News and World Reports America's Best Colleges. U. S. News* bases its rankings on Christendom's freshman retention rate (84 percent), alumni giving (34 percent), and average SAT scores (1130-1330)—which are the highest in its tier.[7]

And, like Franciscan and Christendom, Thomas Aquinas College has been recognized for its excellence in secular circles as well as orthodox Catholic ones. The 2008 edition of the prestigious *Princeton Review* featured Thomas Aquinas College as "one of the nation's best institutions for undergraduate education" and 1 of only 8 new schools receiving the *Best 366* designation out of more than 3,500 institutions across the country. A spokesman for *The Princeton Review* said, "only about 10% of all of the colleges in America are included in this book. It is our flagship guide to the crème of the crop institutions for undergraduates. We chose them as our best based on several criteria including our regard for their academic programs and other offerings, the institutional data we collect from the schools, and the opinions of students, parents and educators we talk to and survey . . . Each one is an outstanding institution."[8] Thomas Aquinas was also named as one of the top one hundred liberal arts colleges highlighted in the *2007 U. S. News and World Report's America's Best Colleges*; Thomas Aquinas College was one of only four Catholic liberal arts colleges to break into the top one hundred. This most recent accolade is the result of steady progress in terms of recognition by ranking sites. As far back as 1991, the *National Review College Guide* declared Thomas Aquinas "one of America's Top 50 Liberal Arts Schools." By 1995, the *Los Angeles Times* called the college one of the nation's best liberal arts schools. In 1997 the Intercollegiate Studies Institute's book, *Choosing the Right College* indicated that Thomas Aquinas offered a curriculum virtually unparalleled in providing students with a rigorous liberal arts education. And in 1999, *U. S. News and World Report* ranked Thomas Aquinas the third "Best Buy" of all national liberal arts colleges nationwide. In addition, the college routinely makes "top 10" best college lists published by conservative Catholic publications like the *Catholic Register, Crisis,* and *Insight.*[9]

Inclusion within the list of the top one hundred liberal arts colleges in the 2007 edition of *U. S. News and World Reports America's Best Colleges* and in the "2008 Best Colleges" edition of the *Princeton Review* was especially gratifying for Thomas Aquinas College because of its historic struggles with regional accreditation committees who do not understand the rationale behind the curricular decisions the college has made. Concerns about a "lack of a commitment to diversity" threatened a loss of accreditation during the years that the Western Association of Schools and Colleges (WASC) began mandating a more culturally diverse curriculum for colleges and universities located in the western area of the country.[10] And concerns about academic freedom for faculty emerged from the fact that, in keeping with the requirement of *Ex Corde Ecclesiae,* faculty members at Thomas Aquinas pledge their fidelity to the magisterium by taking the Oath of Fidelity to Catholic teachings, and making a Profession of Faith.[11] Yet, this acknowledgement by the elite *Princeton Review* is described by Thomas E. Dillon, the president of Thomas Aquinas College, as "yet another indication that it is possible for a Catholic college to achieve academic excellence—and recognition for its excellence—while maintaining fidelity to the teaching Church."[12]

Christendom touted its "top ten" inclusion on the Young America's Foundation list on its website and in news releases. Tom McFadden, Christendom's director of admissions, acknowledged that although the college had been honored in the past by Catholic organizations, "it's always nice to be acknowledged by the secular groups too."[13] Unlike so many Catholic colleges, which have "defined down" their Catholicity, Christendom's mission statement proudly proclaims that it is a "Catholic coeducational college institutionally committed to the Magisterium of the Roman Catholic Church."[14] The college maintains that a Christendom education "prepares students for their roles as faithful, informed, and articulate members of Christ's Church and society" and it asserts that Christendom's goal is "to restore all things in Christ by forming men and women to contribute to the Christian renovation of the temporal order."[15]

To win a place on the list on Young America's "top ten," the college's curriculum had to contain what the foundation considered to be rigorous courses that challenged students. For example, in the "Great Books" curriculum at Thomas Aquinas College in Santa Paula, California, students read Homer, Locke, and Shakespeare. There are no majors or minors—students take courses in music, mathematics, science, philosophy, language, and theology—and all students graduate with the Bachelor in Arts degree in liberal arts.[16] In praising the Thomas Aquinas College curriculum, Jason Mattera, a spokesperson for Young America's Foundation asked. "How many students in today's colleges even know what the great books are? You have departments like queer studies and multicultural studies . . ."[17] Despite the absence of trendy course offerings—or perhaps, in part, because of the absence of such courses—Thomas Aquinas welcomed the largest class in the school's history last year with 103 new students arriving from 35 states, as well as Canada, Ireland, Scotland, and South Africa. Most of the new students are drawn to the school because they know that campus life follows traditional Catholic morality and teachings.

Even with their commitment to rigorous academic initiatives, students enrolled at Thomas Aquinas, Christendom and Franciscan do not remain isolated from the rest of the world. Many of these students are actively involved in community service and advocacy initiatives as part of their commitment to Catholic teachings on social and moral issues. In fact, the Young America's Foundation cited Franciscan University in Ohio for its "student body's devotion to activism on traditional religious values."[18] Volunteering to assist the needy in the community is often coupled with pro-life advocacy and political activism. But, unlike their now secularized Catholic college peers who tout their commitment to social justice by promising to "crush heterosexism" or advocate for reproductive choice and equal rights to ordination for women, students on orthodox Catholic campuses remain especially concerned about social justice for the unborn. When John Kerry held a campaign rally near the campus in 2004, more than four hundred students from Franciscan University marched to protest his appearance.[19]

It is the pledge of institutional obedience to the Vatican that is the defining characteristic of the orthodox Catholic colleges. Each was founded or re-dedicated to this obedience to papal authority. While Christendom and Thomas Aquinas were founded in the seventies, Franciscan was founded in the forties. But, by the mid-seventies, what was then called the College of Steubenville was in "critical condition" with fewer than one thousand students, a heavy debt, and a rebellious student body. Choosing the secularizing route of so many of the Catholic colleges described throughout this book, Steubenville had become best known as a "party school." Three of the candidates for the open position of president in 1974 suggested that the school be closed or merged with a state university. The students had presented a non-negotiable demand for open dorms, and campus ministry recommended an end to Sunday Masses because none of the students were attending.[20] But, Fr. Michael Scanlan, a third order Franciscan accepted the presidency and courageously refused to acquiesce to the student and faculty demands. Instead, Fr. Scanlan divided the dorms into sex-segregated "faith households" intended to facilitate community and prayer. He decided that not only would Sunday Mass remain, he would personally celebrate it. Most importantly, Fr. Scanlan redefined the campus as a center for the charismatic movement by recruiting those with a charismatic Catholic orientation. Faculty and students who disapproved of his re-organizational approach were encouraged to leave. Some did—but many more were drawn to the more traditional Catholic college, and although the charismatic component is less visible, student and faculty growth has been continuous since 1974. *National Catholic Reporter* author, Robert McClory wrote in 1996: "When people ask him how Franciscan differs from other Catholic schools Fr. Scanlan said he tells them to look at the schools' various mission statements: 'Notre Dame says it's in the Catholic tradition,' while Franciscan presents the mind of the Church as it is today, as interpreted by the Magisterium."[21]

Likewise, Thomas Aquinas College maintains that the mission of a Catholic college is to organize its curriculum to help its students "perfect their intellects under the light of the truths revealed by God through the Catholic Church." In fact, Thomas Aquinas College believes that "revealed truths should guide students in making a good beginning on the road to wisdom and informing the intellectual virtue characteristic of well-educated men and women."[22] On that journey, the college maintains that although the major subjects comprehended by a curriculum of classical liberal education are worthy of the attention given them because of their intrinsic merits, these subjects are not all of equal importance. Wisdom includes discerning their relationships and relevance to one another. In describing its curriculum, Thomas Aquinas College cites Pope John Paul's encyclical, *Fides Ratio*: "Faith and reason are like two wings on which the human spirit rises to the contemplation of truth."[23]

Indeed, it is the pursuit of Truth on these orthodox Catholic campuses that differentiates them from their more secular peers. The orthodox founders acknowledge that the dogmas of postmodernism, radical feminism, historicism, and Marxism on secularizing campuses threaten to undermine the very idea that there is religious truth. For the orthodox colleges, the starting point in theology and all other studies is the maxim, "faith seeking understanding."[24] What this means is best described in a 1996 *National Catholic Reporter* interview with Fr. Giles Dimock, the chairman of theology at Franciscan University at Steubenville. Fr. Dimock said that what differentiates the orthodox Catholic colleges from the others is that in colleges like Franciscan, "the teacher assumes that the learner has faith in Christ and His Church and accepts what the Church teaches as authoritatively true. In contrast, at most other Catholic colleges since Vatican II, the starting point is just the opposite . . . it is understanding (or intellect) exploring the faith."[25]

Under the mainstream model so prevalent on the secularizing Catholic campuses today, theology courses have been transformed into "critical perspectives of religion." There is no presumption of faith as students are asked to examine religious ideas objectively, without commitment and most often with a critical stance. Fr. Dimock believes that the problem with this approach is that many first year students arrive on campus with little grasp of the basics of their faith or any other faith to begin with—one new student asked him to explain the difference between a commandment and a sacrament: "It can be very frustrating—like trying to explain Shakespeare to people who don't know the rules of English grammar . . . Instead of their intellect guiding them to a mature faith, it leaves them so open that they have lost their moorings."[26] Students are then vulnerable to the anti-Catholic ideology that permeates many Catholic campuses.

In contrast to the critical perspective in theology courses offered on the mainstream Catholic campuses, orthodox Catholic colleges like Franciscan have established theology courses that focus on official Catholic teachings. Fr. Dimock asserts that although "scholars may advance interpretations of doctrine, they must freely submit to legitimate Church authority . . . It isn't purely extrinsic loyalty that is desired, but an appreciation for the dogma in providing boundaries—so the truth doesn't go off in rivulets." When asked if scripture courses at Franciscan take note of modern scholarship, Fr. Dimock said "of course, but with the caveats presented several years ago by Cardinal Ratzinger . . . the critical approach to scripture has been taken too far by some." Rather than a critical approach to scripture, Fr. Dimock asserts that Franciscan maintains an overall consistency: "The mystery we celebrate, believe and live is the same mystery we preach and teach."[27]

This commitment to the truth does not mean that all inquiry is suppressed. In his 1996 investigation for the *National Catholic Reporter*, Robert McClory pointed out that Franciscan University's library "held 32 card entries for the works of dissenting theologian, Hans Kung . . . roughly twice as many as for Cardinal Ratzinger." Charles Curran, the dissenting theologian barred by the Vatican from teaching theology on Catholic campuses, had several publications, as well as entries for Rosemary Radford Ruether, Richard McBrien, and even Elizabeth Johnson.[28] In excerpts from an interview with Timothy O'Donnell, Christendom College's president, published in *God on the Quad,* Naomi Schaefer Riley's recent book on religious colleges, O'Donnell suggested that at Christendom, philosophy is a means to achieving the college's mission to "restore all things in Christ. When they're studying classical philosophy—you know, they're doing Plato, they're doing Aristotle—they're recognizing the great achievement that these men have made. But there would also be a Christian critique or a Catholic critique that would be brought there."[29]

As a result of its success in producing students who will understand and articulate a strong orthodox Catholic intellectual voice in the debates over abortion, stem-cell research, gay marriage, and other social issues, the orthodox Catholic colleges are visited regularly by church representatives from around the country seeking to hire their graduates. Franciscan's Fr. Scanlan once claimed that his school "may be a better oasis for vocations than many seminaries today."[30] For example, in an effort to "aggressively bring the faith" to more than fifty thousand Catholic college students at ten secular Long Island campuses, Rockville Centre Diocese chose to replace long-serving campus ministers with orthodox young graduates of Franciscan University and Catholic University of America. According to the *National Catholic Reporter*, Rockville Centre's Bishop William Murphy announced the initiative that was designed to engage young adult Catholics as part of the Holy Father's invitation "to put out into the deep and renew our commitment to evangelize the world by the witness of our words and actions . . . This new campus ministry initiative is intended to look at campus ministry through the lens of the new evangelization."[31]

Thomas Aquinas College proudly reports that the total number of alumni ordained to the priesthood is forty-seven. The college also boasts twenty graduates who are religious brothers and sisters and an additional thirty-five in seminaries preparing for the priesthood. These numbers are especially striking for a small, private college with only 2,100 total alumni and a maximum enrollment of 350 students.[32] Indeed, graduates of Catholic colleges like Thomas Aquinas, Franciscan, Christendom, and a handful of other traditional Catholic colleges like Ave Maria in Naples, Florida, the University of Dallas, and New Hampshire's Thomas More College and Magdalene College are well prepared for this new role of evangelization.

In fact, in her research on the students at the new conservative Catholic colleges and other evangelical colleges, Naomi Schaefer Riley describes these students as part of what she calls a "missionary generation," and concludes that the graduates of these colleges are quite distinctive from their more secular counterparts. The attitude toward converting others to Catholicism is one way that divides Catholic college students into liberal and conservative factions: "The students at Thomas Aquinas fall on one side of this divide and the students at Notre Dame for the most part, fall on the other." This is not to say that these students use explicit proselytization, but as one student told Schaefer Riley, "why shouldn't we try to convert everyone?"[33]

Student attitudes on the newer conservative campuses differ from those on the mainstream Catholic campuses. And, the stronger the religious commitment of the school, the more distinctive it is. Schaefer Riley points out that there is no question that these graduates will be the vanguard of a more conservative generation. But, it will not be the conservatism of their parents and grandparents. While these students focus highly on marriage and family, they have assimilated contemporary attitudes on the role of women in society. And, they are more tolerant of homosexuality than their past counterparts: "While still regarding homosexual behavior as sinful, this does not entail personal contempt for gays."[34] They are strongly pro-life and:

> They reject the spiritually empty education of secular schools. They refuse to accept the sophisticated ennui of their contemporaries. They snub the spiritual but not religious answers to life's most difficult questions. They rebuff the intellectual relativism of professors and the moral relativism of their peers . . . In practical terms, these students challenge what has become, since the sixties, the typical model of college student behavior. They don't spend their college years experimenting with sex or drugs. They marry early and plan ahead for family life. Indeed, they oppose sex outside of marriage and homosexual relationships. Most dress modestly and don't drink, use drugs or smoke. They study hard leaving little time for sitting in or walking out. Most vote, and a good number join the army . . . While they would disagree among themselves about what it means to be a religious person, it is assumed that trying to live by a set of rules, generally ones laid down in Scripture, is the prerequisite for a healthy, productive and moral life.[35]

Students are drawn to orthodox Catholic colleges because they know that these colleges will give them what they need to succeed in the secular world and the strength to do so without compromising their faith. Whether Riley's "missionary generation" will begin to transform the broader secular culture remains uncertain. What is certain, however, is that students who attend these colleges have a very different experience than those who choose to attend the mainstream Catholic colleges. It is also certain that an increasing number of students are drawn to these colleges. To meet this growing demand, new orthodox Catholic colleges have been created in the past decade in San Diego, Cheyenne, Atlanta, and in Naples, Florida.

In the fall of 2006, San Diego's John Paul the Great Catholic University welcomed students for its inaugural class. Committed to orthodoxy, the university is built on three core values that will define its fundamental beliefs: "to put into action in our lives the teachings of Jesus Christ, being faithful to His Word; to develop all students and staff spiritually, personally and intellectually; to put into practice within the university what we will teach, by being innovative in curriculum development, pioneering in our educational niche, and entrepreneurial in defining our future." John Paul the Great University will offer degrees in technology, business, and communications media—all part of its special niche, which is "to answer the call of John Paul II to a new evangelization by changing the world using media and business."

Like Christendom, Franciscan, and Thomas Aquinas, John Paul the Great University is committed to *Ex Core Ecclesiae* pledging that "all teaching faculty will commit to harmony with Catholic Church teachings in speech and actions." The university also states that "all faculty involved with the teaching of faith based classes will be required to take an Oath of Fidelity, pledging their faithfulness and adherence to the magisterial teachings of the Catholic Church."[36]

Likewise, in the fall of 2007, Wyoming Catholic College opened its doors to students at a temporary campus located at Holy Rosary Parish in Lander, Wyoming. Beginning at the grassroots and first launched with a summer program in 2003 with the founding of the Wyoming School of Catholic Thought, the idea of the Wyoming Catholic College grew from the combined efforts of Bishop David L. Ricken, the ordinary for the Diocese of Cheyenne; Fr. Robert Cook, pastor of Our Lady of Fatima in Casper; and Dr. Robert Carlson, professor of humanities and philosophy at Casper College. Unique to the college is its outdoor education program—all first year students participate in a 21-day wilderness trek that involves hiking 100 miles, climbing heights of 11,000 feet, fly-fishing in the lakes of the Rocky Mountains and cooking all their own meals. This focus on the outdoors is done to "counteract modern culture's obsession with technology . . . to immerse students in God's first book, Nature." All Catholic faculty members make a Profession of Faith, and theology teachers seek the mandatum from the bishop of Cheyenne. The college offers daily mass, the daily recitation of the rosary follows the evening meal, and students learn the art of meditative scripture reading known as *lectio divina*. The traditional curriculum requires four years of theology that encompasses the study of the Catechism, sacred scripture, the Church fathers, and the works of St. Thomas Aquinas.[37]

In 2005, Southern Catholic College welcomed its first students. Located within the Archdiocese of Atlanta, Southern Catholic "was founded to be a top-tier Catholic College committed to the authoritative teachings of the Roman Catholic Church." Their website promises that Southern Catholic provides "a fully integrated education grounded in natural and revealed truth—and prepares moral and ethical leaders who will enlighten society and glorify God." Thomas Clements, the founder of Southern Catholic, believed that there was "a need for colleges to return to an emphasis on morality and ethics as part of the overall educational experience of college life, so as to prepare students to be educated and moral leaders in business, professional and civic life." He stated that he founded Southern Catholic to be a "college of distinction."[38] Yet, like other orthodox Catholic colleges, Southern Catholic will not compromise fidelity to the teachings of the Catholic Church to achieve high status.

Building upon this foundation, there are plans for new conservative Catholic colleges in Washington, DC and Lansing, Michigan. The Legionaries of Christ, a conservative Catholic movement active in twenty countries, opened a new university in Sacramento, California and is planning another one in Thornwood, New York. While these new conservative Catholic colleges have experienced tremendous success in terms of attracting students and faculty, this success has also raised the ire of the leaders of mainstream Catholic higher education—apparently angry that the new colleges have set themselves apart not just from secular colleges, but also from most Catholic ones too. In an article published in *The Chronicle of Higher Education* entitled, "Who is Catholic?" Monica Hellwig, the former president of the Association of Catholic Colleges and Universities, complained, "what bothers us is that they think we're not properly Catholic."[39] The Rev. Charles L. Currie, president of the Association of Jesuit Colleges and Universities, regards the new institutions as "very judgmental" and claims, "there's much more authentically Catholic going on at Catholic universities than they give us credit for."[40] And, Alice Gallin, a nun and former executive director of the Association of Catholic Colleges and Universities and scholar-in-residence at the Catholic College of New Rochelle, disparaged the new conservative Catholic colleges by claiming that "they are like overly protective parents in the way that they try to maintain strict campus environments. Rather than allowing students to develop their own intellectual and moral judgments . . . this group places more emphasis on how often the students go to Mass and what kind of films or plays can be shown on campus; all these neurotic points."[41]

Despite the recent accolades from college rankings systems, and the acknowledgement of academic excellence in publications like *The Princeton Review* for these conservative Catholic colleges, it is clear that for some status-conscious faculty members and administrators, there is still a stigma associated with obedience to the magisterium—and teaching on an orthodox Catholic campus that cherishes the Gospel rather than criticizing it. In *God on the Quad*, Naomi Schaefer Riley suggests that "Academia is a club, and professors at religious colleges want to join, too. Not only are they often coming out of the same graduate programs as their counterparts at secular schools, but once they obtain faculty appointments, they want to publish in the prominent academic journals and speak at the well-attended conferences."[42] The influence of postmodernism still haunts most professors—even those on the Catholic campuses—threatening to undermine the very idea that there is religious truth. And, the jealousies and resentments so pervasive within university faculty in general seem to be present even on some of these new orthodox campuses.

An article in *The New York Times* entitled, "Our Lady of Discord," chronicles the recent troubled story of Ave Maria University, one of the most promising members of the new generation of orthodox Catholic Colleges. Founded by Thomas Monaghan, the founder of Domino's Pizza, the leaders of Ave Maria University drew criticism over Monaghan's decision to donate more than $250 million to help build the campus near Naples, Florida. A Detroit-area philanthropist, Mr. Monaghan had started Ave Maria College, a regional Catholic college, in Ypsilanti and founded the Ave Maria School of Law in Ann Arbor. He had originally intended to build Ave Maria University in Ann Arbor Township. But, these plans fell through when Ann Arbor officials denied him the necessary zoning change in 2002. Later that year, he announced that the Barron Collier Company, a Florida developer, had donated 750 acres of farmland to the university on the northwest edge of the Everglades. Monaghan changed his plans for Michigan, and chose instead to build Ave Maria University in Florida, while investing another $50 million in a separate partnership with Barron Collier to build the adjoining Ave Maria town.[43] Promising to continue operations in Michigan until 2007—when current Ave Maria College students would graduate—Monaghan attempted to placate an angry faculty and disgruntled alumni.

Indeed, it was the impending move out of Michigan that created the discord for faculty and some administrators. Ave Maria College's academic dean sued Mr. Monaghan and the school's trustees in 2004 in a bid to stall the Michigan's campus closure, but a state court judge dismissed the suit. Some disgruntled faculty alleged that while Ave Maria University was beginning operations in Florida in 2003, much of the money Mr. Monaghan had been donating to his Michigan projects, including Ave Maria College and School of Law began to diminish. And, although faculty and students at Ave Maria College were reassured that operations would be maintained until 2007 when the college would be merged into the new university in Florida, some of these same faculty claim that they were pressured to move to Florida quickly or risk losing their jobs. Anthony Messaros, an especially bitter former biology professor on the Ypsilanti campus, wrote a scathing account of the Ave Maria Foundation's board decision to move the campus to Florida accusing Mr. Monaghan of "cannibalizing" the original Ave Maria College.[44]

To add to the turmoil, in 2006 Ave Maria School of Law announced that it, too, would be relocating to Florida in 2009. While currently enrolled law students will graduate from the Ann Arbor location, the incoming first year students were advised that they would spend their final year at the Florida location. Some faculty, students, and alumni have complained about the new location: "It is crazy to leave an intellectual center like Ann Arbor, home of the University of Michigan, for an undeveloped outpost on the edge of the Everglades."[45] In a negative report on the board decision to relocate, *The Wanderer* reported that Dr. Charles E. Rice, a distinguished visiting law school professor at Ave Maria School of Law was removed from the board as part of a restructuring that limited board members' tenure. Some faculty and students interpreted Professor Rice's removal as "retaliation" for representing to the board their resistance to moving the law school to Florida.[46]

Despite this turmoil, most Ave Maria College professors relocated to the new Florida campus—and the university continues to attract new professors committed to providing the kind of serious formation in Catholic and theological traditions that are essential.[47] And although there continue to be some residual problems related to the relocation, including the controversial reassignment of the founding Chancellor and former Provost Fr. Joseph Fessio to the position of theologian in residence in 2007, it is likely that Ave Maria University will flourish.[48] There continues to be a need for the kind of orthodox Catholic experience that Ave Maria can provide. Graduates of the Ave Maria School of Law have already distinguished themselves in terms of their superior passing rate for the bar as graduates of the first 3 classes (since the first class graduated in 2003) sat for the bar exam in 33 states, achieving an overall bar pass rate of 88 percent. Those sitting for the Michigan bar have had the highest pass rate in the state for three of the last four years and the second highest bar pass rate for the other year. In 2006, the passing rate was 96 percent, which is the highest overall among all Michigan law schools. Ave Maria gained full accreditation from the American Bar Association in 2005. This was achieved after only five years, the shortest time frame possible. Ave Maria's Moot Court team has won top honors three years in a row for the statewide competition held annually for the last five years. Graduates have secured thirty-four prestigious judicial clerkships, twenty-eight of these with federal courts.[49]

Not surprisingly, in the world of academic status envy, any success that an orthodox Catholic law school might experience is greeted with the usual jeers from dissidents like former Georgetown law professor, Fr. Robert Drinan, who complained that the founding of the Ave Maria School of Law is "simply a vehicle to advance a right wing agenda." Drinan accused Ave Maria of "implying that the other 26 Catholic law schools aren't Catholic enough, so they had to take their pizza money and put it elsewhere . . . Why not contribute to an existing school? Why go off and start this free-floating school that has no university or diocese attached to it?"[50] Likewise, Monika Hellwig dismissed the need for Ave Maria's law school by saying that "Catholic law schools and the Jesuit schools in particular have been offering legal clinics for the poor and addressing Catholic social teachings for years . . . They pride themselves in being extremely Catholic."[51] But, Mr. Monaghan dismisses these criticisms by saying that "there's nothing wrong with most Catholic schools, except they're not Catholic."[52] He defends his academic initiatives by acknowledging that although there are many Catholic institutions addressing social justice issues "there's no one doing the spiritual, morality kinds of things. There's more of a need there."[53] Ave Maria is the only national Catholic law school dedicated to providing students with an outstanding legal education enhanced by the teachings of the Catholic Church.

Some of the problems that have emerged in the fledgling Ave Maria University and the Ave Maria Law School are quite possibly the result of simply taking on too much and moving too quickly. Mr. Monaghan, one of the country's wealthiest philanthropists, seems impatient with the slow pace of decision making within academic life. He is a business man who is unaccustomed to the kind of slow and deliberate pace so characteristic of academics. In a *Wall Street Journal* article published in 2000, even one of Mr. Monaghan's friends, Franciscan University's

Fr Michael Scanlan, said "I don't expect everything he is doing to work . . . He has taken on too much for what you'd consider a normal person." Mr. Monaghan acknowledged, "I worry about that too . . . I have to find where the priorities are."[54] It is clear that Mr. Monaghan's priorities are with Schaefer Riley's "missionary generation" as he stated in a *Chronicle of Higher Education* interview that his own mission is "to help as many people as possible get to heaven."[55] And, it is clear to Mr. Monaghan, and to a growing number of Catholic families, that the best way to do that is to move away from the mainstream model of Catholic colleges and to promote orthodox Catholic higher education.

To assist families in choosing a Catholic College that will be loyal to the Catholic tradition, the Cardinal Newman Society just released a guidebook listing twenty-one colleges that they have determined to be "genuinely Catholic." With categories like "Joyfully Catholic," "Born from the Crisis," and "Fighting the Tide," the authors provide an indication of those that are "most loyal to the Catholic tradition." Included in the guide are detailed profiles of schools, essential data on each institution, and practical advice from eminent Catholic thinkers including Fr. Benedict Groeschel, Fr. John McCloskey, and Dr. Peter Kreeft.[56]

Within the category of "Joyfully Catholic" are three Texas schools including the University of Dallas, the University of Saint Thomas, and the College of St. Thomas More. Franciscan University of Steubenville, Magdalen College in New Hampshire and Santa Paula, and California's Thomas Aquinas are also included among the "joyfully Catholic." The second category contains those described as "Born from the Crisis" because they are the newer arrivals on the orthodox Catholic College scene. Within this group are Ave Maria; Holy Apostles College and Seminary in Connecticut; John Paul the Great Catholic University in San Diego; Our Lady Seat of Wisdom in Canada; Southern Catholic College in Dawsonville, Georgia; and Wyoming Catholic College. And finally, the category described as "Fighting the Tide" includes Aquinas College in Nashville; Belmont Abbey College in Belmont, North Carolina; Benedictine College in Atchison Kansas; the Catholic University of American in Washington; DeSales University in Center Valley, Pennsylvania; Mount St. Mary's University in Emmitsburg, Maryland; St. Gregory's University in Shawnee, Oklahoma; and Thomas More College of Liberal Arts in Merrimack, New Hampshire.

The Cardinal Newman Society maintains that the schools they have listed are places where students can reasonably expect a faithful Catholic education and a campus culture that generally upholds the values taught in their homes and parishes.[57] Although some of the most prestigious schools, from a secular perspective, like Georgetown, Boston College, and Notre Dame, are not listed in the *Newman Guide*, there are some positive signs for the future. The following chapter will look closely at some of the new developments on Catholic campuses as signs of recovery begin to emerge.

Notes

1.   Cited by Jennifer Jacobson. "Conservative Group Cites Colleges of Like Mind." *The Chronicle of Higher Education.* 52 (January 6, 2006): A 48.
2.   "Franciscan University Receives Top Tier U. S. News Ranking." Franciscan University of Steubenville Website. (August 29, 2006): www.franciscan.edu/Home2/Content/main.aspx?id=2115
3.   Robert McClory. "Steubenville: Echo of Old or Glimpse of the Future?" *National Catholic Reporter.* (March 1, 1996): www.findarticles.com/p/articles/mi_m114/is_n18_v32/ai_18082653
4.   "Franciscan University Receives Top Tier U. S. News Ranking." Franciscan University of Steubenville Website. (August 29, 2006): www.franciscan.edu/Home2/Content/main.aspx?id=2115
5.   Mission Statement at Christendom College: www.christendom.edu/welcome/mission.shtml
6.   "Top Ten Conservative Colleges." *Human Events Online.* (May 15, 2006): http://findarticles.com/p/articles/mi_qa3827/is_20060ai_n16431025
7.   *U. S. News and World Report. 2007 America's Best Colleges.*
8.   "Princeton Review Features Thomas Aquinas College." *The Wanderer.* (April 2007).
9.   Thomas Aquinas College Website: www.thomasaquinas.edu/about/catholic.htm
10.   Naomi Schaefer Riley. *God on the Quad: How Religious Colleges and the Missionary Generation are Changing America.* (New York: St. Martin's Press, 2005), 217.
11.   "Bishop Sheridan Tells Thomas Aquinas Students to Live the Truth." *The Wanderer.*
12.   "Princeton Review Features Thomas Aquinas College." *The Wanderer.* (April 2007)
13.   Jacobson. "Conservative Group Cites Colleges of Like Mind." A 48.
14.   Mission Statement at Christendom College: www.christendom.edu/welcome/mission.shtml
15.   Ibid.
16.   "Top Ten Conservative Colleges" *Human Events Online.*
17.   Jacobson. "Conservative Group Cites Colleges of Like Mind."
18.   "Top Ten Conservative Colleges." *Human Events Online.*
19.   Jacobson. "Conservative Group Cites Colleges of Like Mind."
20.   Robert McClory. "Steubenville: Echo of Old or Glimpse of the Future?" *National Catholic Reporter.* (March 1, 1996).
21.   Ibid.
22.   Thomas Aquinas College Website: www.thomasaquinas.edu/about/catholic.htm
23.   Ibid.
24.   McClory. "Steubenville: Echo of Old or Glimpse of the Future?"

25.   Ibid.
26.   Ibid.
27.   Ibid.
28.   Ibid.
29.   Schaefer Riley. *God on the Quad.* 224.
30.   McClory. "Steubenville: Echo of Old or Glimpse of the Future?"
31.   Jeff Severns Gentzel. "Campus Ministry Terminations Draw Fire." *National Catholic Reporter.* (April 22, 2005): http://natcath.org/NCR_online/archives2/ 2005b/042205/042205h.php
32.   The editors. "Not so Much Catechism as Conviction." *California Catholic Daily.* (August 16, 2007): http://www.calcatholic.com/news/newsarticle.aspx?=4fld8bcb- 5986-431a-aeb2-1d8afb075b2e
33.   Schaefer Riley. *God on the Quad. 74.*
34.   Ibid., 261.
35.   Ibid., 5-6. .
36.   John Paul the Great Catholic University: www.jpcatholic.com
37.   "Wyoming Catholic College To Open in 2007." *The Wanderer.* (October 12, 2006); see also Wyoming Catholic College website: www.wyomingcatholiccollege. com
38.   Southern Catholic College Website: www.southerncatholic.org/?view=about_mis- sion
39.   Burton Bollag. "Who is Catholic?" *The Chronicle of Higher Education.* 50. (April 9, 2004): 31. www.chronicle.com/weekly/v50/i31/31ao2601.htm
40.   Ibid.
41.   Ibid.
42.   Schaefer Riley. *God on the Quad.* 227.
43.   Susan Hansen. "Our Lady of Discord." *The New York Times.* (July 30, 2006): www.nytimes.com/2006/07/30/business/yourmoney/30monaghan.html?_ r=180ref=slogin
44.   Andrew Messaros. "Fr. Fessio's Next Educational Disaster? *New Oxford Review.* (March 2005): www.newoxfordreview.org/article.jsp?did=0305-messaros
45.   Hansen. "Our Lady of Discord."
46.   Paul Likoudis. "Ave Maria School of Law Fires Rice on Eve of New School Year." *The Wanderer.* (August 24, 2006).
47.   William Hobbib. "America Style Freedom." *Cardinal Newman Society Mission.* (June-July 2005).
48.   Alan Cooperman. "Magnate's Decisions Stir Controversy." *Washington Post.* (March 25, 2007): A 03.
49.   Ave Maria School of Law. Fact Sheet. www.avemarialaw.edu/news/media/facts. cfm
50.   Katherine Manga. "Ave Maria: a Seriously Catholic Law School." *The Chronicle of Higher Education* 46. (February 18, 2000): A 18.
51.   Ibid.
52.   Lisa Miller. "Pizza Magnate Mounts a Crusade to Restore Orthodox Catholicism." *The Wall Street Journal.* (June 21, 2000).
53.   Ibid.
54.   Ibid.
55.   Bollag. "Who is Catholic?"
56.   Joseph A. Esposito. *The Newman Guide to Choosing a Catholic College.* (Wilm- ington, DE: ISI Publishing, 2007).
57.   Ibid.

10

Looking for Signs of Life

A few years ago, Georgetown University hosted yet another conference on the state of Catholicism in America. One of the attendees, *First Things* editor Joseph Bottum wearily recalled that by the second day, when the conservative Catholic writer Michael Novak began to debate with the progressive Catholic higher education leader Monika Hellwig, "a truly palpable gloom settled over the room." Apparently, Novak and Hellwig have had this same debate so many times, over so many years, that "they began to squabble like an old couple locked in a bickering marriage: forgotten occasions suddenly remembered, dead quarrels fanned back to flame—until we seemed to be back at the 1976 Call to Action conference in Detroit, the low point in post-Vatican II American Catholic unity—nothing learned, nothing gained, nothing advanced in thirty years."[1]

Sadly, these kinds of quarrels are replicated on Catholic campuses throughout the country as the battle lines were drawn decades ago and contentiousness continues to characterize our conversations over controversial issues from Church governance to sexual morality. As the earlier chapters have shown, far too many of these arguments remain hopelessly deadlocked—driven by the emotion and tired rhetoric of the liberationist movements of the sixties and seventies and fueled by a resentful response from the right.

It is difficult to remain optimistic about Catholic higher education when even Notre Dame Law Professor Gerard Bradley, a tireless advocate for restoring the Catholic identity of colleges and universities through the implementation of *Ex Corde Ecclesiae,* sadly acknowledges that "the people in charge—faculty, college administrators, trustees, other intellectual elites, and (judging by what they do) the bishops—do not believe what they need to believe to restore Catholic education to the colleges."[2] Describing *Ex Corde Ecclesiae* as a "sick patient," Professor Bradley recently pronounced, "the patient is now dead."[3] For Bradley, a two-term president of the Fellowship of Catholic Scholars, an orthodox Catholic organization that is faithful to the magisterium, the real crisis on Catholic campuses is a crisis of faith. He believes that many faculty members and administrators have rejected "the defining passage" of *Ex Corde Ecclesiae,* which asserts that "the distinguishing task of the Catholic university is to unite existentially by intellectual effort two orders of reality that too frequently tend to be placed in opposition as though they were antithetical: the search for truth, and the certainty of already knowing the fount of truth."[4]

Rejecting this passage, faculty and administrators have redefined the Catholic university as one in which Catholic themes of social justice or Catholic social teachings may be integrated into student affairs through university ministry and community service, or Catholic symbols may remain exhibited around the campus to remind others of the heritage—yet, Catholicism remains far removed from the actual education of students. Instead of looking at the difference in education one should find at a Catholic university, Professor Bradley suggests that we have adopted the idea that a Catholic university is simply a "generic product in different wrapping." Just as a single laundry detergent is chemically and in every other substantive way indistinguishable from other laundry detergents, Catholic colleges have become indistinguishable from other colleges that you can buy elsewhere. The only difference is that Catholic colleges are "wrapped distinctively and marketed with a lot of hype about the kind of person you must be because you buy Catholic: concerned, caring, different, spiritual." Bradley points out that Catholic should not be a "a separate element added to a university—it is not an aggregate of two things, it is not a term comprised of adjective and noun . . . Rather it is an undivided but complex whole. It is simultaneously and always a faith-filled, real university." In a true Catholic college, "the faith suffuses the entire institution, and transforms it, and causes it to transcend non-Catholic counterparts."[5]

Still, most Catholic colleges compartmentalize their "Catholicity" by relegating it to the margins of the campus in the offices of university ministry, social justice, or community service. When asked how these Catholic colleges differ from their secular peers, administrators and faculty point to their strong commitment to social justice—but in many ways, this is just more evidence of their loss of faith in their educational mission. Father Peter Ryan of Mount Saint Mary's writes, "activism on behalf of social justice and a robust ministry program, important as they are, are extrinsic to the essential activities of a university: teaching and learning."[6] While Professor Bradley supports such social justice activities and acknowledges their importance as one part of the Catholic mission, he reminds us that "you do not set up a university in order to soup kitchens. You do not keep a university going so that young people can go on retreats. Even if every student and staff member works Easter vacation for Habitat for Humanity, that does not make a college Catholic. You need a Catholic *education* for that."[7]

For this reason, some attention must be paid to the faculty. The faculty is the principle of any university and, as Professor Bradley reminds us, the Catholicity of the faculty is the principle of a Catholic university. "No college can be much more, or will be much less Catholic than its faculty . . . Without a solidly Catholic faculty there is nothing a college can do to be Catholic. With a solidly Catholic faculty, there is little more that needs to be done . . . The soul of a university is its faculty." This is especially true in the departments of theology where the subject matter is the faith—and for this reason Professor Bradley believes that "it is essential that only Catholics who hold the faith teach the theological disciplines. Canon Law requires it."[8]

Claiming that "a Catholic education is better because the faith is true," Professor Bradley writes, "critics of Catholic education glibly allege that "truth is the engine of indoctrination." Yet, Bradley counters this by asking, "Is it not intuitively more likely and does not experience confirm that where there is no truth there is more likely to be manipulation? Where there is no truth there can be no genuine common good. There can only be shifting consensus about this or that, implying that 'right' and 'wrong' manifest not things as they are, but interpersonal power relations. This field is ripe for indoctrination."[9] A Catholic college that holds a "Drag Ball" or a "Coming-Out Week" to celebrate the homosexual lifestyle, or that gives an honorary degree to a notoriously pro-abortion politician bears false witness to the truth. These colleges have lost their faith—even though they may keep the crucifixes on the walls and the statues of the saints exhibited on their campuses. These are the trappings of Catholicism—Masses, student retreats, service projects: "The nearly ubiquitous recipe for a Catholic college today is to surround an education indistinguishable from that at other schools with a Catholic collegiate atmosphere."[10] Its constituent elements are good things in themselves.

But, unfortunately, they do not add up to a Catholic education. In fact, Professor Bradley laments, "Sometimes a college which has lost its faith in the Redemption does not wish to highlight it by taking down once hallowed, now hollow signs of lost faith . . . Apostates recognize that appearances matter, especially to parents and donors."[11]

Despite the apparent failure to implement *Ex Corde Ecclesiae*, there are slight glimmers of hope that we may once again recapture the mission that drove the founders of the earliest Catholic colleges. This hope emerges from Naomi Schaefer Riley's new "missionary generation" of students who are beginning to join forces with a few supportive faculty members, trustees, and administrators who are finally gaining the courage to view their own Catholic colleges and universities as what Pope John Paul called the "living institutional witness to Christ and His message." Some of them are even beginning to see that the activities on their own Catholic campuses are connected with the evangelizing mission of the Church. They are recognizing, as the pope had said they must, that "research carried out in the light of the Christian message puts new human discoveries at the service of individuals and society." And, they are beginning to acknowledge that "education offered in a faith-context forms men and women capable of rational and critical judgment and conscious of the transcendent dignity of the human person."[12]

This is not to say that those on Catholic college campuses are again beginning to "impose" their Catholic religion on others. In fact, Robert George, a legal philosopher at Princeton wrote recently: "When Christians insist that human laws line up with moral truth, they are not imposing religion. Instead, they are making the entirely reasonable demand that reason be given its due in human affairs. Unjust law fails to bind the conscience and must be opposed by people of faith."[13] This joining of faith and reason is especially true for life issues as a growing number of Catholic colleges are finally confronting the pro-choice culture that had been allowed to flourish on their campuses.

At the University of San Diego a student-led, pro-life initiative helped to begin the transformation from what was once a strongly pro-choice campus culture—replete with student internships at Planned Parenthood and university honors given to pro-choice politicians and graduation speakers—into one that is supportive of pregnant and parenting students and less supportive of abortion. Built upon the courage of University of San Diego Students for Life, this initiative drew from the strength of three pro-life faculty members and four members of the university's board of trustees, including San Diego's Bishop Salvatore Cordileone. Rather than dwelling on the negative pro-abortion culture that had taken hold on campus and choosing instead to move beyond the unproductive protests over pro-choice campus speakers or honorees, the newly constituted pro-life group decided to take a more positive track toward building a campus culture of life by increasing the number of resources available to students who may be pregnant or parenting.

For example, in an effort to make the San Diego campus more "baby-friendly," diaper-changing stations were installed in several key areas of the campus where there is significant student traffic. A nursing lounge was also added. Other action items included improving the current policy related to campus housing for pregnant and parenting students—in an effort to enable students to continue a commitment to their education as well as to their child. The university has also begun to address the root causes of unintended pregnancy such as substance abuse, sexual assault, and other high-risk behavior choices, and it has begun offering assistance to faculty and staff that might be a first resource for students faced with an unplanned pregnancy. A compassionate statement of support for pregnant students was added to the student handbook—with a list of resources available to students in need. And during the 2007 spring semester, the university hosted an advance screening of the pro-life film, *Bella,* and invited the director of the film to campus.

None of this progress toward creating a pro-life campus culture would have been possible without the support and encouragement from the bishop and the members of the board of trustees. This is not to say that San Diego's administrators would not have been supportive of the pro-life initiatives, rather, it is just to acknowledge that faculty resistance to such initiatives remains so strong that three lone pro-life faculty members and a committed group of students would not have succeeded in overcoming the faculty hostility without the board and administrative involvement. In the future, these campus resources for pregnant students may be supported by federal grants under a bill approved by the US House of Representatives in 2007. This bill, promoted by Feminists for Life of America, offers support for services including on-campus childcare and maternity coverage in student health plans.

It is clear that the greatest opportunity for reclaiming a commitment to authentic Catholic teachings on Catholic campuses remains within the pro-life arena. Yet, if the pro-life advocacy remains on the fringes of the campus, restricted to the student affairs arena, it will remain marginalized.

To create a culture of life, faculty must once again be willing to confront the culture of death within their classrooms by making a commitment to teaching the truth through education on natural law. In an essay included in an edited collection entitled, *Examining the Catholic Intellectual Tradition,* Catholic philosopher, author, and lecturer Louis Dupre reminds faculty members that "by its very nature, the Catholic college has already declared its commitment to certain ideals of perfection and to specific norms distinguishing good and evil." And, he advises that if a college is to maintain its Catholic moral identity, "teachers must be unambiguous about what clearly agrees and what certainly conflicts with those fundamental principles."[14] Most teachers have ignored this mandate.

Still, it appears that the bishops are beginning to recognize the need for teaching the truth. While pro-choice faculty members like Marquette's Daniel Maguire maintain their tenured teaching positions on Catholic campuses, there are hints from the United States Conference of Catholic Bishops of what the future might hold. In 2007, after decades of silence, the Bishops' Committee on Doctrine finally declared that pamphlets published by Maguire (and distributed by Planned Parenthood) "do not present authentic Catholic teachings." In fact, in a strongly worded statement, the bishops wrote that Maguire's claiming that there is a strong theological tradition in favor of the right to choose an abortion, as well as his views about the very nature of Church teaching and its authoritative character, "cross the legitimate lines of theological reflection and enter into the area of false teaching. Such mistaken views should not be confused with the moral teaching of the Catholic Church."[15] The bishops' willingness to finally offer to Maguire what is called a "Public Correction" is a major step forward in addressing the problems of theologians on Catholic campuses—and a hopeful sign for faithful Catholics. The bishops' concluding statement about Maguire was especially strong: "We deplore as irresponsible his public advocacy of his views as authentic Catholic teachings . . . and we trust that this statement will clarify the Church's faith and teaching for all of the Catholic faithful throughout the United States."[16]

A new generation is beginning to emerge. While it is difficult for this new generation to compete for tenure-track jobs on mainstream Catholic college campuses when the hiring committees are comprised of dissident professors like Professor Maguire, some have made it through to entry-level positions where their impact is already beginning to make a difference for grateful students who have looked for authentic teaching. The reality remains that students on Catholic campuses are the real hope for the future of Catholic higher education and its search for truth. Taking the lead in reclaiming a Catholic culture on Catholic campuses, a "Chastity Initiative" is emerging from the student culture on some Catholic Colleges. During the spring of 2007, Cardinal Newman Society Outreach Director Marc Perrington joined students from Loyola University of Chicago and Seton Hall University at a conference at Princeton University to begin to make plans for pro-chastity student efforts.

Beyond the Cardinal Newman initiatives, students are leading the rediscovery of the Catholic mission at DePaul University—the site of the first queer studies minor in Catholic higher education. Last year, *The Wanderer* reported on the disappointment Nicholas Hahn, a first year DePaul student, felt when he arrived on campus to find an anti-Catholic culture that was alien to everything he had been taught: "He noticed there were no crucifixes on the classroom walls. They told him the crucifixes had been taken down a long time ago—because the crucifixes would make students of different faiths uncomfortable. In the dorms he found the lack of supervision from the university, the heavy drinking, the pot smoking, the bisexual fraternization. What had been billed as a chapel for daily Mass was nothing more than a large room with no Blessed Sacrament one could visit during the day but a room that was used for general services, including Buddhism."[17]

In an effort to address these problems, Hahn became a candidate for the student senate and won a seat as a representative of the campus organization known as University Mission and Values. Hahn's first task as senator was to arrange a one-hour conference with DePaul's president, Fr. Holtschneider, so that he could share his vision for reclaiming the Catholic identity at DePaul. Hahn proposed a university conference that would bring nationally known Catholic speakers like Michael Novak, Thomas Woods, and George Weigel. And, although Hahn and other conservative Catholic students have had no influence on academic decisions like allowing the minor in queer studies at DePaul, it is clear that finally students at DePaul will have more diversity in speakers on campus than they have ever had.

The 2007 spring semester brought hope for a newly renewed attempt to recover a new respect for Catholic teachings on sexual morality as a few more college presidents and provosts have barred performances of *The Vagina Monologues* on their campuses. From a high of thirty-two campuses sponsoring *The Vagina Monologues* in 2003, only twenty-one

Catholic campuses offered the sexually explicit play in 2007. After six years, Notre Dame feminists were forced to move the play off campus after the university provost refused to support it and found no academic department willing to sponsor the event. While Notre Dame's sociology department promised to sponsor the play in 2008, students this year were not permitted to advertise the event or hold auditions on campus. St. Louis University has followed suit, placing the blame for the cancellation on "outside complaints." Thousands of complaints were generated since 2003 by the Cardinal Newman Society arguing that "there is no place in Catholic education for *The Vagina Monologues*, a sexually explicit and offensive play that favorably describes lesbian rape, group masturbation, and the reduction of sexuality to selfish pleasure."[18]

Society president, Patrick Reilly, lauded the decision by Notre Dame and St. Louis University claiming, "faith and reason are reunited in harmony at these prominent Catholic universities." While twenty-one colleges (including Bellarmine University, Boston College, Holy Cross, Mount St. Vincent, College of St. Benedict, College of St. Rose, College of Santa Fe, DePaul, Fordham, Georgetown, John Carroll, Loyola of Chicago, Loyola of New Orleans, Marquette, Regis College, St. Mary's College of California, St. Norbert College, St. Xavier University, Santa Clara, University of Detroit Mercy and the University of San Francisco) continue to sponsor the play, a growing number of colleges and universities are refusing to allow it. And, more importantly, college officials are citing reasons of faith and morals as the rationale behind the refusal. The fact that more than half of these sponsoring schools are Jesuit institutions (thirteen of the twenty-one) is especially revealing. There was a time when other Catholic colleges wanted to emulate the higher status Jesuit institutions and although there are still a few who continue to do so, it can be viewed as a positive step that the non-Jesuit colleges are beginning to move away from the status seeking of the past.

In 2006, Providence College President Rev. Brian Shanley stated that the message of *The Monologues* was counter to Catholic teachings and he courageously stood by his decision despite a campus rally opposing the presidential ban and a petition signed by 1,200 students, faculty, alumni, and others. Carlow University, the College of St. Catherine, Seattle University, and St. Joseph's College and Sacred Heart University in Connecticut sponsored performances of the play in 2006 but did not do so in 2007. News that is even more hopeful is that some campuses are sponsoring alternatives to *The Vagina Monologues*. Notre Dame students are offered the *Edith Stein Project,* which addresses themes of women's dignity consistent with Catholic teaching. The Cardinal Newman Society financially supported the *Virgin Mary Dialogues* at Fordham University in an effort to "promote the true Catholic perspective of the dignity of women and oppose the *Vagina Monologues* in a positive way." Boston College students organized *Dignity of Women Week* and included a panel discussion entitled "Chastity and Courage" and a talk on Pope John Paul II's *Theology of the Body.*[19]

Beyond student affairs, there are a number of Catholic colleges that are publicly requiring all Catholic theology professors to have the mandatum—their bishop's recognition of their pledge to teach in communion with the magisterium of the Church.[20] Concerns about academic freedom seem to have lessened as accrediting bodies have actually supported Catholic colleges who have remained true to their Catholic mission—and chastised those that have not. In fact, in an accreditation report for St. Mary's College of California by the Western Association of Colleges (WASC), the accrediting team faulted the college for a failure to allow the Catholic tradition to "truly guide" the institution.[21] In his research on the "dying of the light" on Catholic campuses, James Burtchaell uncovered a report by WASC which implied that St. Mary's College may be misleading potential students and their families about their Catholic identity. In their report, the WASC site review team observed:

> The liberal arts, Catholic and Lasallian traditions which are used to define the character of St. Mary's College are appropriate and laudatory and consistent with WASC standards. However, we found little evidence that these traditions are truly guiding the institution.[22]

Burtchaell concluded that St. Mary's College became so swept up in the diversity and multicultural movement, accepting a $750,000 grant from the Irvine Foundation to "Celebrate Diversity" in all forms, including diversity in sexual orientation, that "it was no longer willing to celebrate the Catholic values that shaped its founding."[23]

It is possible that accrediting bodies beyond WASC will begin to pay attention to whether Catholic colleges are deceiving potential students, donors, and other stakeholders. But, it should not be necessary for an outside accrediting agency to confront colleges with their defection from their announced purposes—especially when Catholic college administrators have made a conscious decision to "market" their Catholic identity. Even St. John Fisher College, a college that has been stripped of its Catholic identity by New York's Bishop because of its failure to maintain its commitment to Catholic teachings, continues to market itself in public pronouncements as "an independent, liberal arts institution in the Catholic tradition of American higher education." In a recent job ad, published in *The Chronicle of Higher Education*, seeking a campus controller, St. John Fisher administrators continued to claim that the college has been "guided since its inception in 1948 by the educational philosophy of the Congregation of St. Basil . . ."[24] There is no mention that the college is considered "no longer Catholic" by the Church. Truth in advertising should compel all Catholic colleges to begin to offer what they are promising.

There are signs that this may be beginning to happen. After years of complaints about controversial campus speakers at Boston College, officials have announced a new policy to balance dissenting speakers with those willing to present authentic Catholic teaching. Other Catholic colleges are beginning to follow suit. Taking a positive step toward improving the Catholic identity on campus, Boston College is attempting to engage students in conversations about faith in a monthly series of discussions about Catholicism. The *Boston Globe* described the program as "intentionally scheduled late at night, over food, and outside of a Church, is also deliberately irreverent; organizers wear espresso colored T-shirts reading 'What Would Jesus Brew?'"[25] Promotional posters feature a philosophy professor with a latte foam mustache and the first topic of discussion on a November night in 2006 was "Who Needs Religion?" Other colleges are beginning similar programs. Some are addressing the faculty hostility directly—but in a positive way. The *Boston Globe* recently reported that Merrimack College, founded by Augustinian friars, brought 40 percent of its faculty to Italy to retrace the steps of Augustine and think about his mission. The Jesuit College of the Holy Cross has invited faculty to Spain and Italy to follow in the steps of St. Ignatius. In Boston, Emmanuel College is launching a new center for mission and spirituality. And Stonehill College has hired a vice president for mission and appointed a committee on Catholic identity.[26] The *Globe* reporter suggested that what all of these programs have in common is that they are attempts to move beyond seeing the Catholic tradition as simply censorious—and to stress the rich and complex heritage that the Church can offer.

In response to alumni concerns about the Catholic identity at Notre Dame, Fr. John Jenkins announced in 2007 that he has launched a presidential effort to identify and hire more Catholic faculty members. This decision by the president emerged from concerns from several prominent alumni who established Project Sycamore and launched a petition urging Fr. Jenkins to address concerns including the decline of Catholic faculty and his willingness to allow the campus production of *The Vagina Monologues*.[27] Project Sycamore leaders include Richard Allen, former National Security Advisor to Ronald Reagan and president of an international consulting agency. While Project Sycamore is encouraging Fr. Jenkins to make changes on the campus, a local Indiana attorney has publicly called for Fr. Jenkins' resignation—arguing that his failure to act has undermined any future efforts to overcome faculty opposition and make serious changes at Notre Dame.

Likewise, prominent alumni from the College of the Holy Cross, joined with the Holy Cross chapter of the Cardinal Newman Society to protest the choice of Chris Matthews as a commencement speaker. In a paid advertisement that appeared in the Worcester Catholic diocesan newspaper, Charles Millard, a prominent graduate and twenty-two-year member of the college's board of trustees criticized the decision to honor a pro-abortion speaker. Fr. Michael McFarland, SJ, the president of Holy Cross, responded to the alumni criticism by saying that Matthews' support for legal abortion is "allowable in Catholic thought" and lashed out at alumni protesters saying that they have "no authority whatsoever to dictate what is Catholic." And, to make matters worse, the president directly attacked the generous donor and distinguished former member of the alumni who led the protest by saying that when the school honors an individual, "if we checked their conformity with every point in Catholic teaching, we would have no honorees—including Charlie Millard."[28]

The alumni of Catholic colleges and universities are in a unique position to respond to concerns about the loss of Catholic identity. But, they often feel powerless to stop the secularization. To help alumni gain a voice on their campuses, the Cardinal Newman Society is currently discussing, with the American Council of Trustees and Alumni (ACTA), options for Catholic college donors to participate in ACTA's Fund for Academic Renewal—which, among other things, manages donor-advised funds by which donors can designate a particular institution or type of program for ongoing support.[29] This way, donors can continue to support Catholic colleges—yet refuse to be part of supporting "coming out week" or the "club for reproductive choice" on campus. By designating where a donation is to be spent, alumni can have a tremendous impact on campus life, especially if they give their gifts directly to support authentically Catholic student clubs and programs like pro-life clubs, prayer groups, or orthodox Catholic speakers' series. Alumni can also help to fund Catholic educational initiatives, including endowed chairs, as long as they remain involved in helping to choose the chair holders.

This is not to imply that there is no role for bishops in monitoring what is taught on Catholic campuses. Pope Benedict XVI has already shown a willingness to reign in theologians during his own tenure as head of the Vatican's Congregation for the Doctrine of the Faith. There are signs that this will continue during his years as pontiff. Most recently, the Vatican took disciplinary action against Jesuit priest, Father Jon Sobrino, a leading proponent of liberation theology in Central America.[30] Although the Vatican censured his writings, he has not been barred from teaching or publishing. And, there are signs, as Rev. Richard John Neuhaus, editor of *First Things* predicted that in the future, Pope Benedict will appoint bishops who are "vibrantly orthodox and strong communicators."[31] This can only be a positive development. But as the concluding chapter will demonstrate, regaining control will be difficult because it will require confronting those who have mobilized in an attempt to depose the established hierarchy of the Church itself.

Notes

1.   Joseph Bottum. "When the Swallows Come Back to Capistrano: Catholic Culture in America." *First Things*. (October, 2006). www.firstthings.com/article.php3?id_article=53598&var_recherche=when+the+swallows
2.   Gerard V. Bradley. "Looking Ahead At Catholic Higher Education." Fellowship of Catholic Scholars Quarterly. (Spring, 2002), 17.
3.   Ibid., 16.
4.   *Ex Corde Ecclesiae*. "Apostolic Constitution of the Supreme Pontiff John Paul II on Catholic Universities." Given in Rome at St. Peter's on August 15, 1990.
5.   Bradley. "Looking Ahead At Catholic Higher Education." 19.
6.   Ibid., 20.
7.   Ibid., 20.
8.   Ibid., 21.
9.   Ibid., 18.
10.   Russell Shaw. "The Future of Catholic Higher Education." *Catholic Herald*. (September 19, 2002) www.catholicherald.com/shaw/shaw02/shaw/0919.htm
11.   Bradley. "Looking Ahead At Catholic Higher Education." 20.
12.   *Ex Corde Ecclesiae*.
13.   Ian Hunter. "Do the Right Thing." *Ottawa Citizen*. (April 2002): www.canada.com/ottawacitizen/index.html
14.   Louis Dupre. "The Task and Vocation of the Catholic College." Included in *Examining the Catholic Intellectual Tradition*. Edited by Anthony Cernera and Oliver Morgan. (Fairfield, CT: Sacred Heart University Press, 2000), 28.
15.   "Doctrine Committee Offers Public Correction of Theologian's Pamphlets on Contraception, Abortion, and Same-Sex Marriage." United States Conference of Catholic Bishops. March 22, 2007.

16. Ibid.

17. Thomas F. Roeser. "DePaul Student Leads Campus Catholic Restoration." *The Wanderer*. (2006).

18. "V-Monologues Pushed Off Campus at Notre Dame and St. Louis." *Cardinal Newman Society Mission*. (Spring 2007).

19. "Cardinal Newman Society Supports Alternatives to Monologues." *Cardinal Newman Society Mission*. (Spring 2007).

20. In March, 2006, *The National Catholic Register* published a list of the US Catholic Universities who have required Catholic theology professors to have the mandatum. The list includes: Aquinas College, Ave Maria, Belmont Abbey College, Benedictine College, Our Lady of Corpus Christi, DeSales, Franciscan University of Steubenville, Magdalene College, Our Lady of Holy Cross College, St. Gregory's University, University of Dallas, and the University of St. Thomas in Houston. In addition, the faculty at Christendom College in Front Royal, Virginia and Thomas Aquinas College in Santa Paula, CA have taken fidelity oaths in lieu of the mandatum because they are in dioceses where the local bishop has not offered the mandatum. www.register.com/articulo.pp?artkod=OFk

21. James Tunstead Burtchaell. *The Dying of the Light: The Disengagement of Colleges and Universities from Their Christian Churches*. (Grand Rapids, MI: William B. Eerdmans Publishing Company, 1998) 688.

22. Ibid.

23. Ibid.

24. Job Advertisement for administrative position at St. John Fisher College. In *The Chronicle of Higher Education*. "Diversity Pages." (October 2006).

25. Michael Paulson. "Across U. S. Catholic Colleges are Searching for Their Identity." *The Boston Globe*. (November 12, 2006): 11.

26. Ibid.

27. "Notre Dame Responds to Alumni Concerns." *Cardinal Newman Society Mission* (Winter 2006-2007).

28. "Catholic College Clashes with Prominent Alumni." *Catholic World News*. (April 28, 2003): www.cwnews.com/news/viewstor.cfm?recnum=22042.

29. Patrick J. Reilly. "Feeling the Pinch: Ten Ways Alumni Can Help Renew Catholic Colleges." *Crisis Magazine*. (September 2005): www.crisismagazine.com/september2005/feature/htm

30. John Thavis. "Vatican To Take Action Against Liberation Theologian." *Catholic News Service*. (March 12, 2007): www.catholicnews.com/data/stories/cns/0701384.htm

31. Eric Gorski. "Pope Set to Make Mark on U. S. church." *ABC News*. The Associated Press. (April 14, 2007): www.abcnews.go.com/us/wirestory?id=3035155

11

Continuing the Catholic Culture Wars

For those who have spent the past few decades fighting for the implementation of *Ex Corde Ecclesiae,* it must appear that the war is over and their side lost. The contentious battles that once surrounded the release of Pope John Paul's 1990 apostolic constitution on Catholic higher education have ended as college presidents quietly refused to implement it, and many of the bishops were reluctant to require it. Most seem to have abandoned the fight. Even University of Notre Dame Professor of Law Gerard Bradley, a longtime proponent of the implementation of *Ex Corde Ecclesiae,* pronounced the document "dead."[1]

Many of those who had spent so many years championing the papal document simply gave up the struggle for a renewed faithfulness to the Catholic mission on their campuses. Those who continued the fight to revitalize the Catholic identity faced the challenge of a campus terrain that in some ways resembled an old battlefield—littered with unexploded mines and eerily silent on many of the issues that have caused so much debate in the past.[2] These weary warriors soon found out that no one fights for hegemony over a dangerous graveyard. For the faithful faculty and students—the apparent losers of the Catholic culture wars—the campus itself stands as a sad reminder of what once was and might have been.

While the once hallowed ground still remains, the sacred symbols, the saintly statues and crucifixes that continue to adorn many of these campuses, have become hollow reminders of what has passed. For Fr. Wilson Miscamble, professor of history at Notre Dame, most Catholic campuses now possess "a certain Potemkin Village quality . . . While their buildings are quite real, what goes on within them has increasingly lost its distinctive content . . . Students emerge from Catholic schools unfamiliar with the riches of the Catholic intellectual tradition and with their imaginations untouched by a religious sensibility."[3] Like the fake

Potemkin Villages that had been built to create an impression of prosperity during Catherine the Great's tours of Ukraine and the Crimea, the Catholic campuses of today create a false impression of a commitment to faithfulness to the truth of the Church that is presented in campus tours to potential students and their parents. And, like the Potemkin villages, Professor Miscamble predicts that for most Catholic colleges and universities, "it will be increasingly difficult to maintain even a Catholic façade in the academic life of these institutions."[4]

Still, there are a faithful few refusing to give up the fight on some of those Catholic campuses. And, although the other side is emboldened by victories in decimating once strong theology and philosophy programs and corrupting the student culture with coming out closets, presentations of *The Vagina Monologues,* and internships at Planned Parenthood, not all is lost. With victory comes complacency—as the aftermath of any war demonstrates. The loyal opposition, those faithful to the spirit of *Ex Corde*, can capitalize on this complacency. But, first, they need to recognize that the culture war must continue, and they need to begin again to enlist others to help with the fight.

Sociology may be a good place to start in helping us understand this war. While contemporary sociology has been silent on the culture wars that have raged on Catholic campuses between those who lament the loss of a Catholic identity and those who insist that Catholic colleges and universities must abandon ties to an antiquated authoritarian model of the past, this does not mean that sociologists have nothing to contribute. Despite the fact that leading sociologists, like Boston College sociologist Alan Wolfe, claim that the culture wars themselves are a figment of conservative imagination, University of Virginia sociology professor, James Davison Hunter, points out that these sociologists have ignored the areas of social life where the conflict is strongest: the culture forming institutions of contemporary society—the colleges and universities, and the elites who lead them, the competing sources of moral authority that animate them, and the symbolic discourse through which much of this conflict takes shape.[5]

Sociology has much to offer to help us understand this culture war. From the earliest days of the founding of the fledgling discipline, sociologists had been concerned with the ways in which social order is maintained—and how social change occurs. Sociologists have always known that "Where there is culture, there is struggle." No culture is static—including Catholic culture. Until his recent death, Philip Rieff was one of the few contemporary sociologists willing to remind us that the struggle over culture is "the continuation of war by other—normative—means." Rieff believed, like many sociologists once believed, that culture is "the form of fighting before the firing actually begins." And, he believed that by its very nature, "the work of culture is the matter and manner of disarming competing cultures."[6]

It is clear that those responsible for secularizing Catholic campuses knew the importance and the benefits of "disarming competing cultures." One of the most effective ways Catholic culture was disarmed on Catholic campuses was through attacking the legitimacy of authority within the Church—and, in many cases, denying the existence of truth itself. Dismissing the idea that the reason Catholic colleges and universities were created was to discover and to teach the truth, this elite culture now embraces what George Dennis O'Brien's new book, *The Idea of a Catholic University*, has identified as "different kinds of truth."[7] In a postmodern appropriation of Cardinal Newman's 1854 classic *Idea of a University,* O'Brien, the former president of Bucknell University and president emeritus of the University of Rochester, dismisses the possibility of what he calls a "single truth." Rejecting the conventional, institutional, juridical, hierarchical model used by the Vatican as "improper both to faith and academic freedom," O'Brien argues that "in an effort to preserve the integrity of both church and university, Catholic colleges must adapt a model that appreciates what he calls "different kinds of truth—each with its own proper warrant and method."[8]

With a strong endorsement on the book jacket from Charles Curran, one of a handful of dissident Catholic theologians to be publicly corrected by the Vatican for his erroneous writings, O'Brien promises that his book questions not only the ideology of the modern Catholic university, but also "the way in which Catholic defenders of the truth of the Catholic faith construe truth."[9] O'Brien claims expertise and impartial outsider status as the former president of two highly ranked secular colleges to make a case for the futility of the kind of truth claims that have been made on a Catholic campus.[10] And, in a classic redefinition of the truth claims of doctrine and dogma, O'Brien argues that on a Catholic campus, "one can uncover academic dogma and Christian freedom, university infallibility and dogmatic fallibility."[11]

The idea of disciplinary infallibility is one that is increasingly cited on both secular and Catholic campuses. In 2007, in response to growing criticisms about the biased behavior of college professors, the American

Association of University Professors suggested a form of such disciplinary infallibility in their report, "Freedom in the Classroom." The AAUP report denies the claims of critics who have complained that professors have used their classrooms to indoctrinate students, present imbalanced perspectives on contentious issues, demean students who disagree, or intrude irrelevant political opinions.[12] And, most importantly, the report claims that the prevailing view held by the faculty within each academic discipline should be viewed as truth.

An analysis of "Freedom in the Classroom" by Peter Wood, the executive director of the National Association of Scholars, suggests that the consistent theme of the AAUP report is that truth on today's college campuses is now defined exclusively by the faculty within each academic discipline. From this perspective, if a faculty member asserts something in the classroom that strikes ordinary people as preposterous, but which is held to be true according to the prevailing view of the faculty member's discipline, the faculty member has engaged in a perfectly worthy example of academic freedom. What Wood calls AAUP's newly constructed disciplinary infallibility is a rejection of the assumption that the best ideas win out over time. From this perspective, "the demand for rational arguments and evidence, and the search for an enduring truth, is just a device to intimidate." From this postmodern standpoint, truth is socially constructed, and academic disciplines like religious studies or even queer studies are free to advance their own disciplinary infallibility.[13] If, as the AAUP contends, the assumptions of a specific discipline provide the criteria for what is academically true, then advocates for any belief—even holocaust deniers—would only have to establish a field or a discipline in order to teach their theories as truth.[14]

It is clear that the culture war on Catholic campuses has moved beyond the *Ex Corde* wars and has escalated to one that is waged between those who assert that there are no truths, only texts, and those who remain dedicated to the proposition that the truths have been revealed and require constant rereading and application in light of the particular historical circumstance in which we live. Like all cultures, issues within Catholic culture are always being re-defined.[15] Still, there are some enduring truths—those that Philip Rieff calls commanding truths—which cannot be changed: "Commanding truths will not be mocked, except to the destruction of everything sacred."[16] Rieff knew, as the sociologists of the past knew, that culture survives by faith in the highest absolute authority and its interdicts. For Catholics, there can be no Catholic culture without authority—or without such commanding truths.

Yet, many Catholic scholars continue to deny the reality of commanding truths. In *Catholic Identity: Balancing Reason, Faith and Power,* sociologist Michelle Dillon argues that those who belong to organizations, like the pro-abortion Catholics for a Free Choice or the gay rights advocacy organization Dignity, are simply engaged in pushing for the elimination of institutional impediments to diversity and the expansion of interpretive and participative equality in the Church.[17] Those Dillon calls "pro-change Catholics" believe that they are simply ahead of the curve of other Catholics. And, for Dillon, conservative Catholics are those who desire to "restrict the intra-church participation of their coreligionists." For Dillon, "pro-change Catholics are committed to remodeling the Church as a more inclusively pluralistic community . . . Pro-change Catholics seek not only to overturn official church teaching de-legitimating Catholics who are gay or lesbian, or advocates of women's ordination, or pro-choice on abortion," they also seek to "reconstruct an inclusive, egalitarian, and pluralist church wherein these identities are validated."[18] While Dillon believes that pro-change Catholics can transform the Church into one that is inclusive in practice and validates as full members in communion with the Church even those Catholics who support abortion or gay marriage, she also believes that these same pro-change Catholics can integrate this change with what they consider to be core aspects of Catholicism as their community of memory.[19]

Most conservative Catholics find Dillon's suggestion impossible, maintaining that the Church cannot allow those who deny authoritative teachings on the "non-negotiable issues" or commanding truths like teachings on the evil of abortion to claim that they are maintaining "core aspects of Catholicism." Yet, even conservatives must acknowledge that the chaos within the Church itself that followed the Second Vatican Council might have led those change-seeking Catholics to think that the Church was indeed going to be more open to women's issues—like female ordination and reproductive rights. These liberal Catholics often point to the documents of Vatican II, especially *The Pastoral Constitution on the Church in the Modern World,* which they believe called for a paradigm shift in our understanding of a theological vision of the world. Instead of conceiving the world as tainted and a place to withdraw from, members of the Catholic community were called to redirect their energies in a quest for holiness and the encounter with God to the world.[20] Some interpreted this engagement with the world as an acceptance of the changing culture of the modern world—an embrace of egalitarianism and a rejection of what they viewed as the archaic hierarchical system of teaching. And, some went even further—maintaining that even our relationship with God needed to be altered from one which was hierarchical to one that is more "horizontal."

Indeed, for liberal Catholics, the abortion debate suggests there is a need to address attention to the "common life" of the individual—moving beyond the authoritarian or "vertical" relationships of the past. As former Jesuit priest, Bernard Cooke pointed out in a series of lectures at the College of the Holy Cross, "the Vatican Council reintroduced an understanding of the divine-human relationship that was more horizontal than vertical. God is less above the people, sending down messages through delegates, than abiding with them."[21] For liberals, even God is not "above" the people. As David O'Brien, Holy Cross historian writes, "The older, now resurgent position leads to a moral teaching that however skilled its intellectual rationalization, remains in essence an articulation of truths handed down from above."[22] Rather, O'Brien suggests that what is needed is a theological method that is anchored in the experience of Christians who "necessarily must be consulted in moral formulations . . . The more horizontal understanding fastens the vision of the church beyond itself, in the historic liberation of the human family."[23]

In contrast, for *First Things* editor, Fr. Richard Neuhaus, the denial of authority and refusal to submit to official Church teachings implicit in O'Brien and Cooke's horizontal formulation and Dillon's argument in favor of pro-change Catholics, is at the heart of the problem on Catholic campuses. Richard Neuhaus argues that a university born *Ex Corde Ecclesiae*—from the heart of the Church—must "decide and then decide again every day, whether or not to keep faith with the Church of Jesus Christ . . . When a university decides not to say that Jesus is the way, the truth, and the life, it is not saying nothing. Rather, it is saying that adherence to this way, this truth and this life is not necessary to, or is a hindrance to being the kind of university it wants to be."[24] The real question for those who lead Catholic colleges is "whether the Christian proposal limits or illumines the university's calling to seek and to serve the truth."[25]

For some of these colleges, it appears that the decision has already been made. In November 2007, the Board of Trustees at the University of St. Thomas in St. Paul, Minnesota voted to remove the bylaw that maintained the sitting archbishop of St. Paul-Minneapolis as the vicar general and priest president of the university—effectively severing all ties to the archdiocese. The St. Thomas Board, which includes Fr. Edward Malloy, the retired president of the University of Notre Dame, voted unanimously to change the university's bylaws and install the soon-to-retire, longtime liberal Archbishop Harry Flynn as chairman for a five-year term. The move is criticized within the conservative Catholic press as "an effort by the university to override the authority of and possible reforms by Archbishop John Nienstedt, Flynn's more orthodox Catholic coadjutor bishop who will fully succeed him as head of the archdiocese next year."[26] Named by the Rainbow Sash Alliance, a gay advocacy organization, as one of the four most "gay friendly bishops" in the United States, Archbishop Flynn has been a favorite of the faculty.[27] With this historic move, St. Thomas University, which describes itself in its mission statement as "inspired by the Catholic intellectual tradition," has chosen to limit the influence of a new and faithful archbishop. At a meeting following the trustee's vote, more than one hundred St. Thomas students vowed to petition the university to reverse the decision. But, the student protest will likely fail in the face of overwhelming opposition from a liberal faculty and an accommodating board stacked with retired Catholic College presidents like Fr. Malloy, Sr. Maureen Fay, the retired president of the University of Detroit Mercy, and the president of Gannon University.

And so the culture wars continue—deadlocked on these very core issues as the aging baby boomers on the faculty and administration remain frozen in time, fighting old battles, holding old grudges, and attempting to recruit new warriors not even born when Vatican II ended and the culture wars began. And, those on the right remain defensive—unable to understand the anger and resentment on the left and unwilling to negotiate on what they see as the non-negotiable issues. Taking the path of least resistance, those on the board who are charged with leading these colleges and universities appear to ally with the left—siding with the faculty against any attempt by faithful bishops to truly lead.

There are no easy answers to the question of how best to help a Catholic college recover its mission—especially when, for many, this is not even a goal. It is often described as a crisis of secularization. But, as these chapters have shown, the real crisis on Catholic campuses is, as Fr. Richard Neuhaus has said many times, a "crisis of faith." While it cannot be denied that part of the reason for this crisis within Catholic colleges is due to status envy—the desire to be the Catholic Harvard or Haverford, or the desire to compete to belong to one of the "upper tiers" in *U. S. News & World Report,* the source of the crisis of faith is much more complex than status strivings.

In *The Secular Revolution*, University of Notre Dame sociologist Christian Smith suggests that something more sinister may have been operating. While not targeting his analysis specifically to Catholic colleges, Smith and the contributors to his book provide a persuasive argument that the secularization of American institutions—including religious colleges—did not happen by accident or happenstance as the natural result of modernization. Rather, the evidence contained in *The Secular Revolution* points out that the secularization process was "an achievement of specific groups of people, many of whom intended to marginalize religion." Instead of an inevitable consequence of modernization on Catholic campuses, Smith asserts that the people at the core of this secularizing movement knew exactly what they were doing—and they wanted to do it.

In many ways, the theoretical framework presented in *The Secular Revolution* helps us understand the culture wars that have continued to rage on Catholic campuses. Drawing from sociological theory on conflict and social movements, Smith opens the first chapter with social theorist, Randall Collins' suggestion that "Secularization is not a zeitgeist but a process of conflict." From that starting point, the authors explore the possibility that the secularization of American public life has been something much more like "a contested revolutionary struggle than a natural evolutionary progression."[28] Even though Smith's analysis is limited to the secularization of American institutions in the last century, his theoretical framework is helpful in attempting to understand the secularization that occurred in Catholic higher education after the 1950s. And, although only God knows the secrets of the heart that have led so many Catholic college administrators and faculty members to make the choices they have made to help their campuses move up and away from their Catholic mission, it is helpful to use Smith's revolutionary model of the secularization process.

Like any revolution, the secularization of Catholic colleges was preceded by an ongoing culture war in which perceptions of an established regime whose institutional privilege and dominance provoked increasing grievances among excluded groups. As the previous chapters have demonstrated, feminists, angry over the Church's stand on women's ordination and reproductive choice, as well as gay men and lesbian women who have felt marginalized by Catholic moral teachings (Michelle Dillon's pro-change Catholics) have had a powerful incentive to challenge the existing order in the Church. Far from valuing the core aspects of Catholicism, these groups have mobilized to depose the established regime from its positions of control. Pseudo-Catholic Organizations like the Women's Ordination Conference, Catholics for a Free Choice, WATER, Call to Action, Dignity, and others have worked closely with those on Catholic campuses—drawing support and influencing others, including students.

Affiliations and alliances with those working on Catholic campuses have brought credibility and attention to the perceived grievances of what has become a growing number of people recruited to assist in the "cause" of giving voice to the perceived powerless. Appealing to the idealism of students and the need for peer approval by junior faculty members, these groups have managed to recruit others to challenge what has become defined on campus as an increasingly oppressive Church. Aided by a set of facilitating forces and events, these insurgent activists have managed to transform the institutions in which the established regime had previously dominated. The creation of women's centers and departments of women's studies on many Catholic campuses and the growing number of gay social clubs and queer studies courses have already transformed Catholic colleges. As the previous chapters have demonstrated, in the process of transferring power and control from the old to the new regime, this insurgency caused a profound cultural revolution that transformed cultural codes and structures of thought, expectations, and practices.[29] Catholic colleges have been transformed from authentically Catholic institutions promoting a general Catholic worldview and morality into places where Catholic concerns were marginalized in favor of a striving for "excellence," a higher tier in the status rankings, and a commitment to egalitarianism that cannot allow the hierarchy of the Church to play a role of authority. Along this journey, conservative Catholic faculty voices were increasingly marginalized by removing them from hiring, tenure, and promotion committees and positions with access to decision making on curriculum or new programs. Some were literally pushed to the fringes of the campus given the smallest offices and the worst teaching schedules.

The process of the secularization of Catholic colleges can be thought of as a kind of revolution because, like all revolutions, it fundamentally concerned questions of power and authority. An identifiable network of insurgents intentionally and largely successfully struggled to displace an established power.[30] Still, the transformation remains unfinished. Unlike the complete secularization of Protestant colleges and universities like

Harvard, Princeton, Yale, and others there is still hope of reclaiming Catholic colleges and winning at least some of the battles for a recovery of a Catholic identity. The real question remains, how to fight this revolution.

Since the secular revolution on Catholic campuses, like the secularization of the Protestant campuses, appears to have been intentional and rational—involving strategic actions by revolutionary insurgents—there is an opportunity that the opposition can employ a counter-insurgency to slow or stop it. Targeting the leaders—the dissident theologians like Marquette's Professor Maguire, Notre Dame's Professor McBrien, or the long list of liberation theologians whose dissidence goes well beyond empowering the poor in Latin America—is a start. This is not to suggest that rooting out the leaders is the answer to ending the secular revolution on Catholic campuses. While it might at first seem to be the easy answer, the reality is that there are now a multitude of partisans and allies that would mobilize to defeat any perceived threat to the leadership. Creating martyrs for the cause emboldens any revolution as battle lines are solidified, warriors begin to dig in, and heroes begin to emerge.

A better strategy for the counter-insurgency is a systematic, well-organized plan to directly address each aspect of the slide to secularization. This plan involves asking the hard questions—the questions that Smith and his colleagues posed when they focused on the secularization of the Protestant institutions:

1. *Targeting the activists* focuses upon identifying the actors and explores the ways in which they constituted a group. This involves, of course, identifying the leaders—but more importantly, identifying the advocacy groups and the organizations who had the most to gain by secularizing the campuses. Fr. Hesburgh's decision to trade a commitment to Church teachings on contraception and abortion for an alliance with the pro-population control Rockefeller Foundation would have to be included in this. Likewise, the "unholy alliances" that several Catholic colleges made with the Ford Foundation or the Irvine Foundation to diversify the campus with pro-choice initiatives or gay and lesbian social activities and pseudo-academic initiatives must also be targeted.

2. Looking closely at the *motivation of the activists* involves looking at the material and symbolic interests that are at stake. It identifies the grievances that may have provoked activists to mobilize and asks, "What did they oppose and what did they seek to change?" While status envy and institutional upward mobility were certainly important goals, many activists had their own individual status strivings—and their own needs for recognition of their own personal issues.

3.   Analyzing the *culture and ideology* helps us to understand the ideologies of moral order that may have shaped the actors. The changing role of women in society and the growing acceptance of homosexuality and homosexual behavior certainly had an effect on the culture of the campus. Removing all legal constraints against homosexual behavior through the Supreme Court decision in *Lawrence vs. Texas,* and the movement to legalize same sex marriage in Massachusetts and elsewhere has contributed to making continued Catholic constraints on same-sex relations seem unreasonable to the activists and their allies. As a result, many of these constraints seem capricious rather than grounded in reason. To begin to change this, the Catholic hierarchy and the informed laity needed to make the natural law basis for such restrictions clear. Yet, few faculty are even aware of such a natural law rationale. A renewed appreciation for Aquinas would be a start.

4.   Looking closely at *political opportunities* reveals the ways in which changes in the sociopolitical environment altered the structure of power relations. These changes increased the opportunities for insurgents to act successfully upon their existing interests and grievances. The removal of the sacred from public life as part of the growing separation of Church and state—what Fr. Neuhaus calls the "Naked Public Square"—has had a negative effect on Catholic college campuses as pressures continue from secular funding sources or accrediting agencies to divest from a strong Catholic identity.

5.   *Identifying Material Resources* points to the shifts in the availability of financial resources that facilitated activism and altered the likelihood of success. Creating an endowed chair for yet another dissident theologian, like Rosemary Ruether, or endowing a center or campus organization that conducts activities counter to Catholic teachings has been one of the most effective ways that Catholic campuses have contributed to the secularization on their campuses. Such resources must be redirected toward ways to strengthen the identity. Endowing a chair for a faithful Catholic scholar would be a start. But, beyond this, the bishops would do well to spend some of these resources on their own assessment initiatives. In 1998, Cardinal Francis George, archbishop of Chicago, suggested that the US bishops form their own Catholic accrediting association. Such an association could operate in a "non-confrontational way, to bring the university into conversation with the body that defines the content of the word 'Catholic' and gives permission to any institution the right to use the name."[31]

6.   Identifying the ways in which *issues were reframed* points to the ways in which activists reframed the agendas, assumptions, issues, and evidence in ways that politically strengthened their cause. Redefining the Church as a site of oppression for women and gay men and lesbian women has been effective in rallying others to the secular revolution on Catholic campuses. This needs to be addressed directly.

7. *Identifying the strategies of the activists* reveals ways to counteract these strategies. One of the most successful strategies of those seeking to displace the authority of the Church has been to enlist the assistance of students through their student life activities. Women's centers have been in the forefront in lobbying for reproductive rights on Catholic campuses. Gay and lesbian student support groups have become powerful on campus by allying with general offices of student affairs to choose gay and lesbian activist guest speakers for student conferences. If faithful faculty members and students protest the honoring of such speakers and simply ask for an "alternative voice," they are marginalized and sometimes ostracized for their faithfulness to Catholic moral teachings. Strengthening student groups that are faithful to the Magisterium including pro-life or pro-chastity initiatives and social clubs would be a start.

8. *Targeting the organizations* reveals the ways in which these organizational structures facilitated the revolution or movement's mobilization. The Catholic Theological Society of America has been instrumental in facilitating the secular revolution by denigrating the clerical authority structure of the Church. One of the most effective strategies liberal theologians like McBrien and McGuire have used to marginalize the clerical authority has been to dismiss the academic theological expertise of the bishops or the clerical administrators on Catholic campuses. McBrien's dismissive suggestion to give the bishops football tickets and "let them sit on the stage at graduation" and McGuire's suggestion that it would take "magic" to bring the bishops up to the level of academic theologians are just two examples of a lack of respect for Church authority. Their success in marginalizing the Catholic hierarchy has greatly elevated the status of the lay theologians in CTSA and the College Theology Society. The only way to counteract this strategy is to enhance the visibility of faithful organizations and articulate, faithful priests and bishops. There are many like St. Louis' Archbishop Burke who can win any theological debate with the smartest secular faculty members—Catholic colleges need to provide a forum for that to happen. Orthodox organizations like the Fellowship of Catholic Scholars or the Society of Catholic Social Scientists would be an invaluable resource to the bishops and priests.

9. *Looking closely at the ways in which both sides in the culture wars have attempted to persuade the public* reveals a continued inability by the Church to effectively communicate her care for her followers. In the past, anti-Catholicism was a serious social problem in this country that resulted in attacks from outside the Church. But the recent clergy abuse scandal within the Church has further negatively influenced public opinion both outside and within the Church—thus emboldening the insurgents. The authority structure of the Church needs to directly address the image they have presented to the public—and begin now to enhance it.

10. *Restoring identity and solidarity* is an important component of restoring the Catholic mission. Activists have been effective in establishing a collective identity of oppression by the Church. Assuming the mantle of victimhood has given great power to the secularizers. This has motivated their insurgency by bringing sympathetic allies to the cause of secularization. To address this, the counter-insurgency needs to identify the rituals, ceremonies, or other identity-building practices that the secularizers have engaged in to sustain their movement relationally. For example, the most recent women's ordination ceremonies have been widely publicized both on Catholic campuses and in the secular media—and it has reinforced the image of the Church as a site of oppression for women. To counteract this, Catholic campuses should first directly confront this issue and, at the same time, begin enhancing the sacred on their campuses. Sacred symbols do work. They are well known as coordinators of moral demand systems and of tone, character, the style and being of life, as well as the picture people have of the way things are in their most inclusive sense of order. Phillip Rieff writes, "sacred symbols render visibly, whether in words or images, what the true way is."[32] Offering the exposition of the Blessed Sacrament for students would be a tremendous start because it would be a visible and physical reminder of the presence of Christ on their campus. Beyond this, restoring crucifixes on the classroom walls and offering masses—rather than "all-faith" services on important occasions—would enhance Catholic cohesiveness and a sense of community.

Underlying Smith's revolutionary theoretical model of secularization are three assumptions drawn largely from the research and writing on intellectuals by Pierre Bourdieu and Alvin Gouldner. The first assumption is that intellectuals, like those teaching on Catholic college campuses, are not any more "above" the pursuit of status, power, and wealth than others. Like other professional actors, these intellectuals pursue their own discernable group interests with the means available to them. The second assumption is that the primary resource of intellectuals pursuing their interests is the power to construct reality through the production and control of knowledge. Through their writings, their lectures, and their very presence on campus, intellectuals "possess a special ability to manipulate symbols, to produce culture schemas, to define and regulate knowledge." Finally, intellectuals, like other social actors, "do not pursue their group interests in a vacuum, but always in relation to antagonists and allies with conflicting and aligning interests."[33] .

Although this theoretical framework is helpful, it remains incomplete. To understand why intellectuals pursuing status and authority struggled so hard and for so long to secularize Catholic colleges and universities, Christian Smith argues that several features of Western intellectuals predispose many of these intellectuals to be alienated from and adversarial toward the established traditions that their societies embrace. Smith believes that certain characteristics of intellectuals also predispose many of them to be antagonistic to religion per se: "Traditional religion often violates what most kinds of intellectuals hold dear."[34] For Smith, the nineteenth-century Protestant establishment stood in the path of upwardly mobile academic and literary intellectuals, in much the same way the magisterium may appear to stand in their way today, blocking their bids for increased group status, autonomy, authority, and income. Displacing this religious authority was required for upward mobility. It is increasingly embarrassing for some Catholic intellectuals to be part of a traditional Church that makes demands on believers and continues to insist that women may not control their reproductive decisions, that homosexual behavior is disordered, and that women and married men are not called to the priesthood. Christian Smith's writings on secularizing Protestants are helpful in understanding this:

> Like children who never want to return to a family and home they remember as suffo-
> cating, such a history naturally tends to make many intellectuals suspicious of religious
> authority and friendly toward secularization . . . Intellectuals love of autonomy easily
> disposes them against the historical religious traditions of the West, for these traditions
> make it impossible to escape that which violates autonomy, namely dependence and
> authority with regard to things beyond and above oneself—on God at least, if not
> also on Scripture, bishops, church teachings, moral commands, and clergy . . . We
> have reason then to think that under the right conditions, many intellectuals would
> perceive a direct relationship between a decline in traditional religion's authority and
> an increase in their own autonomy, and would believe both to be in their interest.

In some ways, it may be less a crisis of faith that has led to the secularization of Catholic colleges, than a sin of pride. Theorist, Alvin Gouldner writes, "Professionalism silently installs the new class as the paradigm of virtuous and legitimate authority—performing with technical skill and with dedicated concern for the society-at-large." Members of this class reject any appeal to established authorities or status positions—beyond themselves. In most ways, faculty on Catholic campuses are not so different than those on secular campuses in terms of pursuing self-interest. When the hostility to religion is combined with the self-interests of the status-hungry, upwardly-mobile professionals and those with specific grievances against specific Church teachings, the decline was inevitable.

While this desire for upward mobility may have required a compromise of the Catholic identity, what truly seemed to have sealed the fate for many Catholic colleges was what Randall Collins identifies as the "breakdown at the top, caused by internal struggles among elites."[35] As Smith has suggested, "insurgent movements enjoy greater political opportunities when institutional political systems become more open for participation; when broad elite alignments that undergird a polity become unstable; when some elite groups ally themselves with the insurgents; and when the established regime's capacity or propensity to repress opposition is reduced."[36] The raised expectations, coupled with the uncertainty and disruption in the Church following Vatican II and the general societal liberalism of the sixties and seventies provided exactly the kind of opportunistic climate that revolutions require. It was a time when some of those at the top, including bishops like Archbishop Weakland, suffering from their own crises of faith, sided with the insurgents further weakening the authority of the hierarchy. And, many within the already weakened hierarchy seemed to surrender their authority during the current clergy abuse scandals.

The complexity of the secularization process on Catholic campuses demands a complex response—one that rejects the "easy answers" of the past. While it is understandable that many have not questioned what seemed to be the "natural" link between modernization and secularization for so many years, it is clear that this must end. It is likely that many Catholic college faculty members and administrators have continued to simply accept this explanation because blaming the natural evolution of modernization for their secularization helps these leaders to avoid making any judgments about those who might have purposely contributed to the decline of their commitment to the Catholic mission. If the secularization of Catholic higher education is simply a "natural" outcome of modernization, it achieves the status of an unavoidable and inevitable occurrence that we should have expected. Besides, if it is simply a natural outcome, there is little reason to even try and recover because it will "quite naturally" occur again.

Sadly, the truth remains that in their pursuit of upward mobility, decision makers at Catholic colleges were unable to resist the tyranny of progressivism, the belief that the present is always better than the past, and we are all better off without it. But, these colleges had plenty of help from Dillon's "pro-change agents" within the Church who had much to gain by discarding the Catholic identity. And, as a result, many colleges and universities have turned from places where faith and reason would be joined, into what *WORLD* magazine editor Marvin Olasky has called "fortresses of bias against faith."[37]

Still, it is possible to recover. The recovery begins by showing respect for the power of the past and the force of authority. It requires one to acknowledge the desire for status, but also our longing for a sacred realm: "Tocqueville believed that the great task facing modernity is not to erase the past and reconstruct the present but to recognize what was best in the past—what was essential—and to carry it forward."[38] Building upon Tocqueville, Philip Rieff reminds us that no culture in history has sustained itself merely as a culture: "Cultures are dependent upon their predicative sacred orders and break into mere residues whenever their predicates are broken."[39]

It is only when decision makers on Catholic campuses are willing to truly embrace the richness of their sacred heritage, and the authority vested in that heritage, that they will once again allow themselves to be guided by Cardinal Newman's founding vision for Catholic colleges and universities. Newman's *Idea of a University* is a place where "the professor is a missionary and a preacher . . . it is a place where the catechist makes good his ground as he goes, treading in the truth day by day into the ready memory and wedging and tightening it into the expanding reason."[40] Newman believed that the university must be "the seat of wisdom, the light of the world, and the minister of the faith."[41] Newman knew, as the founders of the earliest Catholic colleges knew, that without an eagerness to become again a "light of the world" and a willingness to go to war against those wishing to disarm the Catholic culture, the Catholic university will not survive.

Notes

1.   Gerard V. Bradley. "Looking Ahead At Catholic Higher Education." *Fellowship of Catholic Scholars Quarterly.* (Spring 2002): 16.
2.   Colin Sumner. *The Sociology of Deviance: An Obituary.* (New York: Continuum Press, 1994).
3.   Rev. Wilson Miscamble. "The Faculty Problem." *America.* (September 10, 2007): www.americamagazine.org/content/article.cfm?article_id=10176
4.   Ibid.
5.   Philip Rieff. *My Life Amid the Deathworks.* "Introduction" by James Davison Hunter. (Charlottesville, VA: University of Virginia Press, 2006): xx.
6.   Ibid., 2.
7.   George Dennis O'Brien. *The Idea of a Catholic University.* (Chicago, IL: University of Chicago Press, 2002).
8.   Ibid., book jacket notes.
9.   Ibid., 4.
10.   Ibid., 88.
11.   Ibid., book jacket notes.
12.   Peter Wood. "Truths R Us." *Inside Higher Ed.* (September 21, 2007): www.insidehighered.com/views/2007/09/21/wood

13. Ibid.
14. David Horowitz. "The Intellectual Responsibility of Educators." *The Chronicle of Higher Education,* 54. (October 12, 2007): B-4
15. Rieff. *My Life Amid the Deathworks.* 18.
16. Ibid., 59.
17. Michelle Dillon. *Catholic Identity: Balancing Reason, Faith and Power.* (New York: Cambridge University Press, 1999), 2.
18. Ibid., 24.
19. Ibid.
20. Barbara E. Wall. "Mission and Ministry." Included in *Women in Catholic Higher Education.* Edited by Sharlene Nagy Hesse-Biber and Denise Leckenby. (Lanham, MD: Lexington Books, 2003), 146.
21. David O'Brien. *From the Heart of the American Church: Catholic Higher Education and American Culture.* (Maryknoll, NY: Orbis Books, 1994), 148.
22. Ibid.
23. Ibid.
24. Richard John Neuhaus. "A University of a Particular Kind." *First Things.* (April, 2007): 32.
25. Ibid., 35.
26. Hilary White. "Catholic St. Thomas University Votes to Sever Historic Ties with St. Paul Archdiocese." Lifesite News. (November 21, 2007): www.lifesite.net/ldn/200/nov/07/12103.html
27. Ibid.
28. Christian Smith, (editor). *The Secular Revolution.* (Berkeley, CA: University of California Press, 2003), 1.
29. Ibid., 2.
30. Ibid., 4.
31. Cardinal Francis George. "Be Prepared to Give an Account: Today's Catholic Mission in Higher Education." Address presented at Georgetown University. October 20, 1997. Published in *Catholic International.* Volume 9, Number 2. (February, 1998): www.nd.edu/~afreddos/papers/george1.htm
32. Rieff. *My Life Amid the Deathworks.* 43.
33. Smith. *The Secular Revolution,* 38.
34. Ibid., 39.
35. Ibid., 61.
36. Ibid.
37. Marvin Olasky. "Why Liberals Rule Academia and the Media." (September 23, 2004): www.Townhall.com/coumnists/marvinolasky/2004/09/23/why_liberals_rule_aademia_and_media
38. Wilfred M. McClay. "Twilight of Sociology." *The Wall Street Journal.* (February 2, 2007): W 13.
39. Rieff. *My Life Amid the Deathworks.* 24.
40. John Henry Newman. *The Idea of a University.* Originally published 1854. New edition. (South Bend, IN: University of Notre Dame Press, 1990).
41. Ibid.

Index